Getting Started in
Online Day Trading

D1367137

The Getting Started in Series

Getting Started in
Online Day
Trading

Kassandra Bentley

John Wiley & Sons, Inc.

New York • Chichester • Weinheim • Brisbane • Singapore • Toronto

Published by John Wiley & Sons, Inc.

Published simultaneously in Canada.

Library of Congress Cataloging-in-Publication Data:
Bentley, Kassandra
    Getting started in online day trading / Kassandra Bentley.
      p. cm.— (The Getting started in series)
    Includes bibliographical references and index.
    ISBN 0-471-38017-2 (pbk : alk. paper)
    1. Electronic trading of securities. 2. Day trading (Securities) I. Title. II. Getting
  started in

HG4515.95.B462000
332.64'0285–dc21   00-038212

Printed in the United States of America

10 9 8 7 6 5 4 3 2 1

For my stepfather,
A.H. "Spud" Wells

Preface

When I was asked to write this book in the spring of 1999, day trading had already become a hot topic, with dozens of books promising to reveal the secrets of the authors' success. I read many of those books, as I debated the wisdom of adding yet another log to the day trading fire. Although they were helpful in different ways, none of the books took me by the hand and guided me through the basic steps of how to get started in day trading. Most made me feel as if I had walked into a calculus class without ever having cracked a high-school algebra book.

What I needed was a book written by someone who had learned about day trading from the ground up, from the outside in—not books by professional traders who had spent most of their adult life on Wall Street and retained only the vaguest memory of the beginner's needs. Those books could be studied after I learned the basics.

The basics, I felt, should be provided by someone who still remembered the stumbling blocks encountered, the puzzles that had to be solved, all the steps that had to be taken to become knowledgeable in a new field. Such down-in-the-trenches experience allows a writer to approach her subject with a clarity unavailable to one who is an expert going in. Why? Because most experts can't view the area of their expertise with the mind of a beginner, and as a result they often leave out important information or critical steps.

Even though I am an online investor and have coauthored several books on investing, I am a beginning day trader. So I approached the subject as a novice and began to learn the nuts and bolts of day trading. I mined online resources for free and valuable information on the markets, the brokers, the software, and the tools of the trade. I interviewed traders who made their living trading stocks. (This book, by the way, is about trading stocks—not options, futures, commodities, or currencies.) I talked with day trading gurus, owners of day trading shops, and developers of day trading software. I hung out in chat rooms and message boards devoted to day trading. For almost a year I steeped myself in day trading, following every story, every article, every mention of the subject by the media. I continued to read books on day trading; I attended the first International Online Trading Expo and other seminars; I joined a day traders club; I did simulated trading on my home computer; and I sat beside two professional day traders and watched them trade.

The result of these efforts is a book that tells you how to get started in online day trading from someone who did just that.

If this is the first book you've picked up on day trading, it won't be your last, not if you're serious about learning how to trade. Because there is a lot to learn. Day trading is not a road to easy money. It is hard work, brimming with high risk and hang-by-your-fingernails tension and pressure. It is said some 80 percent of day traders fail to make it beyond the first six months. If you expect to be among the 20 percent that become successful traders, you have a long way to go. Consider this book the first step in a lifelong journey.

KASSANDRA BENTLEY

San Diego, California
June 2000

Acknowledgments

There are many people who had a hand in helping me bring this book into being:

- ✔ Mina Samuels, my former editor at John Wiley & Sons, suggested the book and enthusiastically supported my efforts.

- ✔ David L. Brown, my friend and coauthor on previous books (whose presence I sorely missed on this one), was the first person I called whenever I ran into a snag, and my expert source on technical analysis.

- ✔ Mark Seleznov, CEO of Trend Trader LLC, Scottsdale, Arizona, taught me about market makers and trading Nasdaq stocks. I attended his training seminar and then sat by his side for several fascinating hours and watched him trade. He also gave me valuable feedback and advice on the manuscript.

- ✔ Dave Floyd, CEO of CareerDayTrader.com in San Diego, taught me about trading listed stocks, both during an interview and during market hours when I watched him trade. In his shop I witnessed the camaraderie of a day trading shop. Dave also provided valuable feedback on the manuscript.

- ✔ My friends Victoria Lara and Dayle Lyons de Raat had the stamina to read the entire manuscript and made valuable suggestions that helped keep me on track.

- ✔ Dr. Jerome Brams offered his professional expertise on the psychological aspects of trading versus gambling.

- ✔ The International Online Trading Expo in Ontario, California, brought me in contact with dozens of market experts and day traders whose experiences and advice grounded me in the art of day trading. In particular, the traders on the Million Dollar Panel expanded my narrow definition of day trader to encompass the myriad styles described in this book.

✔ DayTraders USA offered valuable workshops at its Irvine, California, location and educational material on its web site that started me off on the right track. I am particularly grateful to the traders who frequented the #daytraders chat group and gave me a glimpse into the mind of the trader.

✔ Jack Gaston, who took over the editorial reins of the book when Mina left, and Pamela van Giessen, executive editor at Wiley, extended my deadline and saved me from complete mental collapse!

✔ My family and my friends—especially Jeanne, Dayle, Brandi, and Taylor—cheerfully endured my litany of "Sorry-I-can't-make-it-I-have-to-work-on-the-book" excuses for many months.

✔ And Phil Hardy, who came into my life just as I began the book, gave me enormous support and encouragement and has managed to weather the storm.

To all, I offer my heartfelt thanks.

K.B.

Contents

Introduction

The Day Trading Game

T he last year of the twentieth century was a banner
year for the stock market. In just 12 months, the
Dow gained nearly 4,000 points, the *Nasdaq* almost doubled in value, and both the Nasdaq and the *New
York Stock Exchange* (*NYSE*) set trading volume records of
more than a billion shares a day. In 1999, more than 540
companies went public, many of which made instant bil-
lionaires of their founders. Things never looked rosier on
Wall Street. But behind the scenes, the markets were in
turmoil, and at the heart of that turmoil, indirectly, were
day traders.

Day traders have been credited with creating the
volatility that exists in today's markets, moving the Dow
or the Nasdaq up one day and down the next in 100-point
swings. They've been blamed for the inflation of Internet
stocks, for the unprecedented gains of dot-com *initial public offerings* (*IPOs*), and for anything that hints of irra-
tionality in a stock move. If in fact day traders have this
power, they get it from their ability to access the markets
directly through a group of *electronic communications networks* (*ECNs*). These networks had been around in some
form for decades, but in 1997 they were incorporated into
the Nasdaq quote system and blessed by Nasdaq as a way
to handle certain kinds of orders for Nasdaq stocks. Now
ECNs are changing the entire marketplace. Like the red-

Dow
the Dow Jones
Industrial Aver-
age, an index
that measures
the performance
of 30 blue-chip
stocks.

Nasdaq
the Nasdaq Stock
Market. Nasdaq
originally was an
acronym for the
National Associa-
tion of Security
Dealers Auto-
matic Quotation
system.

1

New York Stock Exchange (NYSE)
the largest and second oldest stock exchange in the United States (the Philadelphia Stock Exchange is older) where stocks of more than 3,300 companies are traded.

day trader
one who buys and sells securities for short-term gains, usually exiting all positions by the end of the day.

volatility
a measure of a stock's daily price fluctuations. Large swings in stock prices equal high volatility.

headed office boy in the Ameritrade commercial, ECNs have crashed Wall Street's private party, and they've taken the market by the heels, held it upside down, and are shaking the living daylights out of it.

So far, they've shaken over 30 percent of the trading volume out of Nasdaq and have emerged as a driving market force for the twenty-first century. In midsummer 1999 ECNs began offering *after-hours trading*, one-upping Nasdaq and the NYSE—both of which postponed their move to after-hours trading until the year 2000, citing concern with Y2K problems. Then, to improve the *liquidity* in the after-hours market, the ECNs—all competitors—banded together and agreed to share stock quotes during after-hours trading.

All this activity has snagged the attention of some of the biggest names on Wall Street. Goldman Sachs, J. P. Morgan, Merrill Lynch, Morgan Stanley, Donaldson, Lufkin & Jenrette (DLJ), Schwab, Fidelity, E*Trade, even CNBC—all have made multimillion–dollar investments in their favorite ECNs. There is talk of ECN mergers, ECN public offerings, and the creation of superECNs. A couple of the ECNs even have had the temerity to file for stock exchange status.

Meanwhile, the beleaguered Nasdaq and NYSE are trying to keep up. Both are tossing around the ideas of going public or of sharing their regulatory bodies and maybe even their stock quotes. And—in a resigned, if-you-can't-beat-'em-join-'em mood—the NYSE recently announced that it will create an internal ECN of its own.

To a traditional market watcher, it is as if the tail were wagging the dog.

Clearly, this is a market in a state of flux, driven by the power of the ECNs. And, as mentioned earlier, the power that drives ECNs is day traders.

Day trading is not a new phenomenon. It has been around for more than 100 years, beginning with the bucket shops described by Edwin LeFèvre in the classic book *Reminiscences of a Stock Operator.*[1] In those days, traders walked in off the street to buy and sell stocks in the turn-of-that-century's equivalent of our day trading shops. That free-for-all ended after the 1929 stock market crash, although day trading continued at a professional level. It took two revolutions and some Nasdaq rule changes to level the playing field for individual traders.

The first revolution began in the brokerage industry. Until 1974, commissions on stock trades were set at a fixed percentage of the trade, which created three-figure commissions on average trades. Few amateurs could trade with that kind of handicap. But in 1974, the *Securities and Exchange Commission (SEC)* set aside the fixed commission rule, and new discount brokers like Charles Schwab & Co. began to chip away at commission schedules. By the end of 1999, online commissions had dropped to as low as $5 a trade.

The second revolution was technological, beginning with the personal computer in the late 1970s and culminating in the mid-1990s with the advent of the World Wide Web. The Web has shrunk our world to the size of a computer screen, and today's technology lets us navigate that world at warp speed.

But low commissions and technological innovations by themselves were not enough to level the playing field for individual traders. It took the power of the SEC to do that.

The SEC-mandated changes, which are discussed in Chapter 1, forced Nasdaq to change the way it handled trades from individual investors and traders. This created a market in which the *SOES* bandits,[2] as the media dubbed these early day traders, could "steal the *spread*" and make thousands of dollars a day with relatively little risk. In those days, spreads were wider, competition was milder, and the opportunity for big profits was, by some counts, limitless.

Today, day trading is a much different game, thanks to increased competition, narrower spreads, and new rules that hamper the trader. Day traders now number more than 250,000, by one count, with about 5,000 trading in day trading shops and the rest trading from home offices. All are competing for the spread. But spreads have narrowed. In the days of the SOES bandits, stock prices were quoted in "eighths," so the minimum spread was $1/8$ of a point. In 1997, the spread was cut in half when stocks

initial public offering (IPO)
the selling of shares of stock to the public in a privately held company, after which the company becomes a publicly traded company. The IPO is usually underwritten by one or more investment banks that buy the shares from the company and then resell them to the general public.

Electronic communications network (ECN)
a computerized trading system sanctioned by Nasdaq for the display of customer limit orders and integrated into the Nasdaq Level 2 quote system.

after-hours trading
trading after normal market hours, which may be from 4:00 P.M. Eastern Time (when the regular market closes) to 8:00 P.M. Eastern Time.

liquidity
having a sufficient amount of trading volume to accommodate the buying and selling of a security without a large bid/ask spread.

Securities and Exchange Commission (SEC)
the regulatory body of the securities industry.

began to trade in increments of "sixteenths." Spreads could conceivably narrow to a penny after the switch to *decimalization* in 2001. And, the new Nasdaq trading rules, described in Chapter 2, appear to take back some of the benefits of the rules that opened up the markets to day traders in the first place.

All this does not mean the end of day trading. Successful traders can still make in a week the kind of profits that a buy-and-hold investor would be grateful to claim in a year. But day trading is not an easy road to riches, as some have claimed. In fact, here are a few hard, cold facts you should contemplate before you launch a career in day trading:

✔ Eighty to 90 percent of novice day traders are expected to fail. If you fall into this group, you will lose all your money and have to go back to whatever it was you were doing before you tried day trading.

✔ The learning curve can be steep and very expensive. Some estimate that beginners may lose 50 percent or more of their trading capital during the first six months. Even successful traders talk about having lost their entire stake before they learned how to trade.

✔ Losing is part of the game. Successful traders lose 50 to 80 percent of their trades. These are the *successful* traders! So even if you succeed at the day trading game, you'll have more losing trades than winning trades.

✔ Previous success in business or a profession does not translate into success as a day trader. In fact, as you will see in Chapter 8, the very traits that led to your success might be detrimental in a trading career.

✔ The market is driven by fear and greed, and you have to learn how to control your own reactions to both. The best trader is one who can check his or her emotions at the trading room door.

If all this sounds overly cautionary, it merely reflects the atmosphere that has surrounded day trading during the past year.

Early in 1999 Arthur Levitt, head of the SEC, cautioned online brokers to warn customers of the risks of investing in *fast markets*. The Atlanta shootings in mid-summer 1999 were followed by a deluge of negative publicity, and the *National Association of Security Dealers* (*NASD*) quickly proposed that day trading firms be required to screen potential traders for their ability to handle the stress and tension of trading. Early in 2000 the New York Stock Exchange and Nasdaq proposed to raise the minimum level of *margin accounts* for day traders, presumably to eliminate thinly funded traders.

 SOES
short for Small Order Execution System. It is an electronic order delivery system that requires mandatory executions by Nasdaq market makers at the inside quote. Used as a verb, it means to sell shares at the quoted bid or buy shares at the quoted ask. SOES cannot be used with ECNs.

> It is a good idea to read some of the cautionary statements issued by brokerage firms. There is a particularly thorough one at Trend Trader LLC (www.trendtrader.com). The SEC has also posted a caveat for day traders at its web site (www.sec.gov).

 spread
the difference between the bid and the ask prices of a security.

All this caution is meant to protect day traders from themselves, but the best protection must come from the individual trader. If you decide to join their ranks, you must prepare for it as you would any new, highly skilled profession—with education, training, practice, and dedication. And you must learn the rules and mechanics of trading.

Before we begin, you might ask yourself three questions:

1. *Do I have the guts to day trade?* David Brown, my coauthor on previous books, talks about matching your investing (or trading) style with the fortitude of your tummy. As a day trader, you will operate in a highly volatile market that requires constant vigilance, quick judgments, and snap decisions. You must judge the next move of a stock based on a screen full of rapidly changing data, and when the signal says "go," you must react in-

 decimalization
the quoting of stock prices in decimals instead of fractions.

fast markets
markets characterized by rapidly changing prices and extreme volatility.

National Association of Security Dealers (NASD)
the self-regulating securities organization and parent company of the Nasdaq Stock Market.

margin account
a type of brokerage account that allows you to borrow funds against the securities in the account in order to purchase more securities.

stantly or miss the action altogether. If the thought of this puts your tummy in turmoil, you might want to consider another career.

2. *Do I have the humility to day trade?* Learning to take losses is said to be the single biggest obstacle in day trading. Successful traders consider losses simply part of the game. They plan how they will exit a trade *before* they enter it, and when a trade goes against them, they get out quickly and without questioning the why or the how of it. It takes a certain degree of humility to admit you are wrong about a trade. If you are the kind of person who *has* to be right, you'll stick with losing trades far too long, which will turn small losses into big ones. And that can put you out of the game before you even begin.

3. *Do I have the dollars to day trade?* If the current rules proposal before the SEC is approved, the minimum for a day trading margin account will jump to $25,000. Most traders say you need that much *or more* to day trade effectively. Whatever the size of your account, it should be money that you don't need. It should not be your children's education fund. It should not be your retirement account. It should not be a second mortgage on your house or any kind of borrowed funds. You should trade only with discretionary funds that you can lose every last cent of without wanting to throw yourself out a 10th-floor window. Why? Because you will lose money during the learning period. To remain in the game, you have to have a good-sized stake to start with.

Think about your answers to these three questions as you read this book. By the time you arrive at the last chapter, you'll have a pretty good idea of whether you have what it takes to be a day trader.

HOW THIS BOOK IS STRUCTURED

You might think of this book as the CliffsNotes that will prepare you for the subject of day trading. For example, if you read the CliffsNotes to *Moby-Dick*, you will get the plot outline and character sketches of Ishmael and Queequeg and Captain Ahab; you'll read descriptions of the ship and the sea and the great white whale; and you'll learn how the story ends. But to get the full force and flavor of Herman Melville, you'll have to read the sprawling 600-page novel for yourself.

Like CliffsNotes, *Getting Started in Online Day Trading* will introduce you to the markets, tools, and concepts of day trading; it will tell you about broker/dealers and order execution systems; it will delve into the mind of the day trader and help you write a trading plan. But it will not make you a day trader.

This book is just one of many you will read, if you are serious about becoming a day trader. To get the full force and flavor of day trading, you'll need to supplement this book with the books, tutorials, seminars, courses, and tools described in these pages—and with others that you will find on your own.

But here is where you can start.

First, you will learn the nuts and bolts of the day trading game. Chapter 1 introduces you to the markets and the changes that opened them up to day traders. Chapter 2 lays out the day trader's basic tools: *Level 2 quotes*, the *Small Order Execution System (SOES)*, *Select-Net*, and ECNs; Chapters 3 and 4 introduce you to the electronic brokers and trading software that give the day trader direct access to the markets.

> **Level 2 quotes**
> stock quotes that reveal the bids and asks of all market participants (market makers and ECNs), along with the number of shares offered at each bid and ask price.

Italicized terms in the text are defined in boxes and in the Glossary at the end of the book. All the web sites mentioned in the book are listed alphabetically and chapter-by-chapter in Appendixes 4 and 5. Chapter-by-chapter links can be found in the Active Trading Center at the author's web site at www.cyberinvest.com.

Next, you can explore different day trading styles and learn the rudiments of analyzing stocks and the markets. Chapter 5 describes the major trading styles and talks about how to find stocks to trade. Chapter 6 is

Small Order Execution System (SOES)
a mandatory order execution system that requires Nasdaq market makers to execute limit orders of up to 1,000 shares at their quoted bid or ask.

SelectNet
a nonmandatory electronic order delivery system that allows any subscriber to Level 2 quotes to direct (preference) orders to specific market makers and ECNs or to broadcast orders to all market makers and ECNs.

a beginner's guide to technical analysis, which is an important component of many trading styles. Chapter 7 talks about the forces that move the market and a few market analysis tools.

There's more to day trading, though, than mere mechanics. Many experts say that trading is mostly psychological and that to succeed as a day trader you must master its mental and emotional challenges. Chapter 8 talks about the psychological pressures that the market places on traders and how to handle them, and Chapter 9 outlines the steps for managing risk and creating a trading plan.

Then we move on to practical matters. Chapter 10 walks you through setting up a remote office and Chapter 11 summarizes the online and offline resources where you can continue your day trading education. Finally, we wrap up the book in Chapter 12 with a look at the changes that will shape the market of the new millennium.

Becoming a day trader requires a substantial investment of time, effort, and money. If you approach it as you would any new career—doing what is necessary to gain the requisite skills and knowledge—you might end up in that elite group known as successful day traders.

Chapter 1

The Playing Fields: Nasdaq and the NYSE

I f you want to master a new sport, one of the first things you must do is learn about the field on which it is played. If the sport is golf, you'll study the fairways and sand traps and greens of the golf course. If it is tennis, you'll learn the layout of the singles court and the doubles court. If you're learning to sail, you'll study the bay or lake on which you plan to sail. Of course, it is most important to learn the rules, regulations, and etiquette of the sport, but these flow from the field on which the sport is played.

For the equity day trader, the playing fields are the Nasdaq Stock Market and the New York Stock Exchange (NYSE). You can choose to play exclusively on one or the other, or you can play on both. Whichever you choose, you should learn as much as you can about how the markets operate.

SPECIALIST VERSUS DEALER MARKETS

The New York Stock Exchange is commonly referred to as an *auction market*, while the Nasdaq has been called by

> **auction market**
> a market in which traders meet on a trading floor to buy and sell securities through a specialist (such as the New York Stock Exchange and the American Stock Exchange).

negotiated market
a market in which prices are negotiated between buyers and sellers.

specialist
the firm or individual who makes a market in a listed stock and manages all orders for that stock.

market maker
a broker/dealer or investment bank that makes a two-sided market in a Nasdaq security by maintaining a firm quote on both the buy side and the sell side. Market makers are appointed and regulated by the National Association of Security Dealers (NASD).

some a *negotiated market*. In reality, stocks are bought and sold in each market through bids and offers based on supply and demand, which is the basis of an auction. The difference is that the bids and offers at the NYSE are controlled by one person (the *specialist*) and at the Nasdaq by many competitors (*market makers*). In this way, the NYSE can be considered a *specialist market*, and the Nasdaq, a *dealer market*.

The AMEX and the Regionals

The American Stock Exchange (AMEX) operates through specialists, like the NYSE (www.nyse.com). It is not considered a primary playing field for day traders, even for those who trade only listed stocks. It merged with Nasdaq in 1998, but it is not part of the SOES or SelectNet systems, and any orders sent to the AMEX are routed directly to the specialist, just as they are with an NYSE stock. You can learn more about the American Stock Exchange at www.amex.com.

There are also six regional stock exchanges:

Arizona	www.azx.com
Boston	www.bostonstock.com
Chicago	www.chicagostockex.com
Cincinnati	www.cincinnatistock.com
Pacific	www.pacificex.com
Philadelphia	www.phlx.com

None of the regional exchanges can be accessed directly by individuals. *The Intermarket Trading System* (ITS) links all the exchanges and, through the Consolidated Quote System (CQS), displays quotes for listed stocks.

Specialists and market makers must agree to maintain liquidity in a stock by always having a ready buyer for shares that someone wants to sell or a ready seller for shares that someone wants to buy. If a ready buyer or seller cannot be found at any given time, the firm must use its own capital to buy or sell the stock for its own account.

As a day trader, it is important to understand the way specialists and market makers operate because you will be competing with these professionals for every dollar you make. The better you know your opponents, the more profitable you're likely to be.

The New York Stock Exchange

The New York Stock Exchange operates from a 36,000-square-foot trading floor at 11 Wall Street in New York City.[1] Each of the 3,000-plus stocks listed on the NYSE is assigned to one of 27 specialist firms that are members of the exchange. Each specialist firm hires individuals—the specialists—to manage the stocks assigned to the firm. An individual specialist may manage from 2 to 10 stocks (the mixture is balanced between high-volume and low-volume stocks), but each stock is represented by only one specialist.

The specialist operates out of one of the 17 *trading posts* on the floor of the exchange. Each trading post is manned by several specialists and their assistants and outfitted with dozens of computer screens. One post can accommodate more than 150 different *securities*. Views of the trading posts and the floor of the exchange can be seen at the NYSE web site at www.nyse.com (and also in the background of live television broadcasts from the floor of the exchange).

Along the perimeter of the floor of the exchange are about 1,400 *trading booths* (also called *broker booths*) owned and run by member firms and independent brokers. Formerly referred to as "seats" on the exchange; they're now called "memberships." They are purchased by broker/dealers or investment banking firms like Goldman Sachs, Merrill Lynch, or Salomon Smith Barney for the privilege of doing business at the New York Stock Exchange. Members may also purchase physical or electronic access rather than a seat.

Floor brokers, the individuals who trade stocks on the floor of the exchange, communicate with the specialists face-to-face, while brokers who are not on the trading floor

specialist market
a market, such as the New York Stock Exchange or American Stock Exchange, in which a single firm or individual is assigned the responsibility of maintaining the market and handling the order flow for each stock listed on the exchange.

dealer market
a market, like Nasdaq, which has competing broker/dealers who make a market in each stock, each using its own capital and other resources.

Intermarket Trading System (ITS)
the system that electronically links all U.S. stock exchanges.

trading posts
the 17 computerized structures on the floor of the NYSE from which specialists trade their securities.

securities
a general term that encompasses equity instruments (stocks) and debt instruments (bonds), although the term is often used interchangeably with stocks.

communicate with the specialists directly through *Super-Dot*, the NYSE's electronic order-handling system. There are also independent floor brokers not associated with a broker booth—known as "free agents"—who represent nonmember broker/dealers.

All orders for a stock flow through the specialist, who is responsible for matching buy orders with sell orders—or, as mentioned earlier, if no buyers or sellers can be found, to trade the stock for his or her firm's account. Obviously, this gives the specialist enormous control over the price of the stock. That control is most obvious whenever a specialist calls a *trading halt*. If an unusual news event is expected to greatly impact the price of a stock, the NYSE specialist can stop trading in the stock—sometimes for hours—until he or she can sort out the orders and arrive at a "reasonable" price.

SuperDot

SuperDot is the *Super Designated Order Turnaround System* used by the New York Stock Exchange since 1976 (originally called DOT and renamed SuperDot in 1984). It links member firms directly to the specialists and is used primarily for smaller orders (orders less than 2,100 shares have priority). Some 40 percent of all shares traded on the NYSE go through SuperDot, but it handles more than 80 percent of all NYSE orders. SuperDot is not directly accessible by individuals, but when a day trader routes an order to the NYSE, it goes through SuperDot.

Execution of an NYSE Trade. Day traders' orders are routed directly to SuperDot, but to see how brokers and specialists work together, let's do a little role-playing as an ordinary investor.

- ✔ Let's say you just placed an order with your broker at Merrill Lynch to buy America Online (AOL), an NYSE-listed stock.
- ✔ Your ML broker transmits the order (either by phone or electronically) to the Merrill Lynch bro-

ker booth on the floor of the exchange. The order is printed and handed to a floor broker. The floor broker then becomes your agent for the purchase or sale of the stock.

✔ If your order is a *market order*, the floor broker carries it to the trading post of the specialist that represents AOL and tries to get the best price from other floor brokers who are holding sell orders at the AOL trading post.

✔ If the order is a *limit order*, the AOL specialist enters it into a computerized *limit order book* where it will stay until it becomes a *marketable limit order*—that is, until the stock price reaches the limit price, at which time the limit order becomes a market order and is executed—or until the order expires or is canceled.

✔ Once a trade is executed, the process is reversed. The specialist enters the trade in the system, where it appears instantaneously on tickers around the world. The floor broker transmits the information to the Merrill Lynch trading booth, which relays it to your ML broker, who calls or e-mails you with a confirmation.

 trading booths
the structures (about 1,400) along the perimeter of the floor of the NYSE from which member firms and independent brokers operate.

 broker booth
a trading booth.

 floor broker
brokers who work on the floor of the New York Stock Exchange, either as employees of brokerage houses (commission brokers) or for themselves (independent brokers). The latter execute orders for both member brokers and non-member brokers.

Big Brother Sees All

Stock Watch is a computerized system on the floor of the NYSE that helps guard against manipulation and insider trading. The system continuously monitors trading activity and automatically flags unusual volume or price changes in any listed stock. If no legitimate explanation is apparent, such as a company announcement or industry trend, the NYSE will launch an investigation. For more on its investigative approach, click Regulation, then Market Surveillance at www.nyse.com. There is a similar regulatory eye at the Nasdaq Stock Market called MarketWatch. (Click About Us, then MarketWatch at www.nasdaq.com.)

SuperDot
the electronic
order handling
system used by
the New York
Stock Exchange,
primarily for
small orders. It
was originally
named the Desig-
nated Order Turn-
around (DOT)
system and re-
named SuperDot
in 1984 after
certain enhance-
ments.

**trading
halt**
a pause in the
trading of secu-
rity, initiated by
the specialist,
that occurs when
significant news
is released about
the security, to
give the market
time to absorb
the impact of the
news.

This is a very simplified overview of a trade, and in reality, this sequence takes place only on large institutional orders. Small orders, from day traders and ordinary investors, are entered directly into the SuperDot system by the brokerage firm and routed automatically to the specialist's booth.

Despite the apparent chaos on the trading floor during market hours, the NYSE is an orderly, highly regulated machine and less volatile than Nasdaq. Some day traders prefer to trade only NYSE stocks for that reason, but others consider the specialist system slow and cumbersome. For most day traders, Nasdaq is where the action is.

NYSE Mini-Fact Sheet

Founded: The forerunner of the NYSE was founded in 1792 when 24 brokers signed an agreement to trade only with each other, initially conducting business under a buttonwood tree on what is now Wall Street.

Renamed: The New York Stock Exchange in 1863.

Location: 11 Wall Street, New York, New York.

Chairman and chief executive officer: Richard A. Grasso.

Listed securities: 3,300.

Specialists: 27 firms employ approximately 460 specialists.

Order handling: SuperDot.

Seat on the exchange: In 1817 a seat on the New York Stock Exchange cost $25. In August 1999, a seat was sold for $2.65 million.

Source: www.nyse.com.

The Nasdaq Stock Market

The Nasdaq Stock Market is an electronic network of broker/dealers. It is sometimes referred to as the over-the-counter or OTC market, a name that originated in its past.

Prior to 1971, all stocks not listed on an exchange were traded "over the counter" in brokers' offices. In 1971, the National Association of Security Dealers (NASD) launched an automated quote system, which formalized and automated quotes for OTC stocks. That system was known as NASDAQ, which stood for the National Association of Security Dealers Automated Quotation system.

Four years later, listing standards were initiated, which effectively separated Nasdaq stocks from other OTC stocks.[2] Today, even though Nasdaq stocks go through a formal listing procedure, the terms listed stocks and OTC stocks are still used to distinguish between stocks traded on the NYSE (or other exchange) and those traded on Nasdaq.

A further distinction is made within Nasdaq stocks between the *Nasdaq National Market* (NNM) and the *Nasdaq SmallCap Market* (SmallCaps). These are two separate markets within Nasdaq. The NNM stocks have more stringent listing requirements and consequently include the largest and most actively traded securities. The Small-Caps are primarily *emerging growth companies*.

Nasdaq Market Makers. The driving force of the Nasdaq Stock Market is its cadre of market makers who compete with each other for the stocks in which they make a market. Any of the NASD's 500+ broker/dealer firms may register with the NASD (the parent company of Nasdaq) to become a market maker in any stock, if the firm meets certain net capital, staffing, and supervisory requirements. In its broker capacity, the market maker acts as an agent for its clients; in its dealer capacity, the market maker buys stock for and sells stock from its own inventory. Nasdaq market makers, like NYSE specialists, must agree to make a *two-sided market* in the stock they represent. That means the market maker must be both buyer and seller of the stock.

For each stock in which it makes a market, the market maker quotes a price at which it is willing to buy the stock (the *bid*) and the price at which it is willing to sell the stock (the *ask* or offer). There may be dozens of market makers competing for the bid and the ask on a high-

market order
an order to buy or sell a stock at the current market price, whatever that price may be when the order is executed.

limit order
an instruction to a broker to buy or sell a specified number of shares of a stock at a specific price, or better.

limit order book
a collection of unfilled limit orders held by an ECN or exchange.

marketable limit order
a limit order that can be executed because the stock price has reached the limit price.

Nasdaq National Market (NNM)
Nasdaq stocks that have market caps of more than $75 million; includes about 4,400 stocks.

Nasdaq SmallCap Market
Nasdaq stocks, numbering about 1,800, which have a minimum market cap of $50 million; includes primarily emerging growth companies.

emerging growth company
a small-cap company in a relatively new high-growth industry.

Pink Sheet and Bulletin Board Stocks

Pink sheet stocks or bulletin board stocks are considered over-the-counter (OTC) securities, but they are not listed or traded on Nasdaq or any other exchange. They are traded through broker/dealers who use quotations from two competing services: the OTC Bulletin Board (OTCBB stocks) and the National Quotation Bureau (the pink sheet stocks). Pink sheet stocks got their name from the long pink sheets on which quotes were formerly printed. Today, both the pink sheet stocks and the bulletin board stocks are quoted electronically.

The confusion between OTC and Nasdaq stocks arises from the fact that over-the-counter securities existed long before Nasdaq came into being as a quotation and listing service (as mentioned previously). Confusion also comes from the fact that the OTCBB is regulated by the NASD, and the material at the OTCBB web site is copyrighted by the Nasdaq Stock Market. (Little wonder we're all confused.)

In the past, companies issuing OTC securities were not required to file financial statements with the Securities and Exchange Commission. But as of January 1999 all companies desiring to be "listed" on the OTCBB are required to meet certain eligibility standards, including SEC filings. By June 2000, all preexisting OTCBB companies will be required to have their filings up-to-date or be dropped from the OTCBB.

For more information, go to the OTCBB at www.otcbb.com and the National Quotation Bureau at www.nqb.com.

volume stock like Microsoft. The important thing to remember is that each market maker's goal is make a profit on each trade. It does this by pocketing the spread—the difference between the bid and the ask prices.

A market maker may be willing, for example, to buy Microsoft at $105^{1}/4$ and sell it at $105^{3}/8$. The $^{1}/8$ difference is a $125 profit on a 1,000-share trade. This doesn't sound like much, but multiply that by hundreds of thousands of shares a day and you'll see the kinds of profits at stake.

Who Are Nasdaq Market Makers?

Some of the best-known names on Wall Street are Nasdaq market makers: Goldman Sachs, Lehman Brothers, Merrill Lynch, Morgan Stanley, PaineWebber, and Salomon Smith Barney. A list of the top 35 appears in Appendix 3. A full list can be downloaded at the Nasdaq Trader web site (www.nasdaqtrader.com).

As a day trader of Nasdaq stocks, you are competing for those same profits.

Execution of a Nasdaq Trade. To see how an ordinary investor—one without direct access to the markets—trades a Nasdaq stock, let's role-play again. Let's say you just placed a market order with an online (Web-based) broker to buy 1,000 shares of Microsoft (MSFT). Here's how it will get filled:

✔ Let's say the best bid (buy quote) for MSFT is $107^1/_2$ and the best ask (offer to sell) is $107^3/_4$.

✔ Your broker (most likely) routes your order to a specific market maker that has agreed to pay the broker so many cents a share for the privilege of filling the order. This is called "payment for *order flow*," and it is a common practice among brokers.

✔ If the market maker doesn't have the shares in inventory, it can buy the shares at $107^1/_2$, the best bid, and then sell them to you at $107^3/_4$. The $1/_4$-point spread—$0.25 per share—goes in the market maker's pocket, minus the penny or so per share that is paid to the referring broker.

✔ Once the trade is completed, the market maker enters the trade into the quote system, where it appears on computers around the world as a buy.

 two-sided market
a market in which the firm making the market in a security is both buyer and seller and must maintain firm bid and ask prices. Nasdaq market makers and NYSE specialists both make a two-sided market in the stocks they handle.

 bid
the price at which a market maker, specialist, or ECN is willing to buy a stock.

 ask
the price at which a market maker, specialist, or ECN is willing to sell a stock. (Also called offer.)

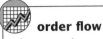

order flow
refers to orders directed by a broker to a market maker for execution. The market maker pays the broker X cents per share for this order flow because it can make a healthy profit on the spread. Electronic brokers do not (for the most part) sell order flow; most Web-based brokers do.

buy at the bid
the ability to buy stock at the inside bid price. Ordinary investors have to buy at the ask, which is higher than the bid.

✔ The market maker notifies your broker that the trade was executed, and your broker confirms the trade on your trading screen, via e-mail, or both.

Market makers, like NYSE specialists, make money on the spread. They can *buy at the bid* and *sell at the ask* (something the ordinary trader couldn't do until the advent of ECNs). The wider the spread, the greater the market maker's profit. In the old days—prior to 1987—market makers could negotiate prices with other market makers over the telephone. They were not required to give customers the best prices, and in fact often ignored customer orders to maintain artificially wide spreads. The NASD had rules against this, but the market makers were playing by their own rules.

Nasdaq Mini-Fact Sheet

Founded: 1971.

Location: Headquarters: Times Square, New York. The Nasdaq Data Center (main computers): Trumbull, Connecticut.

Chairman and chief executive officer: Frank G. Zarb.

Listed stocks: 6,200.

Nasdaq National Market (NNM): 4,400 stocks with capitalization of over $75 million.

Nasdaq SmallCap Market: 1,800 stocks with minimum market capitalization of $50 million.

Parent company: The National Association of Security Dealers (NASD).

Market makers: 500+ firms.

Order handling: SOES, SelectNet, and OptiMark.

Merger: The Nasdaq Stock Market merged with the American Stock Exchange in October 1998, but each continues to operate separately.

Source: www.nasdaq.com, www.nasdaqtrader.com, www.nasd.com.

THE CHANGING OF THE RULES

Rules of a game, like laws of a country, rarely change until they have been abused to the point that people rise up in outrage. That's what happened, essentially, after the market crashed with a 588-point drop on October 19, 1987.

In 1987 telecommunications was in its infancy. Fax machines had just begun to reach critical mass. Cell phones were still a novelty. The Internet was still a World Wide Web–less communications network for academics and government agencies. There was no such thing, in 1987, as direct access to the markets for the individual investor. Granted, Schwab and Fidelity had begun offering a primitive type of online investing through proprietary networks, but 1,200-baud modems and DOS-driven PCs made the process slow and clunky.

It was a world in which investors had no choice but to communicate with their brokers by phone. And on Black Monday, as it was called, investors were unable to sell their shares, which were tumbling like rocks down a mountain. The telephones rang and rang and rang in the brokers' offices. But the brokers refused to pick up.

In the wake of this debacle, the rules began to change.

✔ In 1987, the Securities and Exchange Commission (SEC) made its Small Order Execution System (SOES) mandatory, to protect small investors and prevent another debacle like Black Monday.

✔ In 1988, Nasdaq introduced the SelectNet system to facilitate electronic communications among market makers.

✔ In 1997, the Securities and Exchange Commission issued its revolutionary *SEC Order Handling Rules*, which forced Nasdaq market makers to display their best quotes to the public.

✔ In 1999, the Firm Quote Rule was adopted to prevent market makers from *backing away* from a quote.

Let's take a closer look at these changes.

sell at the ask
the ability to sell stock at the inside ask price. Ordinary investors have to sell at the bid, which is lower than the ask.

SEC Order Handling Rules
two rules that govern the handling and execution of limit orders (the Limit Order Display Rule) and the display of such orders on ECNs (the Quote Rule). These rules were effective in January 1997 and are responsible for the emergence of ECNs and the flourishing of the day trading industry.

backing away
a term used to indicate that a market maker is not honoring its displayed quote. As in: *PRUS is showing 107¹/₂, but he keeps backing away.*

 inside quote
the highest bid and lowest ask prices on a particular stock at any given time.

The Latest Rule Changes

In January 2000, the SEC approved Nasdaq's proposal to combine the functions of the SOES and SelectNet systems, and ultimately to replace both. The new system is called the Nasdaq National Market Execution System (NNMS) and is scheduled for implementation in mid-2000. For details see Chapter 2.

The SOES and SelectNet

Nasdaq's Small Order Execution System—SOES—had been introduced two years earlier, in 1985, as a way to streamline the execution of small trades at the *inside quote.* The intention was that orders of 1,000 shares or less were to be executed automatically, electronically, without negotiation between market makers who, as we've noted, had traditionally negotiated trades by phone. The market makers, for the most part, ignored the system because it was not mandatory, and when they ignored customers' phone calls on Black Monday, the SEC stepped in.

Although the Nasdaq is a self-regulating agency, the SEC has the authority to initiate and enforce such rules and regulations as may be required to protect the investing public. After the 1987 crash it became apparent that the public who invested in Nasdaq stocks needed a great deal of protection from Nasdaq market makers. So the SEC made the SOES mandatory. As a result, a market maker must now execute an order routed to it on the SOES, or risk disciplinary action from the SEC.[3]

SOES was the first crack in the market makers' armor. (In those days, a few ECNs existed but their quotes were not posted in the Nasdaq system.) SOES became the execution method of choice for the early day traders, who gained notoriety in the media as SOES bandits.[4] They could SOES a market maker—that is, route an order directly to a market maker who was at the inside quote—and the execution took place automatically and without negotiation. This enabled a wily SOES bandit to "steal the spread" from the market maker—buy at the bid and sell at the ask. (We'll cover the many rules governing the SOES in the next chapter.)

About the same time that SOES was made mandatory, SelectNet came into being. In January 1988 this electronic order routing system was introduced as a way to reduce the market makers' reliance on the telephone for negotiating trades. With SelectNet, they could negotiate trades electronically. SelectNet, which was used only for limit orders, was not mandatory, but it offered several advantages to the increasingly computerized Nasdaq market: It provided anonymity for larger orders and the opportunity to negotiate for more shares or improve the prices over those listed in the system.

Traders saw SelectNet as the market maker's way to continue to hide orders from the public, but almost a decade later it would become one of the day trader's primary order execution tools, as we shall see in the next chapter.

The Order Handling Rules

The next leveling of the Nasdaq playing field came in 1997, with the SEC again rapping the knuckles of the Nasdaq market makers.

Three years earlier, the Justice Department and the SEC had begun an investigation into 37 market making firms for manipulating the market over a six-year period from 1989 to 1994. Some of the biggest names on Wall Street were accused of conspiring to keep trading spreads artificially wide to increase their profits.[5]

The spread, remember, is the difference between the bid and the ask prices. One way a market maker could maintain an artificially wide spread was to *trade ahead* of a customer's limit order.

For example, assume the best bid for XYZ stock is $47^1/_4$, and the best ask, $47^1/_2$. If I want to buy 1,000 shares, I have to buy it at the ask—$47^1/_2$—the price at which the market maker will sell me the stock. But suppose I don't want to pay $47^1/_2$. Suppose I want to pay only $47^3/_8$. I can submit a limit order to buy 1,000 shares

trade ahead refers to a market maker ignoring a customer's order that is priced better than the inside quote and continuing to trade at the inferior quote.

at 47³/₈. So now the market maker is sitting there with my order to buy stock at 47³/₈. It *should* display that quote as its bid—because at this point, the market maker is acting as my agent. My quote would narrow the spread by ¹/₈ point—making it 47³/₈ bid, 47¹/₂ ask. But SOES didn't apply to limit orders, and market makers frequently would ignore such orders and continue to trade at the inferior price. That little trick was called "trading ahead of the customer."

The Ambiguity of Bid and Ask

These two little three-letter words—bid and ask—harbor a lot of ambiguity, because *each* has to do with both buying and selling. On the quote screen, the bid is the price at which a market maker or ECN will buy a stock—but it is the price at which you and I have to sell a stock. The ask is the price at which the market maker will sell a stock, but it is the price at which you and I have to buy the stock. If you still find this confusing, see "Deconstructing the Bid and the Ask" in Chapter 2.

Instinet
the oldest electronic communications network. Identified by the symbol INCA on the Level 2 quote screen.

Another trick that market makers used in the past was to place orders on private quote systems such as *Instinet*. Prior to 1997, the Instinet ECN was available only to professionals, who used it to offer quotes better than those being displayed to the investing public. In effect, professionals got one price for a stock; individual investors got another (worse) price. These practices sparked the 1994 class-action lawsuit against dozens of Wall Street firms, which led to the investigations by the Justice Department and the SEC.

Out of this unsavory chapter in Nasdaq's history came the SEC's Order Handling Rules:

    ✔ The *Limit Order Display Rule* states, in essence, that market makers must display the price and full size of customer limit orders that are superior to (meaning a higher bid or a lower ask) the inside market. This rule—also called the Limit Order Protection Rule—was intended to prevent market makers from trading ahead of customer orders.

✔ The *Quote Rule* states that market makers must display their most competitive quotes to the public (for orders of 100 shares or more). In other words, they can't display their best quotes on a private system (such as Instinet was at that time) that is not accessible by the public.

There was, however, an important exception to these rules. A market maker was not required to display a customer's superior quote under its own name or ID. Instead, the SEC allowed an exception, which stated that market makers could send customer limit orders to any NASD-sponsored electronic communications network (ECN) and not be in violation of the rules.

This exception to the SEC rules opened the gate through which several ECNs promptly marched, and Wall Street has never been the same.

THE NEW KIDS ON THE BLOCK

As a result of the exception to the SEC Order Handling Rules, the National Association of Security Dealers sanctioned nine ECNs and networked them into the Nasdaq quote system. Now, a market maker that doesn't want to display a quote under its own name can route it to an ECN and let the ECN display it.

The original purpose of ECNs was to facilitate Nasdaq's handling of limit orders, but ECNs have evolved into serious competitors of Nasdaq. Broker/dealers (and thus day traders) can now trade stocks directly through the ECNs (which match buy orders with sell orders and post nonmatching orders in their limit order books). As a re-

Limit Order Display Rule
one of the SEC Order Handling Rules, which states that if a market maker receives a limit order priced better than its current quote for that security, that limit order becomes the best bid or best ask and must be displayed on the Level 2 screen (with the size of the quote).

Quote Rule
a rule passed by the SEC in 1996 (effective January 1997) requiring Nasdaq market makers to display their most competitive quotes on a public quote system, such as Level 2.

sult, ECNs have siphoned off more than 30 percent of Nasdaq's trading volume and are expected to control more than half of that volume by 2001.

Inroads into the NYSE have been less dramatic because of NYSE trading rules, specifically Rule 390, which prohibited members from trading NYSE stocks off an exchange floor. Rather than matching NYSE buy and sell orders, the ECNs simply route all NYSE orders to the appropriate specialist at the exchange. As a result, less than 5 percent of the NYSE volume is routed through ECNs. That too is destined to change since the repeal of NYSE's Rule 390 in late 1999.

Whether or not the repeal was a direct result of the growing influence of ECNs, it is an example of how Wall Street is changing the way it does business. Another area of change is *extended-hours trading*.

extended-hours trading refers to trading before and after normal market hours. (Normal market hours are 9:30 A.M. to 4:00 P.M. Eastern Time.)

While Nasdaq and the NYSE pondered the matter, the ECNs acted. In early summer of 1999, they began, one by one, to extend their trading sessions past traditional market hours. By late summer they had announced an agreement to pool their limit order books during the extended sessions to increase liquidity. By year-end, extended-hours trading was firmly entrenched. Nasdaq and the NYSE are scheduled to join the after-hours party in mid-2000. (More on this in Chapter 3.)

Another area undergoing major changes is the structure of the exchanges and the ECNs. The NYSE is a private corporation owned by its member firms; Nasdaq is a subsidiary of the National Association of Security Dealers. Each is currently self-regulated, under the watchful eye of the SEC. Now both the NYSE and Nasdaq are making plans to go public, and, as mentioned earlier, the NYSE just announced that it will launch its own ECN in 2000. (It is called the NYSeDirect+ and will provide for automatic execution of orders of 1,099 shares or less.) To make things really interesting, three ECNs are also planning to go public and have filed for exchange status, partly to escape the regulatory arm of Nasdaq, whom they consider a competitor.

The whole area seems to be going through an identity crisis.

Meet the ECNs

All you really need to know about ECNs is how to use them to display and execute your order, which we'll talk about in the next chapter. But it helps to put a face, so to speak, on each of the ECNs.[6] Keep in mind that some may not survive the shakeout that has begun, or they may survive under different names or be joined by new super-ECNs. If you learn the original nine, however, you'll be able to track the changes as they occur. Table 1.1 summarizes the salient features of the ECNs.

You may also find the flowchart in Figure 1.1 helpful in sorting out the order routing systems (SOES, SelectNet, and SuperDot) from the ECNs. Each ECN is an independent entity, a corporation in most cases, while SOES and SelectNet are Nasdaq systems and SuperDot is an NYSE system.

Instinet (INCA). Instinet (www.instinet.com) is the original ECN, predating the display rule by almost 20 years. Instinet began in 1969 as a way for institutional investors to trade directly, privately, and anonymously with each other so that their large block trades would not unduly influence the markets. Bought by Reuters in 1987, it is affiliated with several online brokers including E*Trade. Instinet trades both listed and Nasdaq stocks, as well as global equities in over 40 countries, and it is open for business 24 hours a day.

Island (ISLD). Island (www.island.com) is the most ubiquitous of the ECNs, with virtually every trading platform offering an ISLD button for direct access. Its trading volume surpasses that of the original ECN, Instinet (Table 1.1), and in mid-1999 it filed for exchange status with the SEC. It is also rumored to be contemplating an IPO.

Island was the first ECN to publicly display its limit order book, which shows all its buy and sell limit orders on each stock (Figure 1.2). To see the real-time book, go to the Island web site during market hours and enter the security symbol for your favorite stock. Keep in mind that Island's book displays only the orders held by Island; it is not the

	1999 Trading Volume		
ECN	*(000,000)*	*Owners*	*Of Interest*
Island (ISLD) www.island.com	12,421	Datek, TD Waterhouse, Vulcan Ventures	Displays limit order book at web site; filed for stock exchange status; headed for IPO
Instinet (INCA) www.instinet. com	7,816	Reuters	Oldest ECN, since 1969; designed to allow institutional money managers to trade listed stocks directly with each other
REDIBook (REDI) www.redi.com	2,439	Spear, Leeds & Kellogg*, Fidelity Investments, Charles Schwab & Co., Donaldson, Lufkin & Jenrette	Trading software: REDIPlus, REDIPlus Online
TradeBook (BTRD) www. bloomberg.com/ products/trdbk. html	2,136	Bloomberg LP, Investment Technology Group	Primarily institutional; building superECN with ITG and others
Archipelago (ARCA) www.tradearca. com	1,975	E*Trade, Goldman Sachs, J. P. Morgan, Reuters' Instinet, American Century, Merrill Lynch, CNBC, Townsend Analytics	Merging with Pacific Exchange; headed for IPO; formerly known as Terra Nova (TNTO)
Brut (BRUT) (no web site)	BRUT: 1,586.0 STRK: 437.0	Bear Stearns, Bridge Trading Company, Goldman Sachs, Knight-Trimark, Lehman Brothers, Merrill Lynch, Morgan Stanley Dean Witter, Salomon Smith Barney	Brass Utility and Strike Technologies, two of the original nine ECNS, merged in February 2000 to become Brut.

TABLE 1.1 The Electronic Communication Networks (ECNs)

	1999 Trading Volume		
TABLE 1.1 (Continued)			
ECN	(000,000)	Owners	Of Interest
Attain (ATTN) www.attain.com	54	All-Tech Investment Group	Direct access with the Attain software
NexTrade (NTRD) www.nextrade1. com	34	Professional Investment Management, Inc.	Affiliated with GlobalNet Financial; founding member of MatchBookFX
MarketXT (MKXT) www.marketxt.com	.5	Tradescape.com, SOFTBANK, Morgan Stanly Dean Witter, Salomon Smith Barney	After-hours ECN
Optimark (OPTI) www.optimark. com	Not available	General Atlantic Partners, SOFTBANK, American Century, Goldman Sachs, Merrill Lynch, PaineWebber	Uses a flexible pricing mechanism

*One of the largest NYSE/AMEX specialist firms and a Nasdaq market maker.
Note: The nine ECNs are listed in order of trading volume obtained from www.nasdaq-trader.com. The MMID (market maker identifier), the symbol that identifies the ECN in the Nasdaq Level 2 quote montage, is shown in parentheses.
Source: ECN web sites and press releases; trading volume from www.nasdaqtrader.com.

Level 2 quote screen. Level 2 displays only the best bid and best ask from the Island book for a particular stock. This will become clearer after you read the next two chapters.

Online brokers Datek and TD Waterhouse, and Paul Allen's Vulcan Ventures are owners of Island. Island is headquartered in New York City.

Archipelago (ARCA). Archipelago (www.tradearca.com) is backed by some heavy hitters: Goldman Sachs, J. P. Morgan, Merrill Lynch, American Century, E*Trade, CNBC, and the Instinet ECN (which is owned by Reuters). This

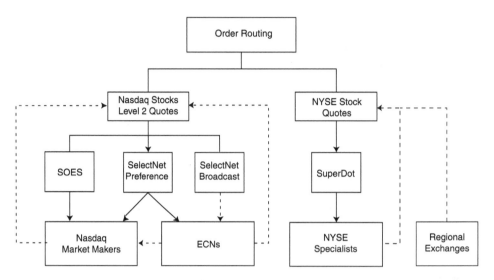

FIGURE 1.1 This flowchart shows the order flow to Nasdaq market makers and ECNs via SOES and SelectNet and to the NYSE via SuperDot. It also shows the flow of stock quotes into the Level 2 quote system. The new Nasdaq National Market Execution System will combine the SOES and SelectNet systems for Nasdaq National Market stocks.

lineup practically guarantees that ARCA will be one of the survivors in the upcoming ECN shoot-out—in one form or another.

This Chicago-based firm uses proprietary software to route orders internally or externally for the best price. Traders may access ARCA, via their brokers, using RealTick™ trading software. ARCA, by the way, was developed by Townsend Analytics (the developer of RealTick™); the ECN was formerly known as Terra Nova and identified as TNTO on the Level 2 screen.

ARCA recently announced plans to join with the Pacific Exchange to create a fully electronic, national stock exchange (subject to approval by the SEC). It also plans to go public, although a date has not yet been set.

REDIBook (REDI). The third largest ECN, REDIBook, is owned by Spear, Leeds & Kellogg, a leading specialist at the NYSE and a major Nasdaq market maker (SLKC on the Level 2 screen). Its trading platform REDIPlus is

refresh | island home | system stats | help

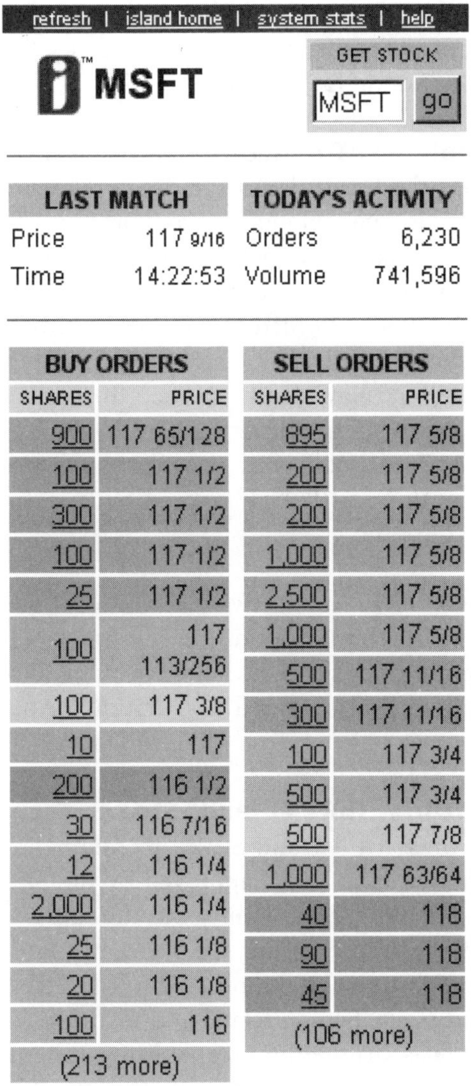

ⓘ™ MSFT

GET STOCK

MSFT go

LAST MATCH		TODAY'S ACTIVITY	
Price	117 9/16	Orders	6,230
Time	14:22:53	Volume	741,596

BUY ORDERS		SELL ORDERS	
SHARES	PRICE	SHARES	PRICE
900	117 65/128	895	117 5/8
100	117 1/2	200	117 5/8
300	117 1/2	200	117 5/8
100	117 1/2	1,000	117 5/8
25	117 1/2	2,500	117 5/8
100	117 113/256	1,000	117 5/8
100	117 3/8	500	117 11/16
10	117	300	117 11/16
200	116 1/2	100	117 3/4
30	116 7/16	500	117 3/4
12	116 1/4	500	117 7/8
2,000	116 1/4	1,000	117 63/64
25	116 1/8	40	118
20	116 1/8	90	118
100	116	45	118
(213 more)		(106 more)	

FIGURE 1.2 The Island limit order book can be viewed with real-time quotes at www.island.com.

aimed at professional traders while REDIPlus Online is designed for amateur traders. (See them both at www.redi.com.)

REDIBook may soon give Instinet and Island a run for their money. Owner Spear, Leeds & Kellogg is forming a new ECN (presumably to be the successor of REDIBook) with investors Fidelity Investments, Charles Schwab, and Donaldson, Lufkin & Jenrette.

TradeBook (BTRD). TradeBook is owned by Bloomberg LP and has the fourth largest trading volume of the nine original ECNs (www.bloomberg.com/products/trdbk.html). It is used primarily by institutional and professional investors who use the Bloomberg trading terminals. The Global TradeBook, formed in May 1999, provides access to 65 markets worldwide.

TradeBook may also be headed for superECN-dom. According to a press release in May 1999, Bloomberg is combining TradeBook with two alternative trading systems (QuantEX and POSIT) owned by Investment Technology Group, Inc.

Attain (ATTN). Attain (www.attain.com) is the ECN founded by Harvey Houtkin, the self-proclaimed "Father of Day Trading." It is accessed directly by the broker/dealer All-Tech Direct (also owned by Houtkin). Attain trading software is available through All-Tech Direct.

Brass Utility (BRUT) and Strike Technologies (STRK). Brass Utility and Strike Technologies were two of the original nine ECNs approved by the SEC in 1997. At the end of 1999, Brass Utility was the sixth largest ECN in trading volume; Strike, the seventh largest. Their merger in February 2000 moved Brut, the surviving ECN, up to third place, behind Island and Instinet.

Brut was originally an operating unit of SunGard Data Systems, Inc. Owners of the new Brut ECN include, among others, Bear Stearns, Bridge Trading Company, Goldman Sachs, Knight-Trimark Group, Lehman Brothers, Merrill Lynch, Morgan Stanley Dean Witter, and Salomon Smith Barney. There is no web site at present.

NexTrade (NTRD). NexTrade (www.nextrade1.com) is the smallest of the ECNs. It is a wholly owned subsidiary of Professional Investment Management, Inc. and a founding member of MatchBookFX (www.matchbookfx.com), an electronic matching system for spot foreign currency trading. NexTrade offers its own ProTrade trading software, which you can demo at its web site, and is affiliated with broker/dealer onlinetradinginc.com and GlobalNet Financial. NexTrade offers 24-hour access to the markets.

MarketXT (MKXT). Market XT (www.marketxt.com) is the most recently authorized ECN. Formerly an Alternative Trading System (ATS), it was the first to offer extended-hours trading in August 1999, and currently functions as an extended-hours ECN.

MarketXT was founded by two SEC enforcement lawyers and is managed by the former chief executive officer of Reuters' Instinet. The ECN is being acquired by TradeScape.com, which owns the TradeScape.com electronic brokerage described in Chapter 3. Investors in the new venture include SOFTBANK, Morgan Stanley Dean Witter, and Salomon Smith Barney.

OptiMark (OPTI). While not exactly an ECN, OptiMark is nevertheless integrated into the Level 2 quote system under the symbol OPTI. Designed for institutional investors, it is a market optimization system that matches buy and sell orders based on the intensity of the trader's desire to make the trade. For example, an investor who wants to sell, say, 100,000 shares of a stock priced at $90^{1/4}$ to $90^{3/8}$ can enter a range of prices and sizes. He or she may be willing to sell 20,000 shares at $90^{1/16}$ and price the rest in 20,000-share increments at, say, $90^{1/8}$, $90^{3/16}$, $90^{1/4}$, and $90^{5/16}$. OptiMark allows investors to structure an order this way without losing their anonymity.

Coinvented by Bill Lupien, past chairman and CEO of Instinet, OptiMark was launched in June 1999 on the Pacific Exchange and on Nasdaq in August 1999. Major shareholders include General Atlantic Partners, SOFTBANK, American Century, Goldman Sachs, Merrill Lynch, and PaineWebber.

To learn more about OptiMark, read the press releases at www.optimark.com.

As their ownership structure demonstrates, ECNs are firmly entrenched in the financial establishment. They are currently used strictly for limit orders, but that will change for the ones that become full-fledged exchanges. But for now, all you need to be concerned with is how to use them for the best trade execution.

COMING UP . . .

Now that we've surveyed the playing fields of the day trading game, let's take a look at the tools of the trade: specifically, the Level 2 quote montage and the rules for using SOES, SelectNet, SuperDot, and the ECNs.

Chapter

2

The Tools of the Trade

The most common tools of day traders—at least those who trade Nasdaq stocks—are the Level 2 quote montage, SOES, and SelectNet. But contrary to what you might have heard, these tools are not essential to all types of day trading. Some traders—especially those who trade listed stocks—use streaming, real-time *Level 1 quotes*. Others opt for a trading system that uses artificial intelligence to select the best order execution.

Your choice of tools will depend on your trading style and preferences, but if you want to trade Nasdaq stocks, you should have a passing acquaintance with Level 2 quotes, even if you opt not to use them. This section will introduce you to Level 2 quotes and order routing through SOES and SelectNet.

> **Level 1 quotes**
> stock quotes that reveal the best bid and best ask. Level 1 usually includes the last trade, the open, the high and low for the day, and the cumulative volume for the day.

THE MULTILEVEL NASDAQ QUOTES

In any given Nasdaq stock, there are as many bid and ask prices as there are market makers in the stock. The average stock has 11 market makers, with two or three times as many on a high-volume stock like Microsoft. Being able to see all the quotes from all market makers is what Level 2 is all about.

Nasdaq quotes are displayed on three different levels:

33

Level 3 quotes

available only to market makers, these quotes include Level 1 and Level 2 quotes and allow market makers to enter and change their quotes.

best bid

the highest price quoted among all competing market makers and ECNs for the purchase of a specific stock at a given time.

best ask

the lowest price quoted among all competing market makers and ECNs for the sale of a specific stock at a given time. (Also called best offer.) The best ask and best bid make up the inside market or inside quote.

Level 1: The best bid and best ask (inside quote) for the stock.

Level 2: All bid and ask quotes from all market makers in the stock. Includes Level 1.

Level 3: Available only to market makers. *Level 3 quotes* include Level 1 and Level 2 and allow market makers to enter and change their quotes.

Let's look closer at Levels 1 and 2.

Level 1 Quotes

A Level 1 quote is a "snapshot" of the trading in a stock at a particular moment in time. It consists of the *best bid* and *best ask*—the *inside market*. It may also include additional information such as size of the bid and ask, high and low for the day, the latest trade, and the cumulative volume for the day. The free quotes that are available on the Web are usually *delayed quotes*—they have been delayed 15 to 20 minutes by the exchanges.

Free real-time quotes are offered by many web sites, but the term *real-time quotes* can be confusing. Most web sites that advertise "free real-time quotes" offer one quote at a time, on demand—a *snap quote*. Enter the stock symbol and get a quote that is "real-time" as of that second. On a fast-moving stock, the quote can change a second later.

Day traders who use Level 1 quotes need real-time streaming quotes, which means the quotes are automatically updated—refreshed—when the inside bid or ask changes (they are also called continuous, updating, or self-updating quotes).

Subscriptions start at about $30 a month for nonrefreshing real-time quotes and $80 to $100 a month or more for streaming real-time quotes.

Figure 2.1 is a Level 1 quote screen from online broker A. B. Watley (www.abwatley.com).

Every broker formats its quotes differently with different pieces of data. The quote screen in Figure 2.1 shows the following:

QUOTE		As Of 1/25/00 11:48:39 AM	
Cmgi Inc.		**Industry:** Advertising	
Last	110 1/32	Change	- 19/32
Open	112	% Change	-0.54%
High	112 5/8	52 Week High	163 1/2
Low	106 3/4	52 Week Low	20 1/8
Volume	3,512,800	Bid	110
Earnings P/Share	1.31	Ask	110 1/16
Shares Outstanding	245.94M	Mkt Capitalization	27.21B
P/E Ratio	N/A	Exchange	NASDAQ

FIGURE 2.1 This Level 1 quote screen for CMGI is from online broker A. B. Watley. *Source:* Reprinted with permission of A. B. Watley, Inc., www.abwatley.com.

✔ "Last" is the price of the most recent trade. After market hours, this is the closing price of the day.

✔ "Open" is the price at which the stock opened for the day.

✔ "High" and "Low" are the highest and lowest prices of the trading day.

✔ "Volume" is the cumulative number of shares traded during the day.

✔ "Change" and "% Change" show the change from the previous day's closing price in points and percentage.

✔ "52 Week High" and "52 Week Low" are the highest and lowest prices the stock has reached in the past 52 weeks.

✔ "Bid" and "Ask" are the current highest bid (*inside bid*) and lowest ask (*inside ask*) prices.

✔ "Extras": A. B. Watley, like many online brokers, offers extras with its Level 1 quotes, such as *earnings per share (EPS)*, *outstanding shares*, *price-to-earnings (P/E) ratio*, *market capitalization* and the exchange on which the stock is listed. At top of the table it also tells you the industry group of the stock.

inside market
the highest bid and the lowest ask (offer) on a particular stock at any given time.

delayed quotes
quotes delayed by the stock exchanges, usually for 15 or 20 minutes.

real-time quotes
stock quotes that include the most current bid and ask and the most recent trade.

snap quote
a stock quote at a single point in time—a snapshot of a quote—as opposed to continuous or streaming quotes.

inside bid
the highest quote among all competing market makers and ECNs for the purchase of a particular stock. Also called best bid.

inside ask
the best or lowest quote among all competing market makers and ECNs for the sale of particular stock. Also called best ask or inside offer.

Level 1 quotes are sufficient for trading listed stocks, if they are real-time *streaming quotes*, but they don't tell the whole story, particularly on Nasdaq stocks. For that, you need Level 2 quotes.

Level 2 Quotes

If Level 1 is a snapshot of a quote, Level 2 is a live, unscripted motion picture of the second-by-second trading in a stock. The bid and ask prices of *all* market makers in the stock—and the best bid and best ask of all ECNs—are displayed, along with the number of shares offered at each price. In Figure 2.2, you can see a frozen moment in time on a Level 2 screen. To experience its true impact, though, you'll need to view a Level 2 screen during market hours (which you can do with one of the software demos discussed in Chapter 4). On a volatile stock, the screen will be in perpetual motion as trades are executed and market makers and ECNs refresh their bids or move from the bid to the ask or ask to the bid.

What do you see on a Level 2 screen? Different trading systems format the quotes differently, but the bid will always be on the left, the ask on the right.

✔ *Name.* On a Level 2 screen, the market maker or ECN is identified by a four-letter symbol called a *market maker identifier (MMID).* Many systems, such as the TORS system shown in Figure 2.2, incorporate the entire limit order book of the Island or Archipelago ECNs, as well as the best bid and ask of all ECNs. Island's best bid and ask are

---

MMID

A list of symbols for the top market makers appears in Appendix 3, along with symbols for the ECNs. To find the identity of a market maker not listed, check the symbol listing at www.nasdaqtrader.com.

CMGI INC _ □ ×

CMGI		110 3/16	↑ -7/16	400		11:46
High	112 5/8	Low	106 3/4	Acc. Vol.	3489100	
Bid ↓	110	Ask	110 1/16	Close	110 5/8	

Name	Bid	Size	#Best	Name	Ask	Size	#Best
HMQT	110	100	0	INCA	110 1/16	600	340
PERT	110	200	17	ISLAND	110 1/8	200	0
MASH	110	200	34	REDI	110 1/8	600	77
SBSH	110	100	3	ISLD	110 1/8	200	374
HRZG	110	100	26	ISLAND	110 5/32	64	0
ISLD	110	300	291	ISLAND	110 3/16	1800	0
ISLAND	110	243	0	HRZG	110 3/16	100	18
SLKC	109 7/8	100	46	BRUT	110 3/16	300	25
INCA	109 13/16	300	357	SHWD	110 1/4	500	9
ISLAND	109 3/4	700	0	ISLAND	110 1/4	600	0
ISLAND	109 5/8	20	0	ISLAND	110 5/16	200	0
ISLAND	109 1/2	20	0	ISLAND	110 3/8	800	0
PRUS	109 1/2	100	12	ISLAND	110 1/2	650	0
REDI	109 1/2	200	55	FACT	110 5/8	100	38
ISLAND	109 3/8	100	0	PRUS	110 5/8	100	2
BTRD	109 3/8	100	101	ISLAND	110 5/8	2100	0
ISLAND	109 5/16	300	0	SLKC	110 11/16	100	75
LEHM	109 1/8	100	0	MASH	110 7/8	100	22
BRUT	109 1/8	100	55	ISLAND	111	290	0

FIGURE 2.2 This Level 2 screen for CMGI shows the bids and asks from all market makers and ECNs who make a market in this stock. The inside quotes on the first line are included in the Level 1 quotes on the top panel. _Source:_ From Trend Trader's TORS system. Reprinted with permission of Trend Trader, LLC, www.trendtrader.com.

identified by ISLD, but other quotes (_outside quotes_) from the Island book are identified as IS-LAND. Archipelago's inside bid and ask are identified as ARCA and the rest of its quotes are identified as _ARCHIP_.

✔ _Bid column._ In the bid column, the price at which the market maker or ECN is willing to buy shares of a stock appears next to its MMID, along with the number of shares (size) being sought at that price. Notice that the bid prices go from highest

earnings per share (EPS) a company's net earnings divided by the number of outstanding shares.

outstanding shares
in a publicly held company, the number owned by the public, as opposed to shares in reserve but not issued.

price-to-earning (P/E) ratio
a company's current stock price divided by its earnings per share for the past 12 months.

market capitalization
a measure of the size of a company by multiplying the number of outstanding shares by the price per share; also called market cap.

(best bid) to lowest. (Use the scroll bar to see all the quotes.)

✔ *Ask column.* In the ask column, the ask is the price at which the market maker or ECN is offering to sell shares of this stock, along with the number of shares (size) being offered at that price. Notice that the ask prices go from lowest (best ask) to the highest.

✔ *#Best.* Some systems, like TORS, offer additional information. The #Best column shows the number of times a market maker or ECN has been at the inside bid or ask. This helps you find the *ax*—the dominant player in the stock. This is important in a particular Level 2 trading strategy called *shadowing the ax.* (See Chapter 5.)

✔ *Color coding.* There may be only one market maker or ECN at each price level, or there may be several. The Level 2 screen is color coded to distinguish the different price levels. Most execution systems allow you to choose the colors you want to display.

✔ *Highlighting.* Many systems allow you to highlight one market maker or ECN. For example, you may be interested in what Island (ISLD) or Instinet (INCA) is doing, or you may wish to highlight the market maker you've identified as the ax. The only purpose of the highlight option is to make it easier to follow the actions of a particular market maker or ECN.

Level 2 quotes show the depth of the market—the number of players who are willing to buy the stock and the number willing to sell the stock, and the prices they are bidding or asking. Thus, these quotes present a truer picture of demand and supply than Level 1 quotes reveal.

Level 2 and the NYSE. New York Stock Exchange stocks do not have Level 2 quotes because there is only one "market maker," the specialist, who controls the bid and the ask. However, there may be competing quotes

:: AMERICA ONLINE

AOL	62 5/8	↑	-2 1/8	100	M	13:57
High	65 15/16	Low	62 3/8	Acc. Vol.	14867500	
Bid	62 9/16	Ask	62 5/8	Close	64 3/4	

Exch	Bid	Size		Exch	Ask	Size
NYS	62 9/16	9000		CSE	62 5/8	100
BSE	62 9/16	300		NYS	62 5/8	10500
NAS	62 1/2	100		NAS	62 5/8	200
CIN	62 7/16	200		BSE	62 5/8	900
CSE	62 3/8	3300		CIN	62 3/4	100
PSE	62 3/8	3500		PSE	62 7/8	3000
PHS	62 5/16	100		PHS	63 1/16	100

FIGURE 2.3 This Level 2 screen shows multiple quotes for AOL, an NYSE-listed stock. The competing quotes are from the regional exchanges. *Source:* From Trend Trader's TORS system. Reprinted with permission of Trend Trader, LLC. www.trendtrader.com.

from regional exchanges, from the American Stock Exchange, and from Nasdaq. When you enter an NYSE stock symbol into a Level 2 system, you'll see a screen similar to the one in Figure 2.3, displaying quotes from all exchanges that trade the stock. But there is no NYSE equivalent of SelectNet that will let you trade directly with the regional exchanges. When you buy or sell an NYSE stock, your order is routed directly to the NYSE specialist via SuperDot.

 **streaming quotes**
quotes that automatically change on your screen when the actual bid or ask is changed by the market maker or specialist.

Deconstructing the Bid and the Ask

Bid and *ask* are the two most important terms in the day trader's vocabulary. They seem like simple terms, but they can be confusing. Why? Think about an auction. The owner of the item being auctioned is offering to sell it at a certain minimum price. This is the ask (asking price). When you bid on the item, you're offering to buy it. This is your bid.

Continued

market maker identifier (MMID)
the four-letter symbol that identifies a market maker or ECN on the Level 2 screen.

outside quote
any quote that is inferior to the inside or best quote; on bid prices, outside quotes are lower than the best bid; on ask prices, outside quotes are higher than the best ask.

ARCHIP
the symbol on the Level 2 quote screen that identifies outside quotes from the Archipelago limit order book.

That's simple enough. Bid equals the buying price; ask equals the selling price. In an auction where buyers and sellers rarely change roles, there is no confusion. But, when you switch back and forth between buyer and seller, as market makers and traders do, the terms become fuzzy.

Consider the bid-and-ask format for a stock quote. The bid is the price the market maker (or specialist) is willing to pay for the stock; the ask is the price at which the market maker is willing to sell the stock. The difference between the bid and the ask is called the spread, which, as discussed elsewhere, goes into the market maker's pocket as profit.

But if *you* want to sell a stock, can you sell it at the ask price? No. You have to sell it at the bid price. You're selling it to a market maker that is willing to buy it at its displayed bid. And vice versa: If you want to buy a stock, you'll pay the market maker's asking price—or offer, as it is frequently called. (Day traders have a way around this by broadcasting a quote through SelectNet, as described later in this chapter.)

The following may help you sort out the bids and the asks.

The Bid (Buy)	The Ask (Offer)
Price market makers will *pay* for a stock.	Price at which market makers will *sell* a stock.
Price at which an average trader *sells* a stock.	Price at which an average trader *buys* a stock.
Bid prices go from high (the best bid) to low.	Ask prices go from low (the best ask) to high.
Bid prices represent demand.	Ask prices represent supply.
Bids represent buyers.	Asks represent sellers.

Continued

ax
the dominant
market maker in
a specific stock.
(Also called the
hammer.)

**shadowing
the ax**
mimicking the
trades of the
dominant market
maker (the ax) on
a stock.

Sample	
Bid	**Ask**
$30^{1}/_{4}$	$30^{1}/_{2}$
$30^{1}/_{8}$	$30^{5}/_{8}$
30	$30^{3}/_{4}$
$29^{7}/_{8}$	$30^{7}/_{8}$
$29^{3}/_{4}$	31

Thinking of the quotes as supply and demand puts the situation in perspective. The bid prices on the left side of the Level 2 screen represent buyers; the ask prices on the right side represent sellers. Buyers represent demand; sellers represent supply. When demand exceeds supply—more bids (buyers) than asks (sellers) at the inside quote—the stock price should increase. And when supply exceeds demand—more asks (sellers) than bids (buyers) at the inside quote—the stock price should decrease.

Of course, it is not that simple. Market makers go to great lengths to disguise their true intentions. Nevertheless, it helps to know your bid from your ask.

INTERPRETING LEVEL 2

Interpreting Level 2 quotes is either an art or an act of futility, depending on who's doing the interpreting. A very simplistic interpretation of CMGI, Inc., in Figure 2.2 reveals more buyers than sellers at the inside quote—a bid price of $110 for a total of 1,243 shares versus an ask price of $110^{1}/_{16}$ for 600 shares. Based on supply and demand, the stock should head up.

But take a look at the next three price levels. On the bid side there are 1,100 shares at prices from $109^{7}/_{8}$ to $109^{3}/_{4}$, while sellers are offering 3,264 shares at prices from $110^{1}/_{8}$ to $110^{3}/_{16}$. In this view, supply outweighs demand.

As it turned out, CMGI did head up, closing the day at $112^{1}/_{2}$. But you can't rely on such a simple interpretation,

market impact cost (MIC)
the increased cost of acquiring a position due to the rise in the price of the stock that is directly related to the large size of the buyer's orders (usually an institution).

 gap
a situation that occurs when a stock price skips several price levels between one trade and the next. This usually happens with the release of good or bad news after the market closes and the stock will either gap up (on good news) and open higher than the previous day's close or gap down and open lower than the previous day's close. Intraday gaps can also occur.

because what you see on the Level 2 screen does not necessarily reflect an accurate picture of what is going on.

First of all, on an actively traded stock, the Level 2 screen changes with dizzying rapidity. It takes a quick eye and a lot of practice to be able to figure out what is really going on in the stock.

Second, the Level 2 screen doesn't reflect the activity of institutional traders. Their large block trades go on behind the scenes, and you can learn about them only after the trade is made. All executed trades, including block trades from institutional traders, are reported on the Time & Sales (or Print) screen (see Figures 4.1 and 4.2 in Chapter 4).

Third, market makers, like poker players, don't show their hands. They do not necessarily reveal all the shares they have for sale or that they're willing to buy at a particular price. A market maker may be sitting on a buy or sell order for 10,000 or 20,000 shares, but chooses to dribble out the shares 1,000 at a time to control the *market impact cost (MIC)*. Or they may try to convince inexperienced traders that demand or supply is greater or lesser that it appears by selling stock from their own accounts to start a run, so to speak, on a particular stock, at which time they will switch to the buy side and pick up the stock at bargain prices. (If you don't think this is possible, read about the games that were played almost a century ago in *Reminiscences of a Stock Operator.*[1])

Another game market makers play is to post a lower bid or higher offer than the stock's close (or last trade), in anticipation of reaction to good or bad news, rather than let the orders themselves dictate the market's reaction to the news. That's why you'll sometimes see a huge *gap* up or down with very quick *retracement*.

Such games run counter to the spirit, if not the letter, of Nasdaq's rules and regulations under which market makers operate. But market makers are consummate gamesmen, and they have very deep pockets with which to finance their games.

This is why many traders put very little credence in Level 2 quotes. As you'll see in Chapter 5, there are many different trading styles. Some use Level 2 and some don't.

Those that do rely heavily on the Time & Sales screen or on a tick-by-tick chart of the stock, or both.

    If you want to try to beat the market makers at their own games, check out the various Level 2 tutorials and seminars described in Chapter 11. The free online tutorials at MTrader.com (www.mtrader.com) and Pristine Day Trader (www.pristine.com) are good introductions. Meanwhile, I will show you how to use Level 2 and your trading software to execute a trade, whatever trading strategy you use. But first, let's talk about the kind of orders you'll be using as a day trader.

retracement
a technical pattern on a stock chart made when a stock falls in price and then recovers most or all of its loss. The recovery is the retracement.

UNDERSTANDING ORDERS

To accomplish the objective of a trade, you must use the proper order. A market order is appropriate in some situations, a limit order in others; and *stop orders* can be used in a variety of ways. It is important to understand the different types of orders and to know when to use what.

Market Orders versus Limit Orders

A market order is an order to buy or sell a stock at the current price being offered by the market. That does not mean the order will be *filled* at the price you see on your quote screen. Market orders are filled on a first-come, first-served basis, and if the stock price has dropped or risen by the time your order reaches the head of the queue, it will be filled at the current market price, whatever that is. Market orders ensure that your order will be filled but not the price at which it will be filled.

    A limit order is an order to buy or sell a stock at or better than a specified price. On a buy limit order, you may get the stock for less than the limit price, but you'll never pay more than the limit price. On a sell limit order, you may be able to sell the stock for more than the limit price but never would receive less than the limit price. The disadvantage of limit orders is that you may miss buying or selling the stock altogether in a fast-moving market. Limit orders are also filled first-come, first-served, and by the time your order is up for execution, the price

stop order
a market order that instructs your broker to sell a stock if it declines to a specified price. (Also called a stop loss order). A stop order will not protect you from a gap down, as the stock will be sold at the first available price, however far that may be below your stop price.

fill
order execution. As in: *I got a fill at 20¹/₂.*

stop limit order

a stop order that limits the price at which the stock will be sold. For example, if the stock gaps down below your stop price, the stock will not be sold. This gives you a chance to evaluate the conditions that caused the gap and give the stock a chance to recover from a temporary setback.

stop

the price at which you will sell a stock (if long) or buy a stock (if short) in order to cut your losses.

trailing stop

a stop that is moved in the direction of the trend to protect profits.

move may have exceeded your specified price. A limit order will prevent you from paying more (or selling a stock for less) than the specified price, but it doesn't guarantee that your order will be filled.

Nevertheless, remember the adage: Missed money is better than lost money. Limit orders can protect you in volatile situations, and the market will always present other opportunities.

Stop Orders

A stop order is used to limit losses and protect profits. It may be called a stop order, a stop loss order, or a *stop limit order*. On a long position, a stop order is an order to sell the stock at a specific price that is lower than the current market price. On a short position, a stop order is an order to buy the stock at a specific price that is higher than the current market price.

When you set the initial stop, the intention is to limit your losses. As the stock price increases (on a long position), the *stop* can be moved up to lock in your profits; this is a *trailing stop*. You can also use a trailing stop to protect your profits in a short position.

Here's the catch with stop orders. First, you shouldn't set them so tight that you'll be taken out of the stock prematurely. One of the games market makers play is to figure out the most logical positions for stops and then deliberately trigger the stops to take out the competition, after which the stock resumes its original path. You may want to consider a *mental stop* instead, which is simply a reminder to yourself to reevaluate the stock at a certain price level.

Second, you can't set a *hard stop* on Nasdaq stocks, as you can on NYSE stocks. Electronic brokers help you get around this by incorporating in their trading software stop orders that mimic hard stops, triggering a buy or sell order should the stop price be reached.

Buy Stop Order

The *buy stop order* is different from the stop orders just described. It is not really a stop order, but a unique type of limit order that is used to buy a stock after the stock has exhibited trading strength.

Ordinary buy limit orders, remember, instruct the broker to buy a stock at a specified price or better (i.e., lower). If a stock is trading at 20 and you don't want to pay more than 19, you'd use a limit order for 19; if you got filled at $18^3/4$, you'd be happy with the *price improvement*.

A buy stop order, however, tells the broker to buy a stock if and only if it reaches a specified price. For example, if a stock is trading at 20, you might enter a buy stop order for $20^1/2$ to make sure the stock has enough upward momentum to keep on moving. The buy stop keeps your order from being executed if the stock is too weak to reach that stated price.

Stop orders can be rather confusing, so be sure you understand the types of orders that your trading software offers.

Priority and Duration

Dozens of orders may reach a market maker or ECN at the same time, so the orders are filled on a first-come, first-served basis, based on price, time, and size:

- ✔ Price is the number one priority: The best (highest) bid or best (lowest) offer is first in line.
- ✔ Time is the second priority: On two orders of equal price, the order that arrives first gets filled first.
- ✔ Size is the third priority: In general, larger orders take precedence over smaller ones.

You may also want to specify how long your order remains open and the conditions for filling it.

- ✔ *Day order.* Unless you specify otherwise, your order will be a *day order*: If not filled, it will be canceled at the close of regular market hours.
- ✔ *GTC.* A *good till canceled* (*GTC*) order means the order will remain open until it is executed or canceled by you. Also called an open order.

 mental stop
a reminder to yourself to consider selling a stock (if long) or buying a stock (if short) if it reaches a predetermined price.

 hard stop
an instruction to a broker to sell a stock (if long) or buy a stock (if short) if and when the stock reaches a predetermined price.

 buy stop order
a type of limit order used to buy a stock after the stock has exhibited trading strength. The buy stop order instructs the broker to buy a stock if and only if it reaches a specified price—not at a better (lower) price.

price improvement
refers to making a trade at a price better than the quoted bid or ask.

day order
an order to buy or sell a security that expires at the end of the day.

good till canceled (GTC)
an instruction to leave an order open until it is canceled.

All or none (AON)
an instruction that specifies that the order must be filled in its entirety or none of it should be filled.

partial fill
an order that is not filled in its entirety.

✔ *AON.* An *all or none (AON)* order means no *partial fills.* Like the FOK, the order must be filled in its entirety; but it can be done at any time before the end of the trading day.

✔ *FOK.* A *fill or kill* (FOK) order is one that must be filled within a specified time in its entirety or it is canceled.

A WORD ABOUT SHORT SELLING

Short selling allows you to profit from a stock's downtrends as well as its uptrends. To *short a stock* is to sell a stock you don't own, in anticipation that the stock will decrease in price. In effect, you borrow the stock from your broker, sell it, then buy it back at some point to *cover* your position and return it to the broker from whom you borrowed it. Hopefully, you will buy it back for less than you sold it for and be able to pocket the difference.

There are several rules that govern short selling:

✔ Short sales can be made only in a margin account, not a cash account.

✔ Only stocks on your broker's short-sell list can be shorted. This is because the broker must either have the stock in inventory or be able to borrow the stock from another customer or broker before it can be shorted.

✔ Both SOES and SelectNet may be used for short sales, based on Nasdaq and NYSE short sale rules.

✔ On NYSE stocks, shorting can be done only on a plus *tick* or a *zero-plus tick.* A plus tick is an *uptick*—the last trade is higher than the one before. A zero-plus tick is when the last trade is the same as the previous trade, but that trade was higher than the one before.

✔ On Nasdaq stocks you may short a stock only on an uptick or a zero-plus tick. Specifically, a Nasdaq stock cannot be shorted at or below the in-

side best bid when that price is lower than the previous inside best bid. For example,

> If the current spread is $1/16$ point or greater, the short sale must be at least $1/16$ point above the current inside bid.

> If the current spread is less than $1/16$ point, the short sale must be equal to or greater than the current inside offer (ask).[2]

Short selling intimidates some traders who consider it is riskier than buying long, which it is. If you're wrong about a long position, the stock can only fall to zero; your potential loss is finite. If you're wrong about a short position, there is no limit on how high the stock may go; at some point you will have to buy it back at the market price to cover your position or cover your margin calls. The way to protect yourself in a short position is to set very tight stops.

EXECUTING A TRADE WITH LEVEL 2

To appreciate the difference between executing a trade with Level 2 quotes from an *electronic broker* and executing a trade with Level 1 quotes from a *Web-based broker*, take a look at these comparisons (we'll discuss brokers in more detail in Chapter 3):

Electronic Broker	**Web-based Broker**
Uses Windows-based trading software.	Uses browser-based entry screen.
Level 2 quotes are standard.	Level 1 quotes are standard.
Market orders are executed automatically via SOES at the best inside quote.	Market orders are (usually) routed to a market maker who pays the broker for the order flow, which can slow the execution and increase the cost.

fill or kill (FOK)
a type of order that instructs the broker to cancel the order unless it can be executed within a specified time.

shorting a stock
selling a stock you do not currently own (you borrow it from your broker) in the belief that the stock price will drop.

cover
to buy a stock in order to close out a short position.

tick
an incremental move in a stock price. There are upticks (plus ticks), downticks, and zero-plus ticks.

zero-plus tick

when a stock upticks on a trade and the following trade is executed at the same price level.

uptick

a quote that is higher than the preceding quote; a trade executed at a price that is higher than the preceding trade.

electronic broker

a brokerage firm that allows customers direct access to the markets through an ECN. Also referred to as a direct access broker.

Executions and confirmations are virtually instantaneous (within certain limits) and readily visible on your screen.

You can direct a limit order to specific ECNs and market makers with SelectNet.

There is a smaller risk of slippage in a fast market.

You can narrow the spread between the bid and ask.

Canceling an order is easier because of the instantaneous executions.

It can take up to a minute or more to find out if your order was filled and at what price.

There is no direct access to ECNs or market makers.

There is a greater risk of slippage in a fast market.

You can never narrow the spread; you must always buy at the ask and sell at the bid.

Canceling an order is difficult when confirmations can take up to a minute.

This is not to say every order will be executed instantaneously with an electronic broker. Delays can happen for a variety of reasons, but direct access through SOES and SelectNet gives day traders considerably more control over their trades.

SOES Executions

As you will recall, SOES stands for Small Order Execution System, a mechanism for executing Nasdaq orders instantaneously and automatically. To "SOES a market maker" is to send your order directly to a market maker at the inside quote. You do this by completing the order entry screen and clicking an SOES button on your trading system. The order goes directly to the market maker first in line at the inside quote.

Your broker will advise you of the numerous execution rules that govern the use of SOES, many of which are programmed into the trading system. Here are a few general rules.

Web-based broker

an online discount stock broker whose trading screens are accessed via its Web page on the Internet. Orders placed with Web-based brokers are generally routed by the broker to affiliated market makers for execution.

- ✔ You can use SOES only at the inside bid or ask.
- ✔ Either market orders or limit orders can be SOESed, but limit orders must be marketable, that is, priced at the inside quote.
- ✔ You cannot SOES an ECN.
- ✔ The size of SOES orders was previously governed by tier size, which was based on trading characteristics of the stock (200, 500, or 1,000 shares). The NNMS modifications will do away with tier sizes. The maximum order size for Nasdaq SmallCap stocks will remain 500 shares.
- ✔ SOES fees are $1 per transaction and $0.25 to cancel a SOES order. Either or both of these fees may be absorbed by the broker/dealer.
- ✔ After filling a SOES order, a market maker does not have to accept another SOES order for 17 seconds.
- ✔ A market maker is required to honor an SOES order only up to the tier size. Once filled, the market maker can remove its bid or offer at that

SOES and SelectNet to Be Modified by Nasdaq

The newly approved Nasdaq National Market Execution System (NNMS), which will establish a SuperSOES and a modified SelectNet system for trading Nasdaq National Market stocks, is scheduled to go into effect in June 2000. The current SOES and SelectNet rules (described in this chapter) will still apply to Nasdaq SmallCap stocks. See a recap of the new rules at the end of this chapter.

refresh
to restate a quote at the same price. Used when a market maker has filled an order at the bid or offer and remains willing to continue to buy or sell stock at the quoted price.

price. If it wishes to stay at that price, it must *refresh* the quote.

✔ SOES orders are executed on a first-come, first-served basis, which means that even though SOES is mandatory, your order may not necessarily be filled.

SelectNet Executions

SelectNet was designed to help market makers communicate with each other, but you can use it to beat the market makers at their own game or to beat the crowd when everyone is running for the bandwagon or the exit.

There are two ways to use SelectNet: (1) You may broadcast an order, which means routing it to an ECN that will display it on the Level 2 quote screen (if the order is at or better than the inside quote) or (2) you may route an order to a specific market maker or ECN at its advertised price, which is called preferencing. Before we go further with broadcasting or preferencing, let's look at a few SelectNet rules:

✔ SelectNet can be used with market makers or ECNs.

✔ Only limit orders can be routed via SelectNet.

✔ There is no limitation on size.

✔ There is no time restriction with regard to making a subsequent trade.

✔ SelectNet is not mandatory. The market maker or ECN has 27 seconds in which to fill or reject the order. And, it doesn't have to formally reject it but can simply wait out the 27 seconds.

✔ A market maker must fill the full size of a preferenced order or go to an inferior bid. (This is the result of the 1999 Firm Quote Rule described in Chapter 1.)

✔ A SelectNet order cannot be canceled for 10 seconds.

✔ SelectNet can be used during extended hours trading, as well as during regular market hours.

✔ SelectNet fees are currently $2.50 to broadcast an order, $1 to preference an order, and $0.25 to cancel an order.

Broadcasting a SelectNet Order. SelectNet can be used to broadcast a better-than-inside quote over the Nasdaq Level 2 screen. This means you can (1) step ahead of a market maker and narrow the spread, and (2) buy at the bid or sell at the ask, rather than the other way around like the average Joe.

This was made possible by the SEC Order Handling Rules, which require a market maker to display its best quote (on the Level 2 screen), regardless of whether the quote is a client order or its own proprietary quote. As mentioned earlier, market makers are allowed to pass such quotes on to an ECN, and the ECN must display its best quotes. If you, the trader, send a better-than-inside quote to the ECN, it is required to display that quote as its best bid or ask.

Let's look at how this would work. Say Microsoft is trading at an inside quote of $107^{1}/_{4}$ to $107^{1}/_{2}$. You can send a buy limit order with a price of, say, $107^{3}/_{8}$ directly to Island. Because your price is better (higher) than the bid of $107^{1}/_{4}$, Island must display the bid (per the SEC Order Handling Rules).

Your bid will appear on the Level 2 quote screen under the ISLD symbol. The inside quote then becomes $107^{3}/_{8}$ to $107^{1}/_{2}$. In one fell swoop you've accomplished three things: You've (1) donned the role of market maker by (2) narrowing the spread by $^{1}/_{8}$ point, which allows you to (3) buy at the bid, rather than at the ask.

Broadcasting a better-than-inside quote through an ECN is one of the ways traders "scalp teenies" from the market makers, but it's not quite as cut-and-dried as it might appear. There are thousands of day traders and market makers trying to do exactly the same thing, and with a fast, volatile stock, scalping small profits becomes increasingly difficult.

ECN Hot Buttons

If your trading platform has a hot button for a specific ECN, you don't have to use SelectNet to broadcast or preference an order. Just send the order directly to the ECN. If the price is superior to the inside market, the ECN is required to broadcast the order (post it on Level 2). Otherwise, it will match the order, if possible, with a corresponding buy or sell order, or add the order to its limit order book.

Preferencing through SelectNet. You can also use SelectNet to direct an order to a specific market maker or ECN in order to buy or sell shares at its advertised price. This practice is called preferencing. It's like tapping a market maker on the shoulder and saying, "You wanna sell Microsoft for 107, I wanna buy Microsoft for 107." (Or vice versa.)

Preferencing can be used to buy or sell a stock at any of the prices quoted on the Level 2 screen. For example, if there are half a dozen market makers at the inside bid, you may want to preference the fifth or sixth listed market maker, rather than SOESing it. Why? For any of the reasons listed in the SelectNet rules, such as the size of the order or the ability to immediately make another trade on the same side.

Another use of preferencing is to buy or sell a stock at the *outside market*. For example, if you want to make sure you get in on a fast-moving stock, you might be willing to pay more for it. If so, then you could preference a market maker that is asking a quarter or half a point more than the best ask. On the other hand, if a stock is tanking and you want to get out as quickly and painlessly as possible, you can preference a market maker at a price lower than the inside bid.

In either case, using SelectNet to buy or sell quickly at the outside market beats queuing up behind a thousand SOESed market orders. Why? Because a fast-moving stock could rise or fall several points by the time your market

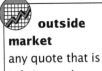
outside market
any quote that is inferior to the inside or best quote. Traders may make a trade at the outside market in order to get into or out of a fast-moving stock.

Smart Keys

If routing an order through SOES or SelectNet sounds too complicated, take heart. Many trading systems use artificial intelligence to seek the best possible execution among market makers, exchanges, and ECNs. All the user has to do is click a so-called smart key—one for limit orders and one for market orders—and the system will do the rest. You'll still get direct and virtually instantaneous executions but with less hassle.

---

order gets to the head of the SOES line, and you could end up losing more (or paying more) than the $1/4$ or $1/2$ point you paid to preference at the outside market.

ECN Rules

As mentioned earlier, ECNs are networked into the Nasdaq quote system. Their sole function is to facilitate Nasdaq's handling of limit orders.

These ECN orders come from three sources: (1) from market makers who don't want to display a customer's order under their own IDs, (2) from affiliated broker/dealers, and (3) indirectly from day traders using SelectNet or ECN hot buttons on their trading systems. Here are a few general ECN order execution rules:

✔ When an ECN receives an order, it attempts to match a buy order with a corresponding sell order within its system, or a sell order with a corresponding buy order.

✔ Orders that can't be matched are listed in the ECN's limit order book. These books are private, although Island, ARCA, and MarketXT display their limit order book at their web sites.

✔ The best bid and best ask within each ECN are displayed in the Nasdaq Level 2 quote montage under the ECN's symbol. The rest of the ECN's quotes are maintained in the ECN's limit order book.

✔ ECNs aggregate orders by price. Thus, the size displayed for an ECN quote on the Nasdaq quote screen (or on the ECN's limit order book) may represent several orders. For example, a bid for 2,000 shares of Microsoft at 107$\frac{1}{2}$ may represent a 1,000-share order from one customer and two 500-share orders from two other customers.

✔ Some ECNs will reject orders that create a *crossed market* or a *locked market*, in adherence to Nasdaq's requirement that they take "reasonable steps" to avoid crossing or locking the market.

✔ ECNs currently charge fees of a penny or more per share, although many brokers absorb all or part of the ECN fees.

The question now becomes: How do you put it all together? How do you send an order to an ECN? How do you SOES or preference a market maker? We'll talk about that in Chapter 4 when we examine an order execution system close up.

crossed market
a situation in which the best bid is above the best ask.

locked market
a situation that occurs when the best bid is the same price as the best ask.

Crossing or Locking the Market

The terms "crossing the market" and "locking the market" are important to understand, if you use SelectNet for routing an order. In a normal market, the best bid is lower than the best ask. In a locked market, the best bid is the same price as the best ask. In a crossed market, the best bid is higher than the best ask. Here are examples of a normal, a locked, and a crossed market for Microsoft:

	Bid	Ask
Normal market	107$\frac{1}{2}$	107$\frac{5}{8}$
Locked market	107$\frac{1}{2}$	107$\frac{1}{2}$
Crossed market	107$\frac{1}{2}$	107$\frac{3}{8}$

NEW RULES FOR
SUPERSOES AND SELECTNET

During the final editing of this book, Nasdaq announced SEC approval of its proposal to implement a new Nasdaq National Market Execution System (NNMS) that entails modifications of the SOES and SelectNet systems. The purpose of the changes is to eliminate potential dual liability for market makers, which can happen when simultaneous orders reach a market maker through different systems. The NNMS is scheduled for implementation in June 2000, although it has been postponed several times and could be postponed again.

Nasdaq Trader (www.nasdaqtrader.com) has a webcast presentation that provides an overview of the changes. Here is a recap:

✔ The modifications will apply only to Nasdaq National Market stocks. Previous SOES and SelectNet rules will continue to apply to Nasdaq SmallCap stocks.

✔ Modifications to SOES—nicknamed SuperSOES— include:

> Increasing maximum order size for auto-execution to 9,900 shares.

> Reducing current 17-second delay between executions against the same market maker to 5 seconds.

> Allowing market makers to use SuperSOES for proprietary (their own accounts) and agency (customer) orders. (See "More Nasdaq Changes on the Way?" at the end of this chapter.)

> Enabling SuperSOES orders to interact with a market maker's reserve size, after taking out other displayed quotations at the same price.

> Eliminating SOES *preferencing*. (Previously, you could direct an SOES order to a specific market maker.)

✔ The major modification to SelectNet is the implementation of the "oversized order requirement."

preferencing
directing an order to a specific market maker or ECN.

This states that the order must be designated as either all or none (AON) or minimum acceptable quantity (MAQ) and be at least 100 shares greater than the displayed quote of the market maker to which it is directed. In addition, SelectNet orders will not be subject to the Firm Quote Rule, which means that market makers don't have to execute them.

The Effect on ECNs

An ECN will have two options in the short run with regard to these changes. (1) It may opt to be an order-entry ECN, in which case it will continue to participate in Nasdaq much as it does now, or (2) it may become a full-participation ECN, in which case it would be subject to all the Super-SOES rules and SelectNet modifications. In the long run, Nasdaq may require the full participation of ECNs in the NNMS and do away with the dual system.

The current SOES and SelectNet rules outlined in this chapter will still be applicable to Nasdaq SmallCap stocks. If the SEC approves the agency quote rule described in "More Nasdaq Changes on the Way?" additional changes will be required.

direct access broker a broker that allows customers direct access to the market through an ECN, as opposed to brokers who sell order flow to market makers. Also referred to as an *electronic broker*.

You can count on your *direct access broker* to have the most up-to-date rules and regulations at the time you open an account. You can also read the rules for yourself at www.nasdaqtrader.com.

MORE NASDAQ CHANGES ON THE WAY?

Nasdaq has proposed that market makers be allowed to display two sets of quotes—one for the market maker's own account and one on behalf of its customers. If the market maker is buying or selling shares for its own account, it will display the quote under its own MMID, just as it does now. But if it is buying or selling stock on behalf of a customer, it can display the quote under a special MMID and charge access fees, just as ECNs do.

One broker/dealer called this agency quote proposal

"an ECN killer" and a return to "an environment much like that which existed before the Order Handling Rules."

The proposed rules must be approved by the SEC, and it is unclear whether the new NNMS will preclude the proposed agency quote rule. For an update on the status of this rule, go to Trader News at Nasdaq Trader (www.nasdaqtrader.com). Notices will be published under Head Trader Alerts or Notices to Members. To view the proposed rule and comment letters, go to www.sec.gov and select Current SEC Rulemaking, then SRO Rulemaking. The proposal numbers are:

- ✔ Agency quote proposal: file no. SR-NASD-99-09 (file name nd9909n.htm).
- ✔ Agency fee amendment: file no. SR-NASD-99-16 (file name nd9916n.htm).

COMING UP . . .

Level 2 quotes, SOES, SelectNet, and ECNs can be used to route your order directly to the markets. But to use them, you'll need two additional tools: an electronic broker and a direct access trading platform. Let's look at the brokers first.

Electronic Brokers: Cutting Out the Middleman

O ne of your most important decisions as a day trader is which brokerage firm to use. You may be familiar with Web-based brokers like Datek, E*Trade, Schwab, or Fidelity, all of which have traditionally catered to online investors and the less active traders. But there is a new breed of electronic brokers that offer direct access to the markets.

The first thing you need to know about electronic brokers is that you can't access them through your Web browser. They use Windows-based trading software that integrates Level 2 quotes, order execution, charting tools, and a wide assortment of account management tools. Most electronic brokers have proprietary software which you must use if you trade at that firm. In other words, you can't use CyBerCorp.com's software to trade stocks through Trend Trader, just as you can't use E*Trade's Web-based order entry screen to place a trade through Datek.

Choosing an electronic broker, then, presents a chicken or egg problem. Which do you choose first? If you like a particular system, you'll have to go with a broker that offers it. If you want a particular broker, you'll have to use the software supplied by the broker.

In this chapter, we'll look at the brokers—both Web-based and electronic—and in the next chapter, we'll examine the trading software.

WEB-BASED VERSUS ELECTRONIC BROKERS

Traditional Web brokers have been around since early 1995 when the Internet first edged its way into the national consciousness. (Only on Internet time could "traditional" refer to five-year-old firms!) Among the first brokers to establish a presence on the Web were Ameritrade and the former Lombard Securities (later reincarnated as Discover Brokerage and recently as Morgan Stanley Dean Witter). These pioneers began a price war that slashed commissions to single digits and lured more than six million investors online.

With a click of a mouse, investors could buy and sell stocks *directly*, without the hassle of a middleman. Trading stocks was now so easy, so quick, and so cheap that the national media found a new pastime in worrying about the addictive powers of online investing.

What most investors don't realize is that they aren't really connected to the markets at all when they make a trade over the Internet. Their point-and-click orders are basically glorified e-mails that replace the phone calls they used to make to their brokers. And in most cases, the brokerage firm doesn't fill the order at all. It hands it off to a market maker firm, which has agreed to pay the broker a few cents a share for the privilege of filling its orders.

This practice is called payment for order flow, and it is the reason online brokers can offer dirt-cheap commissions—because they are, in effect, receiving paybacks from market makers. Although some brokers such as Schwab and Fidelity own their own market maker firms and can route their orders in-house, it is basically the same. (We're talking about Nasdaq stocks; all NYSE orders go through the NYSE specialist.)

slippage
the difference in the price of the stock that appears on a quote screen at the time you place a trade and the price at which your order is filled. The greatest slippage occurs with non–direct access brokers.

The practice of selling order flow is controversial, although not illegal. Arthur Levitt, chairman of the SEC, has questioned the practice, saying that it presents a conflict of interest between brokers and their customers. Indeed, it can cost you money in terms of *slippage* in a fast market, because of the time it takes to route the order to the middleman. And, it can result in a trade at an inferior price because the market maker is more concerned with pocketing the spread than getting the customer the best price.

By contrast, electronic brokers connect the trader directly to the market. There is no middleman, no payment for order flow, and much less chance of slippage. This direct access requires that customers use Windows-based proprietary software to execute their trades. The software is supplied free of charge, but you'll pay $100 to $300 a month for real-time data, plus a commission of $15 to $30 for each trade. The good news is that data fees and commissions usually are reduced on a sliding scale for active traders.

Electronic brokers differ in other ways, as well. They have stiffer requirements than Web-based brokers for opening an account. Web brokers require from zero to $5,000 to open an account, while electronic brokers require from $2,500 to $75,000, depending on the level of trading activity. Some brokers also insist on proof of a certain level of experience, income, and net worth. Because of the high-risk nature of day trading, the reasoning goes, there is a need for greater experience and understanding of the markets, and they want to be sure you aren't mortgaging your house for day trading capital.

Many electronic brokers offer on-site trading—these are the day trading shops you may have heard about—and most have training classes and seminars (some free, some not) to teach traders about Level 2 quotes, trading strategies, and the trading software.

Based on these differences, it would appear that Web brokers and electronic brokers are targeting very different groups, but some of their differences are beginning to blur.

Can a Day Trader Find Happiness with a Traditional Web Broker?

Like so much in day trading, the answer to this question depends on your trading style. Scalpers absolutely cannot use a Web broker. They need the instantaneous direct access to the markets offered by electronic brokers. If you're a swing trader or a position trader, however, the answer is maybe.

The important things to look for are fast executions and real-time streaming Level 1 quotes. If you can find those, a Web broker may be the way to go. The advantages are:

✔ Low initial account requirements—from zero to $5,000.

✔ Simple browser-based trading screens. Enter the number of shares, the type of order, and the stock price (for limit orders); indicate whether it is a Buy or Sell, and then click the Submit Order button. Voilà! You've made a trade.

✔ Low commissions. Commissions range from $5 to $30.

The leading discount brokers, by market share, are Charles Schwab, E*Trade, TD Waterhouse, Datek, Fidelity, Ameritrade, DLJdirect, Quick & Reilly, Morgan Stanley Dean Witter, and SureTrade. For a comparison of commissions and account requirements, and links to their web sites, go to www.cyberinvest.com.

THE BLURRING OF THE LINES

Brokers on both sides of the Web have started designing programs to attract each other's core investors. Some electronic brokers are offering simpler systems and lower sign-on requirements for the low-end trader, while Web brokers are giving special considerations to active traders.

Consider the changes in the Web brokers.

In mid-1999 E*Trade (www.etrade.com) launched its Power E*Trade, a browser-based product that gives commission rebates to active traders (bringing rates down to $4.95 a trade). But trades are still made over the Internet and E*Trade still sells its order flow.

Another browser-based product aimed at active investors is Fidelity's PowerStreet Pro (www.fidelity.com). (Fidelity defines an active investor as one who makes at least 36 trades a *year*.) PowerStreet investors get reduced commissions—$14.95 a trade, which is half the regular Fidelity commission—and Level 2 quotes. But neither Fidelity nor E*Trade offers the instantaneous executions of electronic brokers. The Web brokers that come the closest in this area are Datek and A. B. Watley.

Datek Online (www.datek.com) is a favorite of active traders because of its speedy executions (trades are commission-free if not executed within 60 seconds). It is the only Web broker to offer free *streaming* real-time quotes, and it has begun to rebate payment for order flow to its customers.

Still, no one has blurred the lines between Web broker and electronic broker as much as A. B. Watley (www.abwatley.com), which has one foot planted on the Web and the other fixed firmly in direct access territory. The Web-based Watley Trader (Figure 3.1) is designed for the ordinary online investor. It has simple, browser-based trading screens, Level 1 quotes, $9.95 commissions, and a $3,000 initial investment to open an account.

Schwab Goes Electronic

In one fell swoop, Charles Schwab & Co. (www.schwab.com), the largest online discount broker, erased the lines between Web broker and electronic broker. In February 2000, Schwab announced the purchase of the biggest electronic brokerage, CyBerCorp.com. No doubt this will be the first of many such mergers.

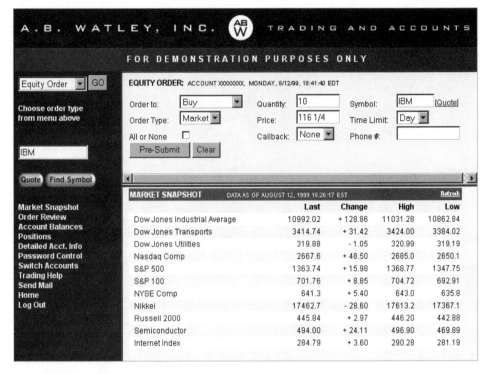

FIGURE 3.1 This Web-based order entry screen from Watley Trader is simple and easy to use. *Source:* Reprinted with permission of A. B. Watley, Inc., www.abwatley.com.

Watley's Ultimate Trader, on the other hand, is right up there with the most sophisticated direct access trading systems (see Figure 3.2). This Windows-based trading software comes with Level 2 quotes, direct access through SOES and SelectNet buttons, four levels of services and commissions, and a $20,000 minimum account requirement.

While Web brokers undergo makeovers to attract active investors, electronic brokers are going mainstream. Their commission structure has always been competitive with Web brokers—at the $15 to $30 per trade level—but now some electronic brokers are offering simpler, lower-cost software to attract less active traders and mainstream investors.

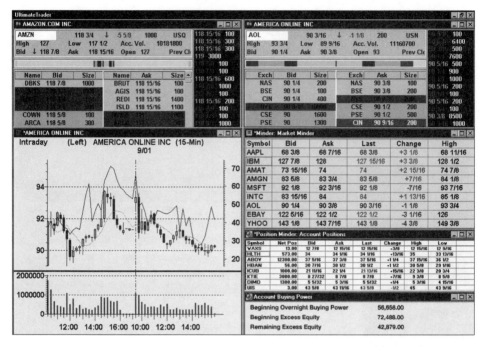

FIGURE 3.2 Watley's Ultimate Trader. Compare the Web-based Watley Trader screen in Figure 3.1 with this full-screen view of the Windows-based Ultimate Trader, both from A. B. Watley. *Source:* Reprinted with permission of A. B. Watley, Inc., www.abwatley.com.

These lower-end systems use streaming Level 1 quotes and simplified trading screens but still offer direct access to the markets with artificial intelligence that automatically selects the best possible price among all market makers, exchanges, and ECNs. The user doesn't have to know anything about Level 2 quotes or games that market makers play. They simply point and click, like the average online investor, but they get instantaneous executions, like day traders. (We'll take a closer look at two low-end systems in the next chapter.)

SELECTING AN ELECTRONIC BROKER

There are several ways to approach the selection of an electronic broker. The first consideration will be your trading style (discussed in Chapter 5). After you define your style, you'll know whether you'll be an active trader making a dozen trades a week or a hyperactive trader making dozens of trades a day. You will need to choose a broker (and trading software) to match your style.

There are many other things to consider. You may want a broker with a local office for on-site trading. You may want the one with the best training program—or the lowest account requirements, the lowest fees, the lowest commissions.

At the end of this chapter are profiles of 15 electronic brokers listing their major features. You may wish to use these profiles to narrow your choices to a short list and then check out the following areas before making your final selection. You'll also want to consider the software tips in the next chapter.

How Good Is Customer Support?

Customer support can make or break your relationship with a broker, so be sure to check this out thoroughly. What are the hours? Is there a toll-free number that you can use? Does it connect you to an actual human for help? If the broker offers an e-mail address for technical support, test it before you sign up to see how long it takes to get a response.

Do You Need a Backup Broker?

What happens when you're not at your computer and you want to make a trade? What happens if the Net is down? What happens if your Internet service provider (ISP) has "technical difficulties"?

Make sure you have an alternate way to place a trade at your primary broker, such as by touch-tone phone or through a live human. Ask if there is an extra charge for broker-assisted trades.

You might want to consider opening a second account at a different broker as a safeguard—or having a backup ISP. In high-traffic periods, it is possible you might not be able to get through to your broker because of congestion at the ISP level. And ISPs do go down. It happened to me on a day that Nasdaq surged more than 100 points to a record high. My ISP, one of the largest national providers and a household name, was out of commission for half of the trading day. Without a backup ISP, I would have been locked out of one of the hottest markets of the year.

An alternate connection can save you a lot of frustration and money.

Can You Trade Both Nasdaq and Listed Stocks?

Most electronic brokers trade both Nasdaq and listed stocks, but be sure you know whether the broker you choose does so. If you've decided to specialize in one, you may not care about the other—at this time. But if you want to expand your horizons in the future, it would be nice to do so without switching software (or brokers).

What Is the ECN Access?

Find out which ECNs are affiliated with the broker, because these can be accessed directly from the trading software with a button or hot key. Otherwise, you have to use SelectNet to preference an ECN. Direct access is quicker (one mouse-click versus two or three) and cheaper (no SelectNet fees).

What Are the Account Requirements?

Check out the minimum to open an account *and* the minimum balance required to maintain the account. The latter is usually smaller, but if your balance dips below that minimum, your account may be closed to further trading unless you pony up the difference. Most trading systems will display a running balance of your available trading capital. You'll also want to know:

✔ If funds in your account earn interest. Some brokers offer an automatic sweep of idle funds into a money market account (which usually offers higher interest rates).

✔ If you can write checks on your account. Many brokers do not allow you to write checks on a trading account; you have to open a separate cash account for this purpose.

What Are the Margin Requirements?

A *margin* account expands your buying power by extending a line of credit based on the collateral in your account. (See "Trading on Margin" in this chapter.) There are two important things you need to know about a margin account: (1) the monthly margin interest charged (*margin rate*) and (2) any special margin requirements. For example, Internet stocks may have a higher maintenance requirement than other stocks because of their volatility.

 margin
the difference between the market value of securities in an account and the amount of money loaned by the broker against those securities.

Do You Understand the Fee Schedules?

Fees can be very complicated at an electronic broker, and they can dramatically change the effective commission rate. The biggest fees are those for the software and data feeds. These usually include exchange fees charged by Nasdaq for Level 2 quotes and by the NYSE. In general, these fees are reduced or waived for hyperactive traders (see next section).

 margin rate
the rate of interest charged for borrowing funds in a margin account.

Fees are also charged by each ECN and by Nasdaq for the use of SOES and SelectNet. Some brokers also charge for canceling an order. A broker may absorb all or part of these fees, so be sure to check out the fee schedule, which is usually posted on the broker's web site.

When Are Rebates Earned for Active Traders?

Active traders usually receive rebates on data fees and sometimes on commissions. The rebates are usually on a sliding scale, with higher rebates for the more active traders.

It is important to find out how long you have to wait for an earned reduction. Some brokers apply the lower

Exchange Fees

All exchanges charge monthly fees for the right to view real-time quotes, fees that will be passed along to you by your broker. In addition, there are fees for using SOES, SelectNet, and ECNs. The broker may absorb part or all of some fees and may add a surcharge to others. Check the fee schedule at the broker's web site. Here are some examples.

NYSE	$5.25/month
AMEX	$3.25/month
Nasdaq Level 1	$2/month
Nasdaq Level 2	$50/month
SelectNet—broadcast	$2.50/transaction
SelectNet—preference	$1/transaction
SOES	$1/transaction
Cancellation	$0.25 to $0.50/cancellation
ECNs	$0.002 to $0.015 a share

rates the minute they're earned. For example, if 100 trades is the cutoff point for a rebate and you make 100 trades by the 15th of the month, all the rest of your trades will be charged at the lower rate. But many brokers wait until the end of the month to calculate the rebate, and some even take another two weeks to apply it retroactively. In this case, you'll always be a month or several weeks behind.

Read the fine print or ask questions to see when the rebates are earned and will be applied. This matters only to hyperactive traders, but it can make a difference in your available trading capital. The rebate schedule is usually posted on the web site.

Does the Broker Sell Order Flow?

Electronic brokers do not sell order flow. Web brokers generally do. But there are some hybrids that appear to be a little of both. If the broker you choose doesn't have Windows-based trading software with direct access via SOES and SelectNet, it is reasonable to ask if the broker sells its order flow. Brokers are required by the SEC and the NASD to inform customers of payment for order flow practices.

Is Your Account Fully Insured?

Virtually every broker insures its accounts through the Securities Investor Protection Corporation (SIPC), an independent, government-sponsored corporation that insures brokerage accounts should the broker/dealer fail. The maximum SIPC insurance is $500,000 for cash and securities in your account, with a cash maximum of $100,000.

If your account exceeds these maximums, find out if the broker has additional insurance. Most brokers (or their clearinghouses) carry additional insurance to cover accounts up to $25 million or more.

Other Questions to Ask Your Broker

Here are other details to find out about your broker:

✔ *Does the broker offer remote or in-house trading, or both?* In-house trading is not important to remote traders, but remote trading may be important to in-house traders who may want to switch back and forth between a home office and a day trading shop.

✔ *What kind of training is available?* And where? If you want to attend a training class in person, you may want to select a broker near you or with a branch office in your city. Be sure to check out the cost of training.

✔ *Which stocks are on the broker's short-sell list?* You can short only the stocks that are on your broker's list (actually, they're on the clearing house's list). If you intend to short stocks, ask your broker for a list of stocks that can be shorted. Some are posted at the web site.

✔ *Is the broker a member of NASD?* All brokers should be. If it's not, don't go there.

✔ *Is the broker licensed in your state?* Many brokers are not licensed in all 50 states. Check the broker's online FAQ (frequently asked questions) for this info.

Answers to most of these questions can be found on the broker's web site. You may have to comb the site to find them, but two good places to look are the FAQ and the site index. If you can't find what you're looking for, call or e-mail the broker. The brokers want your business so they'll be more than happy to respond.

TRADING ON MARGIN

Almost without exception, day traders use margin accounts to expand their purchasing power. A margin account allows you to borrow up to 50 percent of the value of the securities in your account. For example, if you have $25,000 in cash or securities in a margin account, you can buy an additional $25,000 worth of stocks on margin. (With $50,000 worth of securities, the $25,000 margin loan will represent 50 percent of the value of all securities in your account.)

The type of securities in your account will affect the amount of available margin. Internet stocks, for example, have lower available margin at some brokers, and *penny stocks* are not marginable at all.

Once a margin account is established, the minimum maintenance rule comes into play, which means that your equity—the current market value of your holdings minus the loan—must equal at least 25 percent of the current market value of all your shares. (Brokers have some discretion in setting maintenance levels, as long as they're higher than 25 percent.) On a $50,000 account of which half is margin, your equity must not fall below $12,500, which is 25 percent of your total account. If it does, you'll receive the dreaded *margin call* to deposit cash or securities to bring your account up to the proper level.

 penny stocks
stocks that sell for less than five dollars a share; typically, bulletin board and pink sheet stocks.

 margin call
a demand to deposit cash or additional securities to bring a margin account back to the required level (usually 25 percent of total value of the account). Unlike a Fed call or day trading call, a margin call may be met by selling the securities in your account.

Then there is the *Fed call*. This occurs when you take more margin than you're allowed and exceed the 50 percent minimum initial requirement. For example, if you have $25,000 in your account and purchase securities worth $30,000, your equity represents only 45 percent of your total account ($25,000 divided by $55,000). There-fore, you'll get a Fed call for $2,500 to bring the equity up to the 50 percent initial minimum.

Another type of margin call peculiar to day trading is the *day trading call*, which occurs when you exceed the buying power in your account. *Buying power* is calculated as cash plus the marginable amount of securities in an ac-count. Most trading software has built-in safeguards to prevent you from exceeding your account requirements.

Day trading firms have found ways to extend mar-gins beyond these rules. Some brokers arrange loans to extend a customer's purchasing power beyond the cur-rent limits allowed for a margin account. This is very dangerous for the borrower. Trading with borrowed money—especially during the learning curve—can inten-sify the pressure and cause you to ignore good money management rules, which can be disastrous. Another common practice in some firms is overnight lending from trader to trader to cover margin calls, although the pro-posed margin rules may effectively eliminate this practice.

If it is used prudently, margin is great for expanding your buying power. Used carelessly, it can become a nightmare.

The New Margin Rules

In December 1999 the NASD and the New York Stock Exchange proposed new rules that will change margin lending requirements for "pattern day traders."[1] The changes include raising the minimum for margin ac-counts from $2,000 to $25,000, basing margin calls on the cost of all trades made during the day, and shortening the time period in which to meet margin calls from seven to five days.

In addition, the funds deposited to meet a margin call would not be available for withdrawal for two business

Fed call
in a margin ac-count, a demand by the broker to deposit cash or marginable secu-rities to bring the account up to the federally regu-lated margin requirements. A Fed call (or Reg call) occurs when the purchase of securities ex-ceeds the estab-lished margin.

day trading call
a demand to deposit additional cash or margin-able securities, made when pur-chases exceed buying power in a margin account.

buying power
the amount of money available for trading, which is any cash in the account plus the margin-able amount of any securities in the account.

days, which effectively puts a stop to the dangerous practice of overnight loans among traders to meet margin calls.

All this is supposedly to protect the day trader from himself or herself. Inexplicably, the proposal includes increasing the amount that day traders can borrow against their accounts. Margin is currently set at 2:1. With $25,000 worth of securities in your account, you can buy an additional $25,000 worth of securities. The proposed rules would set a 4:1 margin. That means with a $25,000 account you could buy an additional $75,000 worth of securities—putting the trader in an even more precarious position should the market take a hit.

The proposal is very controversial, but the stickiest issue is defining who will be subject to these rules. The proposal seeks to define a day trader as anyone who makes four or more day trades in an account within five business days. A day trade is defined in the proposal as the purchase and sale of the same security in the same day in a margin account. If the shoe fits, the wearer would be subject to the rules.

The SEC must approve the rules, so stay tuned.

EXTENDED-HOURS TRADING

For years, the markets have been open from 9:30 A.M. to 4:00 P.M. eastern time. Only institutional traders traded outside these hours, which they did quietly and anonymously over Instinet. All that has changed in the past year.

Extended-hours trading—which encompasses 60 to 90 minutes before the market opens and up to four hours after the market closes—began for individuals in the summer of 1999. Although Nasdaq and the NYSE both postponed after-hours trading until some time in 2000 (citing concern with possible Y2K problems), ECNs eagerly embraced after-hours trading. Now, most ECNs accept trades in preopening and after-hours trading (thus, the more comprehensive term, extended-hours trading).

Nasdaq and the NYSE have yet to jump in with both feet, however. Nasdaq reports after-hour trades and, in February, began disseminating inside market quotes from

4:00 to 6:30 P.M. eastern time. (Market makers can opt to open their quotations during after hours, or not, as they choose.) But neither the Nasdaq nor the NYSE has begun full-blown trading in pre- or post-market hours. After-hours trading was going to follow decimalization, but now that decimalization has been postponed until 2001, a date for the roll-out of after-hours trading has not been set.

The primary advantage to traders of extended-hours trading is being able to react to corporate news, which is often released after the market closes. Extended hours also allow one to trade on a part-time basis. The major disadvantage is the current lack of liquidity caused by the absence of Nasdaq and the NYSE. This can cause significant price discrepancies. Without liquidity, the difference between the bid and the ask will be "so wide you can drive a truck through it."[2] Which means you won't get the best price for your order.

In this illiquid and volatile environment, many professionals think they are going to eat the amateurs' lunch. Dr. Alexander Elder, author of *Trading for a Living*, put it rather cynically: "Trading is a fairly bloody business—minus the violence—in that it needs a constant influx of new losers. Extending trading hours will allow more losers to enter the game, which is great."[3] (And he doesn't mean great for amateur traders.) Another professional trader was even more blunt: "The individual investor is going to get slaughtered. . . . They are going to do things that are stupid."[4]

If you decide to trade in the preopening or post-close hours, here are some of the rules and considerations that currently govern extended hours trading. Be sure to read the rules for trading during extended-hours posted by your broker.

1. Only limit orders are accepted. (ECNs can't accept market orders.) But that's not all bad. In a low liquidity environment, limit orders protect you from having an order filled at an unacceptable price.

2. If not executed, an order placed during extended hours will be automatically canceled at the end of the session. Good till canceled or all or none orders are not accepted.

The Extended Hours Web Brokers

All electronic brokers offer extended-hours trading as a matter of course because they are affiliated with one or more ECNs, but Web brokers are scrambling to link up with an ECN. (Until Nasdaq extends its hours, traders can access only the ECNs with which their broker is affiliated.) As of April 2000, almost a dozen Web-based brokers were offering extended-hours trading, including Datek, E*Trade, DLJdirect, SiebertNet, Fidelity, Schwab, Dreyfus, Salomon Smith Barney, Mydiscountbroker, Morgan Stanley Dean Witter, A. B. Watley.

round lot
a *lot* refers to the number of shares in a single trade; a round lot is a trade of 100 shares or some multiple of 100.

odd lot
a trade of less than 100 shares.

3. Stop orders and short sales are not accepted.

4. Order size must be in *round lots* only, not *odd lots*.

5. Some ECNs limit the size of after-hour orders. MarketXT, for example, limits the size to 5,000 shares. This is to keep institutions from overwhelming the extended-hours market with large block trades.

6. At this time, a limited number of stocks are available for extended-hours trading. MarketXT offers 300 actively traded Nasdaq and NYSE stocks (the list is posted at www.marketxt.com. Island displays the top 20 most active stocks in extended-hours trading (www.island.com). Your broker may also post similar lists.

7. Some brokers allow a resting period of 30 minutes to an hour between the close of the regular market and the beginning of after-hours trading. This follows the SEC guidelines for extended-hours trading.

8. Brokers may add a surcharge to the commission schedule for orders placed during extended hours.

In 1999, extended-hours trading was a novelty. By the end of 2000, a 12-hour market day—8:00 A.M.

to 8:00 P.M.—will be the norm. The novelty then will be the 24-hour global market that is peeking over the horizon.

HOW TO OPEN A BROKERAGE ACCOUNT

Opening an account at an online broker is a breeze. Fill out the online application, print it, sign it, and mail it along with your check for the initial funding. You'll be notified in a few days that the account is open and you're ready to trade.

Opening a day trading account with an electronic broker can be a bit more complicated, particularly if you're planning on being a hyperactive trader. Some brokers have elaborate qualification procedures to make sure their clients know the risks of day trading and have the minimum levels of income, net worth, experience, and training. (We counted a total of 12 forms at one electronic broker that must be completed, signed, and mailed to the broker to open an account!)

There is a proposal before the SEC that would require brokers to engage in closer scrutiny of potential customers' trading ability and risk exposure. So it is likely that we'll see more, rather than less, elaborate account prequalification.

Here are some general guidelines, as they now stand, for opening a day trading account at an electronic brokerage firm:

1. Almost without exception, day trading accounts are margin accounts, rather than cash accounts. In a cash account, you must pay cash for the securities you purchase (within the three-day settlement period). In a margin account, you may purchase securities on credit up to the limit of your margin. If you plan to do short selling, you must have a margin account.

2. Many brokers offer two or three levels of service—for the active, intermediate, or hyperactive

Adobe Acrobat Reader

Many brokers require the Adobe Acrobat Reader for downloading and printing applications. The Reader is a free software program that allows you to view and print documents in a wysiwyg (what you see is what you get) format. The Reader is required for printing many other documents on the Web, so it's good to have it. You can download it free at any site where it is required for document viewing, or you can go directly to the Adobe web site at www.adobe.com.

trader. Before you open an account, you'll need to decide which type of trader you are in order to open the appropriate account and receive the proper software.

3. Make sure you meet the broker's minimum account requirements. These should be listed on the broker's web site.

4. Make sure your computer system meets the requirements to run the trading software.

5. Complete the account agreement, which usually includes a margin agreement. Be prepared to give very personal information, including your age, Social Security number, business address, and employer. For a margin account, which most day traders want, you'll also have to give income level, net worth, and bank or credit references, and you'll also be subject to a credit check.

   Note: Some brokers allow you to submit this agreement online and then contact the sales department to complete the application procedures; others require you to complete and sign all agreements and mail them in.

6. Complete and sign a short-sell agreement, if you intend to short stocks.

7. Sign the exchange agreements for the NYSE and Nasdaq acknowledging that you're not a professional. This enables you to receive real-time quotes at nonprofessional rates.

8. Complete and sign any "suitability" forms the broker might require, testifying that you meet its requirements. Some of these are more elaborate than others.

9. Mail the signed forms to the broker.

10. The broker will notify you by mail or e-mail when your account has been approved, at which time you'll need to fund it. You can mail a personal check, wire the funds from your bank, or transfer securities from another account.

    To wire funds, obtain the wiring instructions from the broker's web site.

    To transfer securities, complete the form provided by the broker.

11. Once the account has been funded, you'll receive the software link to download the trading platform (if you haven't already downloaded a demo) and a password. Download and install the software and trading manual.

12. Theoretically, you're now ready to trade, although some brokers require that you practice on the software (simulated trading) before trading for real.

Complaints about Your Broker?

To file a complaint about a broker—or to obtain information about a broker's background or history of complaints—go to www.nasdr.com. Or go to the Securities and Exchange Commission (www.sec.gov) and click Investor Assistance and Complaints, then Protect Your Money.

The paperwork to open an account can take a week or longer, and another couple of days to fund the account, if you deposit cash. If you're transferring securities from another brokerage, count on another week to transfer specific securities or more than two weeks to transfer an entire account. This time frame depends on the speed of the transferring broker.

BROKER PROFILES

Here are profiles of 15 electronic brokers. Check out the web site addresses for fee schedules, software demos, and online account applications. For more information on trading software, see Chapter 4. For an updated comparative chart of these electronic brokers, go to www.cyberinvest.com. Please note:

- ✔ All electronic brokers have access to all ECNs via SelectNet.
- ✔ All are members of NASD and SIPC.
- ✔ All trade Nasdaq, NYSE, and AMEX stocks, unless otherwise noted.
- ✔ All have extended-hours trading.
- ✔ Monthly fees do not include exchange fees.

A.B. Watley, Inc.

Location	New York, New York
Telephone	888-ABWATLEY
Web Address	www.abwatley.com
Minimum to Open Margin Account	$10,000 (low-end); $20,000 (high-end)
Min./Max. Commissions	$18.95–$23.95
Trading Software	Low-end: Ultimate Trader Free; high-end: Ultimate Trader Pro

Software/Data Fees	Low-end: free; high-end: $300—free with 50+ trades/month
On-Site Trading or Remote	Remote
Training	Simulated trading
Clearinghouse	Penson Financial Services
Other	Web-based services through WatleyTrader

All-Tech Direct, Inc.

Location	Montvale, New Hampshire
Telephone	888-328-8246
Web Address	www.attain.com
Minimum to Open Margin Account	$25,000 for Attain Pro; $10,000 for Attain Plus
Min./Max. Commissions	Nasdaq: $25; listed: $25 + $0.005 to $0.015/share
Trading Software	Low-end: Attain Plus; high-end: Attain Pro
Software/Data Fees	Low-end: free, with $10,000 account balance; high-end: $250/month—free with 100 trades/month
On-Site Trading or Remote	Both
Training	TrainToTrade.com (see Chapter 11)
Clearinghouse	Penson Financial Services
Other	Home of Harvey Houtkin, the "father of day trading"; owner of the Attain ECN

Broadway Trading

Location	New York, New York
Telephone	212-328-3555
Web Address	www.broadwaytrading.com

Minimum to Open Margin Account	$75,000
Min./Max. Commissions	$0.016 to $0.02/share
Trading Software	High-end: Watcher
Software/Data Fees	No charge
On-Site Trading or Remote	Both
Training	TradersEdge.net (see Chapter 11)
Clearinghouse	iClearing Corp.
Other	Home of Marc Friedfertig and George West; trader statistics posted on web site

CyBerCorp.com

Location	Austin, Texas
Telephone	888-76-CYBER
Web Address	www.cybercorp.com
Minimum to Open Margin Account	$10,000 + minimum income of $35,000 and net worth of $65,000 excluding farm and home, plus experience on a trading platform or a training program
Min./Max. Commissions	$14.95 for low-end; $14.95 to 19.95 for high-end (volume discounts)
Trading Software	Low-end: CyBerX; high-end: CyBerTrader
Software/Data Fees	Low-end: no fees; high-end: $99/month; includes Level 2 quotes; free with 50+ tickets/month
On-Site Trading or Remote	Both

Training Interactive tutorial on CD; user's manual; simulated trading; CyBerChat trading support; affiliated with Trading Places (Chapter 11)

Clearinghouse Penson Financial Services

Other Acquired by Charles Schwab & Co.

EdgeTrade.com

Location New York, New York

Telephone 888-440-EDGE

Web Address www.edgetrade.com

Minimum to Open Margin Account $30,000 ($50,000 to $100,000 recommended)

Min./Max. Commissions $0.02/share to $0.055/share, based on daily share volume

Trading Software High-end: The EdgeTrader (based on TradeCast)

Software/Data Fees $280/month; free with 150,000 shares/month

On-Site Trading or Remote Both

Training Free one-day software tutorial; three-week training seminar

Clearinghouse Southwest Securities, Inc.

Other Cool web site!

The Executioner

Location White Plains, New York (branch of Terra Nova Trading, LLC)

Telephone 877-453-8352

Web Address www.executioner.com

Minimum to Open Margin Account $10,000

Min./Max. Commissions	$18.95 to $22.50
Trading Software	Low-end: Executioner I; high-end: Executioner II (both based on RealTick™)
Software/Data Fees	Executioner I: $175/month—free with 25+ trades/month; Executioner II: $250/month—free with 50+ trades/month
On-Site Trading or Remote	Remote
Training	Live online training room; Pristine.com
Clearinghouse	Southwest Securities, Inc.
Other	Free demos; Spanish version

GRO Corporation

Location	Houston, Texas
Telephone	800-852-3862
Web Address	www.grotrader.com
Minimum to Open Margin Account	$25,000+; $15,000 to maintain; yearly income of at least $35,000 and net worth of at least $65,000 (exclusive of farm and home)
Min./Max. Commissions	$14.95 to $19.95 or $0.015/share to $0.02/share, whichever is greater
Trading Software	High-end: GROTrader Platinum (powered by CyBerTrader)
Software/Data Fees	$89/month—free with 40 round trips/month
On-Site Trading or Remote	Remote
Training	Affiliated with Online Trading Academy
Clearinghouse	Penson Financial Services
Other	Telescan's ProSearch Alerts

MB Trading

Location	El Segundo, California (branch of Terra Nova Trading, LLC)
Telephone	888-790-4800
Web Address	www.mbtrading.com
Minimum to Open Margin Account	$5,000; $2,000 to maintain
Min./Max. Commissions	$14.95 to $22.95 ($5 promotional rate for first 60 days)
Trading Software	Low-end: MBLite; intermediate: MBCustom; high-end: MBTrader (based on RealTick™)
Software/Data Fees	Low-end: $115/month—free with 20 trades/month; intermediate: $200/month—free with 20 trades/month; high-end: $300/month—free with 50 trades/month
On-Site Trading or Remote	Remote
Training	Order routing and software tutorials; RealTick™ software manual; live Internet Relay Chat (IRC) support chat room; technical support staff
Clearinghouse	Southwest Securities, Inc.
Other	Full access to ARCA and Island limit order books; no additional fee for broker-assisted orders; market scanning software—$30/month; free after 30 trades/month

On-Site Trading

Location	Great Neck, New York
Telephone	888-402-0533 or 516-482-9292 ext.190

Web Address	www.onsitetrading.com
Minimum to Open Margin Account	$25,000 + minimum income of $50,000 and net worth of $150,000
Min./Max. Commissions	Nasdaq: $15.95 to $19.95; listed: $10.95 to $14.95 + $0.01/share
Trading Software	The On-Site Trader (based on REDIPlus)
Software/Data Fees	$100/month—free after 40 trades/month; also interfaces to AT Financial, Data Broadcasting Corp.'s eSignal, Trak Data, DTN.IQ
On-Site Trading or Remote	Both
Training	One-on-one in New York, by phone, or over the Internet
Clearinghouse	Spear, Leeds & Kellogg
Other	Free Jag Notes, Wall Street Source, Dow Jones, and xcaliburtrading.com (real-time stock and market analysis)

PreferredTrade.com

Location	San Francisco, California
Telephone	888-889-9178
Web Address	www.preferredtrade.com
Minimum to Open Margin Account	$5,000
Min./Max. Commissions	Nasdaq stocks: $0.02/share up to 2,000 shares (minimum $15) or $7.75/trade (if routed to a specific broker/dealer); listed stocks, up to 2,000 shares: market orders, $0.02/share; limit orders, $0.03/share (minimum $15).

Trading Software	Low-end: PreferredTrade System
Software/Data Fees	No software fees; data must be ordered from third parties: eSignal, DTN.IQ, Quote.com, AT Financial, InterQuote
On-Site Trading or Remote	Remote
Training	User handbook on the PreferredTrade system
Clearinghouse	Preferred Capital Markets
Other	AutoTrade: automatic routing of Nasdaq orders via SelectNet

RML Trading

Location	Bellevue, Washington
Telephone	888-765-4403
Web Address	www.rmltrading.com
Minimum to Open Margin Account	$10,000
Min./Max. Commissions	Nasdaq: $14.95; listed: $14.95 + $0.01/share
Trading Software	Four levels of RealTick™
Software/Data Fees	Four levels with monthly prices of $100, $125, $175, and $250; each level is free after 100 round trips/month
On-Site Trading or Remote	Remote
Training	Real-time support and education through Stock Cam (see Chapter 11)
Clearinghouse	Penson Financial Services
Other	Free access to www.thestockcam.com

Terra Nova Trading

Location	Chicago, Illinois
Telephone	800-258-5409
Web Address	www.terranovatrading.com
Minimum to Open Margin Account	$10,000
Min./Max. Commissions	$14.95 to $22.50 + $0.015/share on orders over 2,000 shares
Trading Software	Intermediate: TNovaPlus; high-end: SuperTNova (based on RealTick™)
Software/Data Fees	Intermediate: $225/month—free with 20 trades/month; high-end: $300/month—free with 50 trades/month
On-Site Trading or Remote	Remote
Training	RealTick™ software manual and tutorials
Clearinghouse	Southwest Securities, Inc.
Other	OptiMark routing available; point-and-click option trading; member of NASD, SIPC, and the Pacific Exchange

TradeCast Online

Location	Houston, Texas
Telephone	877-627-6700
Web Address	www.tradecast.com
Minimum to Open Margin Account	$2,500
Min./Max. Commissions	$9.95 to $19.95 (based on volume)
Trading Software	Intermediate: Revolution; high-end: Elite

Software/Data Fees	Revolution: free with streaming Level 1 real-time quotes (Level 2 upgrade for $60 per month); Elite: with streaming real-time Level 2 data $179.95 per month— free with 50 trades/month
On-Site Trading or Remote	Remote
Training	Seminars throughout United States
Clearinghouse	Penson Financial Services
Other	Trade baskets for making multiple simultaneous trades; options; short sells; wholly customizable Windows-based format

TradeSharp.com

Location	Lake Success, New York (division of Shamrock Financial Services)
Telephone	888-366-8472
Web Address	www.tradesharp.com
Minimum to Open Margin Account	$5,000
Min./Max. Commissions	$14.95 to $19.95 (based on volume)
Trading Software	High-end: Quantum Leap
Software/Data Fees	$199/month, includes Level 2 real-time streaming data—free with 15 trades/month
On-Site Trading or Remote	Remote
Training	Free training CD and free live support staff
Clearinghouse	Penson Financial Services

Other	As a direct data provider, data is supplied directly by Nasdaq, the NYSE, and AMEX; Island limit order book included in Level 2 quotes

Trend Trader

Location	Scottsdale, Arizona
Telephone	888-32-TREND
Web Address	www.trendtrader.com
Minimum to Open Margin Account	$15,000 ($10,000 to maintain)
Min./Max. Commissions	$10 + $0.02/share to $18.95 + $0.01/ share based on number of shares
Trading Software	Low-end: TORS Express; intermediate: TORS Wall Streeter; high-end: TORS Elite (all based on RealTick™)
Software/Data Fees	Low-end: $103/month—free with 20 trades/month; intermediate: $205/month—free with 40 trades/month; high-end: $305/month—free with 80 trades/month
On-Site Trading or Remote	Both
Training	Free on-site training at Scottsdale facility; TORS user guide; free demo and simulation
Clearinghouse	Penson Financial Services
Other	No charge for ECNs, SOES, or cancellations; Island limit order book included in Level 2 quotes

COMING UP . . .

The broker you choose will dictate which trading software you'll use. But you might want to consider the software first—and pick a broker that offers that software. We'll look at what's available in the next chapter.

Trading Software: The Day Trader's Control Panel

I f you use an online broker like E*Trade or Datek, placing a buy or sell order is the essence of simplicity. Enter the number of shares and the kind of order; enter the price if it's a limit order; then select Buy, Sell, or Short and click the Submit button. Voilà! You've just made a trade. No software to install, no Level 2 quotes to monitor, no training or simulated trading. Just point, click, trade.

But to get the instantaneous execution that we've talked about, you'll need an electronic brokerage firm and its trading software to gain direct access to the markets.

In this chapter, we examine the kind of trading software that lets you send an order directly to a Nasdaq market maker, an NYSE specialist, or an ECN. But this software does much more than that. It is a control panel that allows you to monitor market activity in a dozen different ways. You can keep an eye on the Dow, the Nasdaq, and the S&P; monitor real-time stock prices on a dozen stocks; chart a stock or the S&P Futures with real-time, tick-by-tick data; view Level 2 quotes on one or more stocks; watch actual trades as they are posted to the Nasdaq system; track your executions, cancellations, pending

---

Trading Software by Any Other Name . . .

As you read the various day trading literature and tutorials, you'll find that trading software is called by a variety of names: trading platform, order execution system, direct access software, and some I may not have run across. Some names like trade station and workstation refer to the hardware as well as the software. Whatever it is called, it is the software that gives you direct access to the markets.

---

orders, and current positions; and monitor a ticker of real-time news headlines.

All at the same time.

This software turns your computer into a window on Wall Street, and you can open that window as easily in Seattle or Cincinnati as you can in Manhattan.

Because of its complexity, trading software requires a modest level of computer skill to set up the customized screens. But the good news is, most systems come in low-end and high-end versions. Only the full-time hyperactive trader really needs a system with every bell and whistle, and if you opt to trade on-site in the broker's office, your trade station will be set up and maintained for you.

As discussed in Chapter 3, the trading software you use depends on the broker you choose, or vice versa. Most electronic brokers have their own systems branded with their own logos, but most are licensed from one of the Big Three front-end systems (see box). Most systems come in low-end and high-end versions, and some also offer an intermediate version.

✔ *Low-end systems.* A low-end system is designed for the less active trader. It offers fewer features, usually on a fixed screen with Level 1 quotes. Order execution is direct but the routing via SOES, SelectNet, or SuperDot is selected automatically.

Low-end systems can be used with a single monitor and a 56K modem connection.

The Big Three

Many electronic brokers offer private labeled trading software based on one of three front-end systems: CyBerTrader from CyBerCorp.com (www.cybercorp.com); RealTick™ from Townsend Analytics (www.taltrade.com); TradeCast from TradeCast Securities (www.tradecast.com). RealTick™ seems to be the most ubiquitous, offering modules that the broker can use to create its own customized system.

✔ *Intermediate systems.* An intermediate system is usually a fixed-screen version of a high-end system.

✔ *High-end systems.* A high-end system is designed for the sophisticated, more active trader. It is customizable with dozens of screens, Level 2 quotes, real-time news feeds, multiple charts, and other sexy features. Order routing is determined by the trader, although many high-end systems now offer smart keys that use artificial intelligence to automatically select the optimum order routing. Many high-end systems require dual monitors and a high-speed connection via cable, DSL, or ISDN (more on these in Chapter 10).

Electronic brokers usually bundle their trading software with real-time streaming Level 1 quotes, Level 2 quotes, and real-time news, and charge the trader a monthly fee. The cost difference between a low-end and a high-end system is about $200 a month. Rebates based on the number of trades a month can bring this monthly fee down to zero—because the broker is making its profit from increased commissions.

In this chapter we will look at some of the major

components that make up a typical high-end system and then take a closer look at a system that uses artificial intelligence and is promoted as the "next generation" of trading software.

ANATOMY OF A TRADING PLATFORM

High-end trading systems consist of dozens of screens and windows, each customizable by the user. In addition to the Level 2 quote screen, there is the Time & Sales screen, the order entry panel, stock tickers, market tickers, alert windows, top 10 lists, news tickers, charts and technical indicators, position minders, and account management windows. For instructional purposes, I've grouped them under four topics: the Level 2 screen, the order entry panel, decision-making tools, and risk management tools. Examples are included for some of the screens, but the black-and-white renderings lack the visual impact of the actual screens. To see them in full color, check out the demos at the referenced web sites.

Be sure you understand which data is provided by the broker and which will need to be ordered from third parties. For a high-end system, you'll need Level 2 quotes, real-time streaming quotes for charting and other features, and a real-time news feed. You may also want separate charting software. Your broker should have a list of approved third parties whose data can be integrated into the software. See Chapter 10 for more information on data suppliers.

The Level 2 Screen

The Level 2 screen (discussed in Chapter 2) is the primary focus of the Nasdaq trader. Linked with Level 1 quotes, the order entry panel, and the Time & Sales (Print) screen, it is referred to as the stock box by CyBer-Corp.com (Figure 4.1) and as the market maker screen by Trend Trader (Figure 4.2). The vertical Time & Sales screen, shown on the right in both figures, tracks every executed trade of the displayed stock. The price of the

SUN MICROSYSTEMS (no shortable shares)					

File   Options

| Stocks | Options | Fund | News | Other | |

SUNW | 1000 | 91 11/16 | Smart Limit ▼ | DAY ▼ | Sell   Buy

C | 96 5/16 | ↓ T10 | Short   Cancel

O | 91 7/8 | H | 92 1/4 | L | 90 1/8 | * | -4 11/16 | Cancel All

B | 91 5/8 | | A | 91 3/16 | R | 1@1 | T&S | V | 11985900

AANA 91 5/8	10	ATTN 91 3/16	2	91 5/8	1
SBSH 91 9/16	10	JPMS 91 3/8	1	91 11/16	1
DKNY 91 9/16 ↑ 1		GSCO 91 11/16	10	91 5/8	5
SNDV 91 1/2	1	MLCO 91 11/16 ↑ 10		91 5/8	5
DLJP 91 1/2	10	BTRD 91 11/16 ↑ 13		91 5/8	5
SELZ 91 1/2	1	DKNY 91 11/16 ↑ 1		91 3/4	5
NITE 91 1/2	2	FBCO 91 11/16	7	91 9/16	5
PRUS 91 1/2 ↓ 1		PRUS 91 11/16 ↑ 1		91 1/2	5 .
MADF 91 1/2	2	MONT 91 11/16 ↑ 10		91 5/8	5
INCA 91 1/2	55	CWCO 91 11/16 ↑ 1		91 5/8	10
BUCK 91 7/16	1	REDI 91 11/16	44	91 5/8	150
MASH 91 3/8 ↓ 1		HRZG 91 11/16 ↑ 5		91 9/16	150
HRZG 91 3/8	5	ARCA 91 11/16 ↑ 10		91 9/16	150

FIGURE 4.1 CyBerTrader's "stock box" integrates Level 2 quotes with Level 1 quotes and the order execution panel. *Source:* Reprinted with permission of CyBerCorp.com, www.cybercorp.com.

trade is shown on the left, the size on the right (in Figure 4.1, add two zeros). On an actual screen, executions at the bid are shown in green, executions at the ask in red.

The importance of the Time & Sales screen is that you can see every trade made, even those hidden from the Level 2 quote screen. For example, if an institutional investor wants to make a 20,000-share trade on Instinet, it won't show up as a bid or ask on the Level 2 screen, but once executed, it will appear on the Time & Sales screen. This is helpful when you're trying to determine the direction of the stock price based on supply and demand. (Chapter 2 discusses the Level 1 and Level 2 screens.)

If you pursue Level 2 trading strategies, you'll become more familiar with the Time & Sales screen.

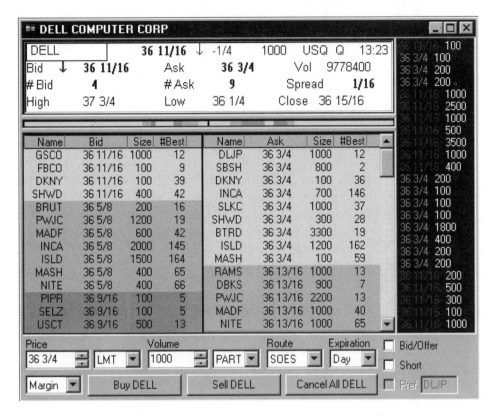

FIGURE 4.2 In the TORS system, the order entry panel is called up automatically when you highlight a market maker or ECN name. The panel can also be anchored to the market maker screen, as it is in the figure. *Source:* Reprinted with permission of Trend Trader, LLC, www.trendtrader.com.

The Order Entry Panel

The order entry panel is where you create and enter your order. Different systems configure the panels differently. Some systems, like CyBerTrader's in Figure 4.1, incorporate the order entry panel into the stock box. Others, like Trend Trader's in Figure 4.2, let it float or hide, depending on the user's preference, although you may also anchor it to the Level 2 screen.

So, how does the order entry actually work? How do you send an order to an ECN? How do you SOES or preference a market maker? It works differently on different systems.

If your system has a smart key, just enter the order and click the market order or limit order smart key. Otherwise, to SOES a market maker, simply indicate whether the order is a buy or a sell and click the SOES button. It will be automatically routed to the market maker at the inside market.

To use SelectNet, you have two choices. (1) You can route your order directly to an ECN if the ECN has a dedicated button or is listed on the pull-down menu; just enter the order details and click the ECN button or highlight the name on the pull-down menu. (2) Otherwise, highlight the name on the Level 2 screen, and click the SelectNet or Preference button. The order will be routed directly to that market maker or ECN, who will broadcast it, fill it, reject it, or let it *time out*, based on SelectNet rules.

Decision-Making Tools

Decision-making tools include stock tickers, market tickers, news tickers, alert tickers, top 10 lists, charts, and technical indicators—anything to help you decide which stocks to trade and when.

✔ Stock tickers track the stocks in which you're interested, displaying tick-by-tick changes in the bid and ask (Figure 4.3). One variation on the stock ticker is the top 10 list that tracks the 10 most active stocks on the Nasdaq and NYSE. Another variation is the alert ticker that seeks out stocks that match some predetermined criteria and displays them in a ticker window.

✔ Market tickers track the Dow, Nasdaq, S&P, and other *indexes*.

✔ News tickers display streaming, real-time headlines linked to the full stories. The news feed may be included with your data fee or may require a separate subscription fee. If a separate subscription is required, it is best to use the one affiliated with the broker since the software has already been programmed to receive the feed.

✔ High-end systems offer a variety of charts (daily, intraday, tick, line, bar, candlestick) and dozens of technical indicators. Figure 4.4 shows an intraday three-

timed out

a SOES or SelectNet order remains live for only a specified time and then is automatically canceled by the exchange if not filled. When this happens, it is said to have timed out. Time constraints vary for each.

index

a grouping of securities to track trends in specific market segments.

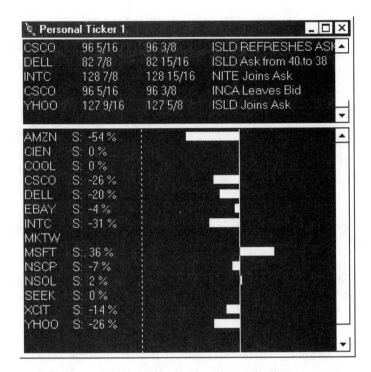

CSCO	96 5/16	96 3/8	ISLD REFRESHES ASK
DELL	82 7/8	82 15/16	ISLD Ask from 40 to 38
INTC	128 7/8	128 15/16	NITE Joins Ask
CSCO	96 5/16	96 3/8	INCA Leaves Bid
YHOO	127 9/16	127 5/8	ISLD Joins Ask

AMZN	S: -54 %
CIEN	S: 0 %
COOL	S: 0 %
CSCO	S: -26 %
DELL	S: -20 %
EBAY	S: -4 %
INTC	S: -31 %
MKTW	
MSFT	S: 36 %
NSCP	S: -7 %
NSOL	S: 2 %
SEEK	S: 0 %
XCIT	S: -14 %
YHOO	S: -26 %

FIGURE 4.3 This dynamic ticker from CyBerTrader tracks stocks of your choice. In the top screen is a Level 1 ticker with notations on market maker activity. The bottom screen presents a graphical display of the stock's trading. *Source:* Reprinted with permission of CyBerCorp.com, www.cybercorp.com.

minute bar chart with an MACD (moving average convergence/divergence) graph.

Risk-Management Tools

Risk management tools help you track the dollars you have at risk.

✔ A position minder (Figure 4.5) tracks all your open positions with real-time quotes. These are stocks you've bought or sold short and have not yet *closed out*.

✔ An account manager (Figure 4.6) tracks all trades, open positions, and executed positions, in-

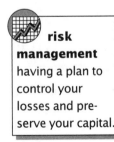

risk management
having a plan to control your losses and preserve your capital.

closed out
exited a position, as in: *I closed out Microsoft.*

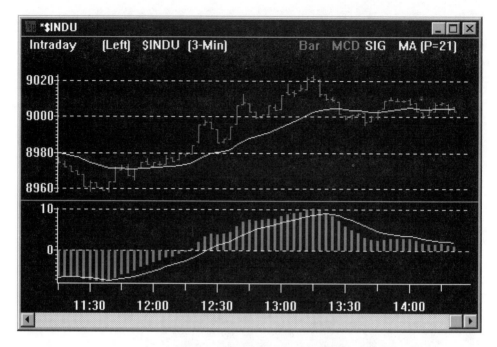

FIGURE 4.4   Intraday three-minute chart with a MACD (moving average convergence/divergence) graph, from the Trend Trader TORS software. *Source:* Reprinted with permission of Trend Trader, LLC, www.trendtrader.com.

Symbol	Last		Change	Bid	Ask	Tot. Vol.	Avg Vol
YHOO	186 3/16	↓	+9 7/16	186 3/16	186 1/4	7457500	8514
INTC	110 1/2	↑	+2	110 7/16	110 1/2	10360800	17751
IBM	159 5/16	↓	+1 5/16	159 1/4	159 3/8	2313100	4765
SEEK	37	↑	+1 1/4	36 7/8	37	3104800	3348
DELL	63 7/8	↑	-7/16	63 13/16	63 7/8	17557100	34013
MSFT	109 11/16	↓	-2 3/16	109 11/16	109 3/4	7444700	16641
EWBX	43 7/8	↓	-7 1/8	43 7/8	44	1891400	7339

FIGURE 4.5   This position Minder from Trend Trader's TORS software tracks real-time changes in open positions. *Source:* Reprinted with permission of Trend Trader, LLC, www.trendtrader.com.

C Account Manager On-Line					
File Options View			Click on Tabs		
Orders	Exec	Trades	Opens	Holds	Stats

Number	Time	Stock	Size	Price	+/-
5	15:42:20	C	1000	51 7/8	3/8
4	15:42:01	INTC	1000	129 1/8	1/4
3	15:40:47	YHOO	1000	273 7/8	+12 1/16
2	15:40:32	DELL	1000	83 3/16	3/16
1	15:40:22	IBM	1000	178 7/16	+1 1/16
0	15:39:53	AMZN	1000	117	+6

FIGURE 4.6 CyBerTrader's Account Manager On-Line tracks different phases of trading activity. The Opens tab, shown here, displays open positions with P&L (profit and loss) marked to market in real time. *Source:* Reprinted with permission of CyBerCorp.com, www.cybercorp.com.

cluding profit and loss (P&L) *marked to market* in real time.

More Bells and Whistles

Trading systems don't stop at the necessities. Here are a few bells and whistles currently offered by some of the high-end systems:

 **marked to market**
to adjust the value of securities in an account based on the current market price.

✔ Integration of the Island, ARCA, or other limit order book into the Level 2 screen.

✔ Full names of market makers, exchanges, or ECNs on the Level 2 screen.

✔ Market maker tickers that alert you to every change in each market maker's bid and ask.

✔ An "ax" or "hammer" window that tracks the dominant market maker in a stock.

✔ The ability to send multiple orders at once.

✔ Linked windows: Change the stock symbol in one window, and all linked windows change instantaneously to that stock.

✔ Ability to use commands of other trading software (handy, if you're switching programs).

✔ Sophisticated alert tools, such as alerts based on technical breakouts.

A high-end system allows you to customize dozens of screens. You can choose the size and location of the windows, the color of the data or highlight, the type and size of the font. Some systems are so complicated that you may need help setting them up. Most brokers have technical support staffs on hand to supplement their user manuals. Some offer free videos to walk you through each screen.

THE NEXT-GENERATION SOFTWARE

If you like the idea of direct access but are intimidated by all those screens and windows, take heart. Electronic brokers are beginning to lure the less sophisticated trader with fixed-screen systems that use artificial intelligence to select the optimum routing for your order.

One of the most talked-about is CyBerX, produced by CyBerCorp.com of Austin, Texas. It is technologically advanced, but looks like a toy when compared with the high-end systems. Its toylike appearance may have something to do with the order execution panel, which sports big red, green, and yellow buttons for buying, selling, or shorting a stock (Figure 4.7), but the main reason for its simplicity is the fixed-screen design. It is very graphical, with few windows, no Level 2 screen, and one tiny chart.

Don't let its simple appearance fool you, because it is very intelligent. Like the smart keys on high-end systems, CyBerX uses artificial intelligence to seek out the best bid or ask among the market makers, exchanges, or ECNs and automatically routes your order for the best execution. That's why Level 2 is not needed; it scans the Level 2 quotes behind the screen.

But just as you can use the automatic setting on a

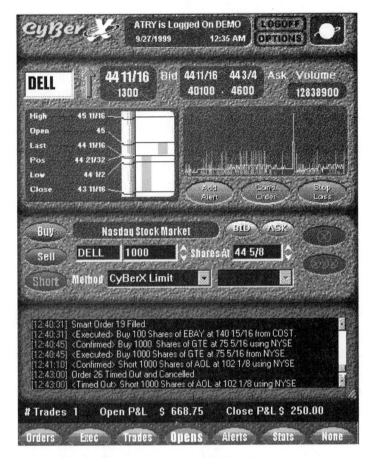

FIGURE 4.7 CyberX, from CyBerCorp.com, uses a graphical display and artificial intelligence to select optimum routing of orders. *Source:* Reprinted with permission of CyBerCorp.com, www.cybercorp.com.

Nikon or control the f-stops yourself, you can control the order routing by setting up the "advanced order entry" feature. Also, a configuration called CyBerX-Plus lets you integrate Level 2 quotes and sophisticated charting software from third-party suppliers.

For a firsthand look at CyBerX, go to www.cybercorp.com and click through the demo pages. Then download the free software for a test-drive.

QUESTIONS TO ASK
ABOUT TRADING SOFTWARE

When you're ready to evaluate trading software, check out the demos of the brokers on your short list. But before you open an account, you might want to add these questions to the list of broker questions in Chapter 3.

✔ *What are the exact requirements for hardware, memory, and storage?* General specs are shown in Chapter 10, but be sure to get the specific requirements for the system you will be using.

✔ *Does the system need multiple monitors or will one monitor do?* Most low-end systems require only one monitor; high-end systems may need two. But ask if you're not sure.

✔ *What kind of connectivity is recommended?* Direct access to the market isn't much good if you don't have a high-speed, dependable connection to the broker. Be sure to discuss connectivity options with the broker and go with its recommendation. Some systems can use your Internet service provider (ISP) and computer modem (at least 56K) to connect to the electronic broker. But that's not sufficient for high-end systems. Also, some systems won't work with cable modems. For more on connectivity options, see Chapter 10.

✔ *Are long-distance fees involved?* Your ISP will usually have a local access number, but there may be a long-distance charge between the ISP and the broker's server. It's good to ask.

✔ *Which ECNs are accessed directly, without using SelectNet?* All ECNs can be accessed via SelectNet, but which can be accessed directly? The more, the better. With direct access to the major ECNs, you'll save on fees and frustration by not having to use SelectNet.

✔ *Can you bypass any smart keys?* Smart keys are based on artificial intelligence and seek the optimal routing for your order. But if you want to do it yourself, make sure there is a way to bypass these keys.

✔ *Does the system trade both Nasdaq and listed (NYSE and AMEX) stocks?* Most trade both.

✔ *Are there any restrictions regarding firewalls or networks?* Trading software uses secure servers. If you're trading from an office that is behind a *firewall*, you may have trouble accessing the server.

✔ *Is additional software required?* Many brokers require special software for remote troubleshooting and customer support, if you trade from a home office. pcAnywhere is the program most frequently cited; it costs $170 at Symantec.com's online store (www.symantec.com).

✔ *Which data feeds are supplied with the software and what are the fees?* Make sure you understand which data are supplied and what the fees are. Level 2 quotes are usually included, but ask about exchange fees, real-time news, and streaming real-time quotes for charting. Usually, the company has agreements with specific data providers. Be sure you know who they are and the cost. (More about third-party data suppliers in Chapter 10.)

✔ *Does the trading software have the charting and technical analysis tools that you need?* If you go with a high-end system, you'll have dozens of charts and technical indicators to choose from. But if you're looking at the lower-end, fixed-screen version, you may want to look into stand-alone technical charting programs (discussed in Chapter 6).

✔ *What about upgrades, both past and planned?* Past upgrades will tell you how "old" the current software is. Planned upgrades will tell you if the company is forward-looking. Specifically, ask if an upgrade is planned if Nasdaq passes the proposed rules for agency quotes and fees (see Chapter 2).

✔ *Is the system expandable?* If you start trading at one level, you may graduate to a higher level down the road. If the system is expandable, you can simply add the desired features, rather than having to switch to an entirely different system.

✔ *Is the software decimal-ready?* Decimalization will arrive in 2001 (see Chapter 12). Make sure the software is ready for the change.

✔ *Will the software run on a Mac?* Unfortunately for Mac lovers, most trading software will not run on the

Apple Macintosh, only on IBM-PC–compatible machines. There is PC-simulation software to get around this, but some trading systems won't work with the simulations.

It is important to have a trading system suited to your style of trading and one with which you're comfortable. The best ones offer demos with live quotes, good training manuals, and customer support to help you with any problems.

COMING UP . . .

The trading system you choose depends on your trading style; the broker you choose depends on your trading style; your trading plan depends on your trading style. Thus your success as a trader depends on finding a trading style that matches your personality and behavioral traits. In the next chapter we'll look at some trading styles that you can try on for size.

Chapter

5

Define Your Trading Style

The classic day trader sits in front of a computer picking off *teenies* like a skeet shooter picks off clay birds. This is the *scalper* who makes dozens of trades a day, looking for small gains on each trade, and closing out all positions by the end of the day.

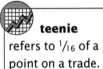

teenie
refers to ¹/₁₆ of a point on a trade.

But the pressure and stress of scalping does not appeal to all those who are referred to as day traders. Some traders—who call themselves active traders, rather than day traders—hold a stock for a week or more, looking for gains of 5, 10, 20 points on a single hot stock. In fact, day trading today encompasses many different styles. Your number one goal, as you contemplate a career in day trading, should be to find the style that best suits your personality, your behavior patterns, and your way of dealing with the world.

scalper
a day trader who makes a lot of quick trades for small profits (often teenies) on each trade.

As Martin Burton says in Alpesh B. Patel's *The Mind of a Trader*, "There is no point in me trying to play tennis like Bjorn Borg if I am John McEnroe."[1]

STYLES TO CONSIDER

When I began writing this book the question I heard over and over from friends was: What *exactly* is day trading? They were aware of the term, often in a negative way, and while the term itself would appear to be self-explanatory, it seemed to be cloaked in an aura of mystery.

In the beginning, I gave the standard answers:

- ✔ Day trading is buying and selling stocks and holding them for less than one day.
- ✔ Day traders don't hold positions overnight.
- ✔ Day traders make dozens of trades a day with the goal of making a lot of quick, small profits.

But the fact is, I had only part of the story.

Since then I have talked with traders who held positions overnight, some for several days. I've talked with traders who trade only Nasdaq stocks, some who trade only listed stocks, and some who trade both. I've talked with traders who are happy to make a teenie on a trade and others who anticipate several points' profit on every trade. The fact is, day traders have many different styles of trading.

This was very obvious at the International Online Trading Expo in Los Angeles in the fall of 1999. Featured at the Expo was a session called "The Million Dollar Panel." The panel was made up of six traders who had made a million dollars or more trading in the prior year—and they did it with very different trading styles. Some traded only NYSE stocks; others traded only Nasdaq stocks; one traded only Internet stocks. Some traded anything that moved; others, a small group of stocks. Some swore by technical charts; others swore that charts were a waste of time. Their styles were different, but their results were the same: a seven-figure income.[2]

The point is, you can make money with any style of trading. As you'll learn in Chapter 8—if you don't already know it—it is how your mind works that will determine your success or failure in the day trading game.

It is important to define your trading style as early as possible because it will dictate the kind of brokerage account you'll need, the kind of trading software you'll use, the kind of training you'll need, and the kind of mentor you'll seek. Each style is a variation on the day trading game with its own rules and idiosyncrasies—and you can't learn the rules until you know which game you're playing.

Nor can you develop a trading plan until you know your trading style, because to write a trading plan you must know what, when, why, where, and how much you're going to trade. When you know these things, you've defined your trading style.

A trading style is defined in part by the time spent in the market—do you close all positions by the end of the day or hold them overnight or longer? Style is also defined by the stocks you trade, whether they're Nasdaq or listed, whether you use technical analysis or base your trades on news events. Many elements go into defining a style and the most important is what is inside your head.

Your mental makeup will (or should) drive your decision about style. For example, if you methodically think through a situation before making a decision, you may never make it as a scalper. Why? Because scalping requires the ability to make split-second decisions based on rapidly changing data. Or if you've spent years as a fundamental investor, you may have a hard time relying on signals issued by a technical indicator. You may prefer instead to trade a small group of fundamentally sound stocks.

The point is to learn about the elements that make up the different styles—and learn about yourself. You will naturally gravitate toward a style that best suits you.

The combination of styles is virtually infinite, but we will look at a few separately and distinctly.

The Scalper

There is a certain kind of day trading style that seems to define the classic day trader: the scalper. A scalper enters and exits a position quickly, staying in long enough to scalp a teenie or an eighth of a point in profit and exiting at the first sign of reversal. The scalper may make 20, 50, 100 trades or more a day, sometimes on just one stock. (One trader on the Million Dollar Panel claimed 700 trades a day.) Scalpers sit in front of their computer

---

What Does a Teenie Look Like?

One-sixteenth of a point isn't much. One point is equal to one dollar, so $1/16$ of a point is $0.0625. So when you're trading for teenies, you're expecting to make slightly over six cents a share on a successful trade. On a 1,000-share trade, that's $62.50; on a 2,000-share trade, $125, and on a 3,000-share trade, $187.50. Commissions, which average between $20 and $30 per round trip, will cut your profits almost in half on a 1,000-share trade. Of course not all trades will be profitable, and you still have to pay commissions on losing or break-even trades. To make money at the game, traders who aim for teenies must make larger-than-average trades and learn to let their profits run.

---

grinder
a trader who seeks small profits on dozens or hundreds of trades a day. Similar to scalping.

screens, grinding out trades (which is why they are also called *grinders*), some trading anything that moves, others concentrating on a small group of stocks.

Scalpers look for intraday trends or momentum (which is why they are also called trend traders or momentum traders). They buy the stock on a dip, sell it on a crest, short it when it turns down, and cover when it heads back up. This style requires volatile stocks, complete emotional detachment, and a good technical strategy to time entry and exit points.

Scalpers sometimes play market maker. When you play market maker, you are "stealing the spread" from the real market makers. How? By buying on the bid and selling on the ask. This kind of scalper uses an ECN to enter a bid slightly higher than the inside bid—which then becomes the inside bid. The instant the buy is executed, the scalper sells the stock at the inside ask, turning a small profit.

To make money scalping, you need to trade at least 1,000 shares, and preferably 2,000 to 3,000 shares or more. Otherwise, commissions will eat your profits.

Is This Style for You? Scalping requires a large amount of capital (some say $100,000 minimum), a full-time commitment (ideally), a professional-level trading platform with a high-speed connection, a thorough knowledge of the markets, and nerves of steel. Dave Floyd, CEO of CareerDayTrader.com, says that scalping tends to be a game for the younger trader. Why? Because you need lightning-quick reflexes and an appetite for risk taking. And let's face it, not only do our reflexes slow as we grow older, but most of us also become more conservative in our thinking and less willing to take risks. Certainly, there are scalpers of all ages, but chances are the older ones have been doing it for many years. You, of course, can always be the exception to the rule.

The Swing Trader

Swing traders deal with a longer time frame than scalpers do. Instead of looking for a teenie or an eighth of a point over the next several minutes, swing traders look for several points over one to five days.

Brandon Fredrickson, one of the head traders at MTrader's Swing Trading Chat Room, believes that *swing trading* takes advantage of a niche overlooked by others. The one- to five-day time frame is "not long enough for large institutions who must move a large number of shares . . . and [it] is too long for most day traders who tend to want to go home *flat*."[3]

Swing trading usually focuses on technical *setups*, so a knowledge of technical analysis is essential. You need not be a dyed-in-the-wool technician, however; you simply need to be able to identify short-term uptrends and downtrends, and support and resistance levels. If you're brand-new to technical analysis, Chapter 6 will lay the groundwork for further study.

Swing traders may also trade on news events such as earnings releases, stock splits, and *upgrades* or *downgrades*, which can present terrific opportunities for short-term profits. For example, after a doubleheader of blowout earnings and a four-to-one stock split on November 4, 1999, Qualcomm gained 30 points in six days (and

swing trading
a style of trading in which a position is held for two or more days.

setup
the conditions, dictated by your trading system, that must occur in a stock before you make a trade.

upgrade
to change a recommendation on a stock to a more positive rating. As in: *The analyst upgraded IBM from a hold to a strong buy.*

downgrade
to change a recommendation on a stock to a less positive rating, as in: *The analyst downgraded IBM from a buy to a hold.*

it kept on going until the end of the year). We'll talk more about trading on news events later in this chapter.

MTrader has a dedicated swing trading site (www.swingtrader.net) with good introductory material and a real-time stock trading chat room. WinningDay-Traders at www.winningdaytraders.com publishes a thrice-weekly newsletter suggesting swing trades for the next day. Also check out two free articles by Linda Bradford Raschke at www.mrci.com/lbr/index.htm: "Notes from a Swing Trader" and "Swing Trading: Rules and Philosophy." And if you're really serious about it, read George Douglas Taylor's *The Taylor Trading Technique.*[4]

Is This Style for You? Swing trading appeals to the more conservative trader who wants short-term profits but doesn't have the stomach (or the bank account) to scalp. The market risk is greater because you are holding positions overnight and sometimes over the weekend, although a cardinal rule of swing traders is never to take home a losing position. The advantages are:

- ✔ You can swing trade on a part-time basis because you don't have to monitor your stock second by second.
- ✔ You can get by with a smaller amount of capital (and smaller trades) because you're going for multiple-point profits, not fractions of a point.

You can also use a Web broker with browser-based order entry screens, because slippage is less critical. In a fast market, however, you may wish you had a direct access broker.

The Position Trader

The primary difference between a position trader and a swing trader is the length of time a position is held (although the terms are often used interchangeably). David S. Nassar, author of *How to Get Started in Electronic Day Trading*, calls position traders those who buy and hold a

---

The Part-Time versus Full-Time Trader

Some say you can't be a part-time day trader, that it requires a full-time commitment, but many think it depends on your trading style and where you live.

Scalping would appear to be a full-time commitment, but on the West Coast, where the market opens at 6:30 A.M. and closes at 1:00 P.M., a scalper might trade for an hour and a half in the morning before going to work. Some say these are the worst hours to trade because of market volatility, but experienced traders prefer the opening and closing hours of the market.

Granted, the ideal commitment is full time, but with the move to extended-hours trading we'll all be part-time traders since few will have the energy to trade 12 hours a day. Meanwhile, pick a style that fits your time frame and initiate a few safeguards like stop loss orders, pager alerts, and an alternative way to place a trade should the need arise.

---

stock for up to 10 days.[5] Some would say that anyone who holds a stock for 10 days cannot be called a day trader, but they are definitely active traders, not investors. Many day traders, in fact, prefer the term active trader to the more pejorative term of day trader.

Position traders might be technicians who enter a stock and wait for a technical pattern to develop, or they might be fundamentalists at heart who stay in a stock just long enough to get the market impact of a news-driven event.

Is This Style for You? Position trading offers the same advantages and similar market risk as swing trading. If you're reluctant to jump in the deep end of day trading, position trading might be a good way to start. In a sense, it is investing with a very short fuse.

The Technician

Most day traders use technical signals for entry and exit points; others use technical analysis as a tool to find stocks to trade, such as breakouts or trend reversals. Some traders, however, are pure technicians, virtually ignoring Level 2 quotes and the games that market makers play and basing all their trades on price trends or on technical signals.

Technicians may use timing signals as simple as moving average crossovers or as complex as *Fibonacci lines*; or they may create their own systems. They may be technical scalpers or technical swing traders or even technical position traders. The important point is that a technician's whole strategy is grounded in technical analysis, and everything else is secondary.

Entire books have been written about single technical indicators. For those who are new to the subject, I've included a technical analysis primer in the next chapter, along with web sites that offer educational sections on technical analysis.

Is This Style for You? The best technicians are those who have an affinity for numbers and who understand the theory behind the indicator. However, any trader will benefit from knowing the basics of technical analysis, such as support and resistance, simple trendlines, and moving averages, all of which you'll discover in the next chapter.

The Level 2 Trader

Some trading styles are based strictly on Nasdaq Level 2 quotes. These traders judge supply and demand for a stock by the bids and offers of market makers and the executed trades on the Time & Sales screen. Some use no technical charts at all; others, like one of the Million Dollar panelists, uses Level 2 and an intraday chart of the S&P futures.

One of the most popular Level 2 strategies is shadowing the ax. The ax is the dominant market maker in a

---

Fibonacci lines
technical indicators based on the studies of a twelfth-century mathematician named Leonard Pisano (nicknamed Fibonacci). Fibonacci numbers involve a sequence in which each successive number is the sum of the two previous ones: 1, 2, 3, 5, 8, 13, 21, 34, 55, 89, 144, and so on. The indicators anticipate changes in trends as prices near the lines created by the Fibonacci numbers.

given stock on a given day, the one that always seems to be at the inside bid. The ax (also called the hammer) returns to the inside bid over and over again because it has a large order to fill. Shadowing the ax means doing exactly what the ax does: buying when it buys and selling when it sells.

There are three things you have to learn with this strategy. First, you have to find out which market maker the ax is. Some trading systems make it easy by indicating on the Level 2 screen how many times a market maker has been at the inside bid. Otherwise, you have to figure it out for yourself.

Second, once you determine which one the ax is, you have to learn how to interpret its movements. This is one of the favorite topics of day trading books, seminars, and tutorials, which you will learn about as you continue your study.

The third thing to keep in mind, as mentioned earlier, is that "Level 2 lies"—which is why many traders don't use Level 2; or if they do, they use it merely to lend support to whatever their technical indicators are telling them.

Is This Style for You? The Level 2 trader seems almost an anachronism, a style that has outgrown its usefulness. Market makers have deeper pockets and more experience than day traders, and trying to beat them at their own game seems like more trouble than it's worth. Nevertheless, there are traders who swear by it and you'll read a lot about it because Level 2 strategies are the main event at many day trading seminars. Before you sign up for one, take the free and low-cost Level 2 tutorials described in Chapter 11. And remember, you can be a day trader without playing the Level 2 game.

The Followers

Some traders have no style of their own—they simply follow someone else's lead. These are the traders who populate the online trading pits—the chat rooms where a head trader calls the plays and the followers try to duplicate

Checking Out the Head Trader

The ideal leader is one whose trading style you want to emulate and who will actually teach you to trade. In a virtual trading room, the head trader's style and biography are usually posted on the web site, sometimes with the trader's track record.

But don't take everything at face value. Sign up for the free trial and observe the action carefully. Ask questions directly of the head trader. Go into a nonaffiliated chat room and ask other traders' opinions of the trading room. Paper trade using the leader's calls (see "The Fallacy of Paper Trading" at the end of this chapter). Keep in mind that if you make a losing trade based on the leader's call, it is *your* loss, not the leader's. In the end, you are still responsible for your own trades.

See Chapter 11 for more on the online trading pits.

them. They buy when the head trader says buy, sell when the head trader says sell.

Some do very well, based on the testimonials posted at the various sites, but there are dangers in being a follower. If you blindly follow the leader without learning the methodology behind the trade, the leader will become a crutch that you can't trade without. By following a leader, you'll never have to take responsibility for your trades, because you can blame the losing trades on the leader. (Will you give the leader credit for the winning trades as well?) And if you never take responsibility for your trades, you'll never develop the mind of a trader that is absolutely essential to successful trading (more about this is Chapter 8).

Consider, too, that as a follower you'll always be a step or two behind, which can be fatal in trades that depend on split-second timing.

One trading coach told me that a trainee who was sitting at the next computer and matching him trade for trade missed the trade that he called. The coach acted the instant he saw the signal and called it to her simultaneously. Yet in the time it took for her to follow his lead, she had missed the teenie he was going for. He was in and out before she could even get in. Granted, it was a fast-moving stock, but timing is critical, especially in scalping. And if you're in a virtual trading room on the Web watching the calls on the chat room screen—instead of at the head trader's side—you may be more than a few steps behind.

Nevertheless, following the leader can be a good way to learn how to trade if you're following an experienced trader who coaches as he or she goes.

Is This Style for You? If you like the camaraderie of fellow traders but don't have access to a day trading shop, a virtual trading room might help you develop your style. Watching an experienced trader in action—even in a virtual space—can be valuable for a novice trader. Most trading rooms provide trade-by-trade analyses (usually after the market closes) and some have formal chat-room lessons on various aspects of trading. In addition, they offer market commentary, which can be helpful to new traders.

 pump and dump
a practice whereby a person or firm that holds an interest in a stock promotes (pumps) the stock to the public, and when the price rises due to increased demand, the promoter sells (dumps) its shares, at which point the price usually plummets.

Let the Trader Beware!

Be sure your trading room isn't hyping a stock in which the leader or the web site has a vested interest. The SEC requires full disclosure by anyone promoting a stock in which he or she owns shares or for which they're receiving monetary rewards of any kind. The disclosure, when made, is in very small type at the bottom of the web page.

Avoid any stock that is promoted in this way, or you might become the victim of a *pump and dump* scheme—after pumping up the price, the promoter will dump the shares and leave you holding a worthless stock. Thinly traded bulletin board stocks are prime candidates for the pump-and-dump treatment.

But check out the trading room carefully (see "Trading Pits" in Chapter 11). They can be expensive—$200+ a month—but most offer free trials to let you experience the trading action before you commit your dollars. Also, subscriptions are on a month-to-month basis, so if you try it and don't like it, you can consider the month's subscription fee part of your day trading tuition.

A TALE OF TWO TRADERS

As part of my research for this book, I sat beside two different professional traders and watched them trade. They have different trading styles, but they are alike in that they both are successful, they are scalpers, and they follow their trading plans to a T.

A Nasdaq Trend Trader

In late August 1999, I visited Trend Trader, an electronic brokerage firm in Scottsdale, Arizona. My first stop was a two-hour training session offered free to on-site traders. Then I sat beside Mark Seleznov, Trend Trader's CEO, in the on-site trading room and watched him trade.

Mark is a highly successful scalper, a technician, and trend trader who is a frequent speaker at day trading events. He likes the volatility of Nasdaq stocks, which he trades exclusively, and he will trade anything that moves, regardless of its name, its industry group, or his personal feelings about the company. The day I watched him, 1-800-Flowers (FLWS) was moving. Mark didn't particularly like the company; he couldn't see why a flower shop should have a market capitalization of more than half a billion dollars, but that didn't affect his trading strategy.

FLWS was moving, and he couldn't care less about its inflated market cap, its earnings potential, or whether it could deliver flowers to his wife in time for their anniversary. He doesn't care whether a stock is moving up or down, just that it is moving. But he doesn't jump on the first stock that moves, either. Like all successful traders, he has a plan for each trade and he follows it faithfully.

His tools are the Level 2 quote montage, the Print (Time & Sales) screen, and a three-minute candlestick chart. He relies mostly on the chart and the print screen because, as he says, "Level 2 lies." He explains that there is no way to know how much supply or demand is really behind each quote on the Level 2 screen, so you can't rely on it. A market maker may have an order for 100,000 shares or more, which it is dribbling out a thousand shares at a time. (As a former market maker, Mark knows whereof he speaks.)

The trades shown on the print screen, however, are de facto; they show what is actually happening in the stock, and they're reflected almost immediately in the changing shape of the real-time candlestick chart.

When the candlestick signal comes, Mark enters his buy order, SOESing the market maker at the inside offer. The buy is executed almost instantaneously, and, much to my surprise, the minute the order is confirmed he prepares to exit the trade.

Part of his plan—maybe the most important part of it—is his exit strategy. Like any good trader, he will let his profits run. As long as the stock is moving as expected, he will watch and wait. But he knows the exact moment he will get out, should the trade turn against him. So as soon as the buy order is confirmed, he sets up a sell order on his order screen. Sets it up and waits.

As FLWS moves upward, Mark watches the chart and the print screen, glancing occasionally at the Level 2 quotes. After a few minutes, the stock reverses and turns down. But he doesn't click the Sell button immediately— it might be a temporary pullback—he waits instead for the candlesticks to form a signal that the stock is indeed reversing its climb.

And when the signal comes, he clicks the Sell button.

There is no "let's wait and see what it does," no hoping and praying it will go back up. He exits the trade without having to think, because he has already thought it through. He has a trading plan and—more important— the discipline to follow it. And that, according to Mark and other experts, is what separates successful traders from the failures.

The Listed Stocks Trader

In early December I visited with Dave Floyd, CEO of CareerDayTrader.com, in San Diego. Dave is a former successful bond trader from San Francisco who discovered that success in the bond market didn't translate directly to success in day trading stocks. This was a different game entirely, a sentiment echoed by other traders, and he lost half his trading capital the first year. How did he turn it around? Perseverance.

"I sat in front of the computer screen every day," he said, "trying to figure it out."

In the end he did figure it out, but it took him a year and a half to make back what he had lost. Now, eight years later, he is a highly successful trader who also mentors a dozen or so on-site traders.

When I walk into the trading room, the first thing I hear is a staccato voice coming from a small speaker atop a monitor. It sounds as if an auction is in progress. (*"ninebid,ninehalfoffer,ninebid,ninehalfoffer,ninebid,ninehalf offer"*). A dozen trading stations, each sporting three or four monitors, line both sides of the long, narrow room. At one end of the room, mounted high on the wall, the anchors of CNBC hold forth.

Dave glances up as I enter the room and motions me to a chair beside him. As he sets up his order screen for the next buy signal he explains the auctioneer's voice coming from the speaker. It is a live feed from the futures pit of the Chicago Mercantile Exchange. It sounds like an auction because it is one—the daily auction of the S&P futures.

"Everything we do is determined by the spooze," says Dave. (That's traders' slang for S&P futures.) "I use S&P pivot numbers, but when the pit announcer yells out 'Big Italy on the offer' I stay put. You don't want to go against an 800-pound gorilla." (Big Italy is the nickname for well-known trader Louis Borsellino; pivot numbers are support and resistance levels.)

Dave is a trend-based scalper who trades only listed stocks and only three at that (Lucent, America Online, and IBM). He's also a technician (he uses stochastics, moving average crossovers, Bollinger bands, and Fibonacci retracements). I count 13 charts spread across his three monitors, but it is the live feed from the futures trading pit that gives him his edge.

"The futures lead the stocks," he says. "If Merrill's on the bid repeatedly, you can see the trend in the making."

Dave trades only for the first couple of hours in the morning and the last hour or so before the market closes. This is when the market is the most volatile, but today it is a choppy, *range-bound market*. He has cut his usual 4,000-share trades to 1,000 shares, and I see fewer than a dozen trades on his daily log.

 range-bound market a market in which the trading is within a general range of prices, with the leaders not moving much.

The stock on which he and his group are focusing today is IBM. When the magic words from the futures trading pit coincide with his technical setups, he clicks the Buy button. A minute or two later, he is out of the trade, pocketing a $3/8$-point profit, a typical profit for a scalper.

It is near the end of the trading day. A low groan goes up as one of the traders sells too soon and misses a big move. Dave's partner, John McConnin, rides the stock another point before jumping out to a round of applause. The closing bell rings on CNBC and the traders—all students of Dave and John—begin to shut down their systems.

I ask Dave what he looks for in a student. "You need to be young and hungry," he says. "And you have to love the game. Unless you love it, you won't stick with it.

"It's not rocket science," he added, with a wry grin. "You just have to be able to sit there until you learn it."

WHAT WILL YOU TRADE?

Part of defining your trading style is deciding what you will trade. In this book, we've limited the trading universe to stocks—as opposed to options, futures, or currencies—but there are more than 10,000 stocks to choose from. How will you narrow it down to a chosen few? Will you trade Nasdaq stocks, NYSE stocks, or both? Will you concentrate on a few stocks or consider the whole universe of stocks as trading candidates? Here are some things to consider.

Nasdaq versus NYSE Stocks

The majority of traders seem to trade Nasdaq stocks, and most day trading courses teach you primarily about the Nasdaq Stock Market, about Level 2 quotes and how to beat the market makers at their own games. Yet many traders trade only NYSE stocks.

With NYSE stocks, you don't have to deal with market maker games or with SOES and SelectNet rules. Small NYSE orders are routed automatically through the Super-Dot system to the specialist on the exchange floor where they are automatically matched and executed. Most listed stocks also have tighter spreads, greater liquidity, and less volatility.

Charles Farrell, author of *Day Trade Online*, trades only listed stocks, mostly utilities. One of the Million Dollar panelists trades just three NYSE bank stocks. Dave Floyd, CEO of CareerDayTraders.com, trades three listed stocks: AOL, Lucent, and IBM.

If you don't already know which you want to trade, try both the Nasdaq and the NYSE before you settle on one or the other. But be sure that the trading software you choose offers access to both. Not all of them do.

The Few versus the Many

There are more than 3,000 NYSE stocks and more than 6,000 Nasdaq stocks. So even after you've decided between Nasdaq and the NYSE, you must still narrow *that* universe to the few stocks that you will trade on any given day.

Many traders trade a group of stocks over and over. These could be considered specialists who learn each stock's trading patterns, which helps them predict future movements. As Dave Floyd, an NYSE trader, says, "Stocks have personalities." Once you learn a stock's personality, you can predict with some accuracy its movements and reactions to news events.

If you trade a small group of Nasdaq stocks, you can learn the trading patterns and games of the major market makers. If you're an investor in trader's clothing, you can trade a small group of stocks with sound *fundamentals* that you wouldn't mind owning long-term, if a trade goes against you. (If you do this, be sure you have two accounts, one for day trading and one for investing.)

fundamentals
factors such as earnings, sales, debt, and other balance sheet items that reveal the basic health of a company.

Some traders find trading just a few stocks boring. They consider the whole universe of stocks as possibilities and use technical screens to find the ones that are moving *today*. These traders are generalists, like Mark Seleznov, who couldn't care less about the name of the stock, much less its fundamentals. They'll trade anything that moves. They might trade a certain stock over and over because it keeps turning up in their screens, but what they're really after is volume and high volatility.

Still other traders pick stock based on certain timely events. For example, some will concentrate on stocks in the *sectors* or industry groups that are currently in favor. Others will select stocks based on recent news events, earnings announcements, upgrades or downgrades by analysts, announcements of stock splits, or initial public offerings. Many traders use screening tools to find stocks that exhibit specific fundamentals or match certain technical patterns. There are dozens of ways to cull the vast universe of stocks—which we'll discuss next—but the decision about which stocks to trade will very likely flow out of your other style choices.

sector
an economic grouping of related industries.

The Top-Down Trader

Many traders narrow the universe of stocks by concentrating on stocks in the best-performing sectors or industry groups. These are top-town traders who first locate the hottest sector and the hottest industry, and then they screen for the hottest stocks in that industry. Some may concentrate on the top two or three stocks in a hot industry; others prefer the less volatile second- and third-tier stocks.

It stands to reason that if some groups or sectors

sector rotation
the movement of sectors in and out of favor with institutional investors, due to economic conditions, demographic trends, technological innovations, or other factors.

industry group rotation
the movement of industry groups in to and out of favor with institutional investors, due to economic conditions, demographic trends, technological innovations, or other factors.

are hot, others are cold and ignored by investors. And, what's hot this week or this month may turn cold as a blue norther next week or next month. This movement of sectors and industries into and out of favor with the market is called *sector rotation* or *industry group rotation*. The rotation may occur because of changing economic conditions, technological innovations, or demographic trends.

For example, in late 1999, mobile communications was one of the top-performing industries by a wide margin because of consumer interest in cell phones and pagers. The tobacco industry, on the other hand, was one of the poorest performers because of the public's changing attitude toward cigarette smoking. Rotation can also occur because of rumors or fears about an industry. In 1992 the health-care industry was shunned by investors because of fears of health-care reform. And the Internet group, which was red-hot throughout 1999, cooled off dramatically in the second quarter 2000.

Sector traders shift their focus as groups rotate upward into favor and downward out of favor.

Sectors and Industry Groups

A sector is a broad economic grouping of related industries. An industry group is a narrow grouping of companies within a similar industry. Industry groups were created by entities such as Dow Jones, Standard & Poor's, and *Investor's Business Daily* as a way of tracking the performance of a related group of stocks. The financial sector, for example, encompasses all industries related to finance: insurance companies, banks, brokerage firms, credit card companies, mortgage companies, and so on. Insurance, however, may be divided into several different industry groups, such as life, property and casualty, accident and health, and miscellaneous. The subgroups depend on who is doing the grouping. The narrower the classifications, the more sensitive the tracking.

Where to Find Rotating Sectors and Industry Groups. There are many places to track sector and industry group rotation: BigCharts.com (www.bigcharts.com), Market Guide Investor (www.marketguide.com), Wall Street City (www.wallstreetcity.com), PersonalWealth.com (www.personalwealth.com), IndividualInvestor.com (www.individualinvestor.com), and Investor's Business Daily (www. investors.com).

Keep in mind that the groups differ, however, depending on whose classification the web site uses. BigCharts.com, for example, uses the Dow Jones classification of nine sectors and approximately 70 industries. In this grouping, Internet stocks are assigned to the consumer services industry, which is one of nine industries in the consumer, noncyclical sector.

By contrast, Wall Street City tracks 24 sectors and more than 200 industry groups. Telescan, the developer of Wall Street City, created its own industry group indexes based on Standard & Poor's industry group divisions. In Telescan's groupings, the Internet is a separate sector *and* the only industry in that sector.

Stocks in the News

Why do traders demand live news feeds and keep one eye cocked on CNBC or Bloomberg TV during market hours? Because stocks that make the news are good candidates for day trading. Just keep in mind that 99 percent of other day traders are also watching the same programs and see the same newsmakers that you see.

News events can include mergers or acquisitions, product releases, new marketing strategies, FDA or other government agency approvals, outcome of major trials—anything that makes a stock newsworthy. These stocks are good day trading candidates because the public's reaction (or overreaction) to the news often causes a sharp spike in the stock price.

For example, a major news event occurred as I was writing this chapter. Amazon.com made a surprise announcement about zShops, a marketing strategy that opened up its e-commerce site to independent retailers. The stock opened at 66½ that day, reached an intra-day high of 85, and closed at 80¾ (Figure 5.1). An astute day trader might have captured several of those 18½ points.

The objective in trading stocks in the news is to take advantage of the spikes caused by overreaction to the news. News events that are surprises (i.e., not rumored beforehand) need to be acted upon instantly and monitored closely with a good technical analysis tool so that you can get in and out quickly. However, news that has been preceded by days or weeks of rumors may generate a different response than you expect.

For example, a stock may drop on good news or rise on bad news, because the smart money—institutional and professional investors—buys on the anticipation of the event and sells once the event is announced. The dumb money (that's us, the investing public, I'm sorry to say)

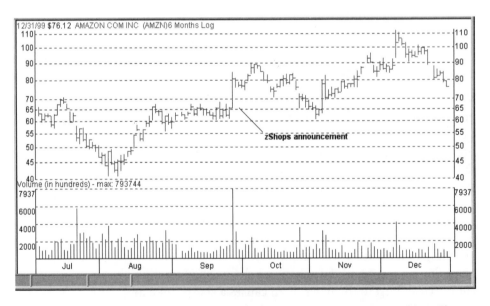

FIGURE 5.1 On September 23, 1999, when Amazon.com announced its zShops feature that opened up the site to small retail boutiques, the stock shot up 18½ points. *Source*: Stock graph fromTIP@Wallstreet, reprinted with permission of Telescan, Inc., www.telescan.com.

waits for the announcement. Thus, the adage: "Buy the rumor, sell the news."

Part of the art of trading on news events is to emulate the smart money and buy (or short) based on the rumor and sell (or cover) on the news. Of course, this presupposes you can tune in to the rumors and discern which have substance and which don't.

Where to Find Stocks in the News. If you have a live news feed on your trading platform, that's all you need to keep up with news events from major corporations. If not, several web sites offer real-time financial news on a subscription basis, including:

✔ The Fly on the Wall (www.theflyonthewall.com) does not use the standard wire services but relies on Wall Street brokers, money managers, research firms, public companies, and "other intermediaries" for their stock-specific news. $49.95/month or $479/year.

✔ TradingMarkets.com (www.tradingmarkets.com) is a robust site that offers, among other things, a feature called Traders Newswire. This is a scrolling, intraday service that provides alerts on breakouts and breakdowns, abnormal option volume alerts, market commentary, and more. (This site was the former TradeHard.com.) Subscription is $12/month or $120/year.

✔ NewsTraders.com at www.newstraders.com offers real-time, streaming news and a service called Screaming Edgar, a real-time feed of SEC filings that could provide early warning signals for upcoming events such as a company's secondary offering or a major shareholder increasing his or her stake in the company. The service is currently free although subscriptions are planned.

With regard to rumors, JagNotes.com (www.jagnotes. com) reports rumors of mergers, acquisitions, and other events that it hears from brokers, traders, and other sources on the Street. It has been right often enough to be a frequently cited source on CNBC, but rumors are wrong more often than right. The challenge is figuring out which ones to bet on. JagNotes is a subscription site: $9.95/month.

Earnings Plays

A public company must file a quarterly financial statement (10Q) with the SEC each quarter. Part of that financial statement is the company's earnings for the quarter, which are released to the public as earnings per share (EPS). Earnings are announced within 45 days after the end of a quarter, but there is no set date for the announcement. Sometimes the company announces earlier or later than the previous quarter. At the end of a company's fiscal year, the company has 90 days in which to file its annual financial statement (10K) and make its earnings announcement.

Earnings announcements create good trading opportunities for day traders. The key to earnings plays is the consensus of *earnings estimates* made by analysts who follow the company.

As part of their research on a company, these analysts make projections about the company's earnings for the current and next quarter and current and next fiscal years. As many as 50 analysts may follow a single company, and it is the consensus of their estimates—the mean—that is reported by sources such as First Call or Zacks.com and picked up by the media.

It is this number—the estimated earnings per share—that a company must meet or exceed each quarter in order to please the investing public and keep its stock price on an even or upward path. If the company exceeds or fails to meet the analysts' estimate, it is called an *earnings surprise*. A positive surprise is good, and a history of positive surprises is especially good. A negative surprise—failing to meet the estimates—is very, very bad.

But sometimes a company will meet its estimates and the stock still tanks. Why? Because of the *whisper numbers*.

It's those rumors again. Whisper numbers are sup-

earnings estimates
projections of future earnings per share (for the next quarter or next fiscal year) made by analysts who write research reports on a company; usually, the consensus estimate (the mean) of all analysts who follow the company.

earnings surprise
when a company's earnings exceed the analysts' consensus estimates.

posedly the Wall Street's *real* opinion about a company's earnings, as opposed to the published estimates. The whisper numbers are the ones to beat if a company wants a good reception on Wall Street.

As with other news-driven events, you need to "buy the rumor, sell the news" or as David Nassar says, "buy rumor, sell fact." In *How to Get Started in Electronic Day Trading*, he outlines five specific earnings plays (long and short): The first is two to seven days before the earnings report; the next three are the day before the release; the fifth play is on the day of the release.[6] He also suggests concentrating on technology stocks with good earnings estimates.

To trade earnings plays, you'll need to track the earnings estimates, the whisper numbers, the date of the earnings announcement, and the earnings announcement itself.

Where to Find Earnings Information. Here are some sources you can use to find earnings plays:

- ✔ *Earnings estimates.* Earnings estimates can be found at First Call (www.firstcall.com), Zacks.com (www.zacks.com), or on almost any company profile, such as the S&P Stock Report or Market Guide Snapshot, which are available at most investing web sites.

- ✔ *Whisper numbers.* Whisper numbers can be found at WhisperNumber.com (www.whispernumber.com), which offers "whisper charts" that show the before-and-after effects of earnings announcements on a company's stock price. EarningsWhispers.com (www.earningswhispers.com) displays the stock's official earnings estimates along with the whisper numbers.

- ✔ *Earnings calendar.* The earnings calendar at ZDNet Inter@ctive Investor (www.zdii.com) tracks the expected dates for earnings announcements (Figure 5.2). The calendar lists the quarterly estimate

---

whisper number

an earnings number that is circulated (rumored) on Wall Street a few days before a company announces its quarterly or yearly earnings. The whisper number may be higher or lower than the official earnings estimate for the company, and it is widely regarded as the number the company must meet or exceed in order to retain the favor of the investing public.

- Tues, Jan 4 - Wed, Jan 5 ►Thur, Jan 6 - Fri, Jan 7 - Mon, Jan 10

Earnings Calendar 01/06/2000

Company	Symbol	Qtr EPS Estimate	Research
AEP INDS	AEPI	0.43	News • Chart • EPS
AMWAY JAPAN-ADR	AJL	N/A	News • Chart • EPS
ATI TECHNOLGIES	ATYT	0.25	News • Chart • EPS
BASSETT FURNITR	BSET	0.45	News • Chart • EPS
CENTENNIAL CELL	CYCL	N/A	News • Chart • EPS
LEHMAN BROS HLD	LEH	1.78	News • Chart • EPS
LAZARE KAPLAN	LKI	0.23	News • Chart • EPS
LO-JACK CORP	LOJN	0.17	News • Chart • EPS
MAXXIM MEDICAL	MAM	0.48	News • Chart • EPS
MEDIA 100 INC	MDEA	0.15	News • Chart • EPS
MORGAN ST DEAN	MWD	1.77	News • Chart • EPS
NAUTICA ENTERPR	NAUT	0.46	News • Chart • EPS
QEP COMPANY INC	QEPC	N/A	News • Chart • EPS
STRIDE RITE COR	SRR	0.00	News • Chart • EPS
TENET HEALTH	THC	0.41	News • Chart • EPS
TSR INC	TSRI	N/A	News • Chart • EPS
XL CAP LTD-A	XL	1.18	News • Chart • EPS

FIGURE 5.2 The earnings calendar at ZDNet Inter@ctive Investor shows companies due for earnings announcements each day, along with each company's quarterly earnings estimates, where available, and links to related news, stock charts, analysts' ratings, and additional estimates. *Source:* Reprinted with permission of ZDNet, www.zdii.com.

and links directly to a stock chart and an EPS table that provides the most recent actual earnings, the consensus estimates, and percentage of earnings surprises in previous quarters.

✔ *Conference calls.* Traditionally, the CEO of a company holds a conference call every quarter to discuss the company's performance with industry analysts who cover the company and to answer their questions. Now these conference calls are being opened to the public on the Internet. There are several web sites that webcast the conference calls; a schedule can be found at www.bestcalls.com.

Upgrades/Downgrades

A research report that contains an analyst's earnings estimate also includes a target for the stock price and the analyst's recommendation about whether to buy, hold, or sell the company's stock. But unforeseen events can impact or enhance the company's prospects, and when this happens, analysts often change their estimates, their ratings, and their target prices.

The analyst's announcement of the change is picked up by the media as an upgrade or downgrade (some call it a *research alert*). The announcement may not state the upgrade or downgrade in precise terms, but it will be clear whether the analyst's change of opinion is a positive change or a negative change. The magnitude of a change in target price is also important.

 research alert
a notice issued by an analyst who has upgraded or downgraded his or her recommendation on a stock.

Interpreting the 'Grades

An analyst's recommendation is made on a continuum:

Strong buy ↔ Buy ↔ Accumulate ↔ Hold ↔ Sell ↔ Strong sell

With regard to upgrades and downgrades, moving two levels is more meaningful than moving one level. For example, moving from hold to buy is a stronger vote of confidence than moving from accumulate to buy. But the position of the upgrade or downgrade on the continuum is also important. An upgrade from accumulate to strong buy has more significance than an upgrade from hold to buy, even though both are two levels.

Trading upgrades and downgrades can be tricky, because the announcement is always a surprise and usually made before the market opens. As a result, the stock may react violently and gap up or down several points. David Nassar recommends selling into the "buying public"—doing the opposite of the "dumb money." In other words, if the stock gaps up, short it.[7]

Where to Find Upgrades/Downgrades. The best source of upgrades and downgrades is your real-time news feed. Lacking that, try these lists, which are not in real time:

- ✔ SmartMoney.com (www.smartmoney.com) lists the date and time of the upgrade, the broker making the call, and the rating.
- ✔ Market Guide Investor (www.marketguide.com) states the new rating and the previous rating, which helps you measure the importance of the revised recommendation.

Stock Splits

When its stock price reaches what a company considers an unaffordable level for the average investor, the company declares a stock split. There is no agreement on what constitutes an "unaffordable level"—some stocks split at around $100 a share, some at $200, some at $400, some—like Warren Buffett's Berkshire Hathaway—never split. Splitting a stock doesn't change the value of a stock, of course. If a company announces a two for one split, shareholders will receive two shares for every share they own and the stock's price will be cut in half. If the stock had been selling at $100 before the split and you owned 100 shares, your holdings were worth $10,000; after the stock split, you have 200 shares that are worth $50 each, which is still $10,000.

Berkshire Hathaway (BRK.A), which has never been split, was selling for $58,700 a share on April 17, 2000.

Nevertheless, the stock price often increases after a split announcement because the public believes it will go up. They buy it on that assumption, and the increase often becomes a self-fulfilling prophecy.

And therein lies the opportunity for the day trader.

Trading splits, however, is tricky. Not every stock generates the enthusiasm of Qualcomm (QCOM), which shot up 30 points during the week following its four-for-one split announcement in early November 1999. There may be weeks or months between the announcement and the time the stock actually splits—the pay date—and some companies don't even announce the pay date when they announce the split. Because the announcement date and the pay date both generate excitement, stock splits can be played in stages. For a detailed stock split strategy, read the free "Stock Split Manual" at www.investmenthouse.com.

Record Date versus Pay Date. In a stock split, the company picks a cutoff date—the record date—to determine the shareholders of record, the ones who are to receive the new shares. The split shares are not distributed, however, until the pay date—the effective date of the split. If the split shares reach your account on the pay date—because you were the owner on the record date—but you no longer own the stock, the shares will be forwarded to the new owner. In other words, whoever owns the stock on the pay date will receive the split shares. It will just take the new owner a little longer to receive them.

Where to Find Stock Splits. Here are some of the best web sites for tracking stock split announcements.

✔ The Online Investor (www.investhelp.com), which supplies split data to CBS MarketWatch (www.cbs.marketwatch.com) and other sites, offers a free e-mail split alert and the stock split calendar shown in Figure 5.3.

✔ InvestmentHouse.com (www.investmenthouse.com) offers a free e-mail alert of split announcements. Its "Stock Split Forecast" report, which costs $49.95 a month, anticipates "possible stock

COMPANY NAME	TICKER	SPLIT	ANNOUNCE DATE	RECORD DATE	PAY DATE
Check Point Software *	CHKP	2 for 1	12/20	1/23	1/28
Cytyc Corp. *	CYTC	2 for 1	12/29	1/14	1/28
Forward Air (H)	FWRD	3 for 2	1/11	1/21	1/28
Human Genome Sciences *	HGSI	2 for 1	1/05	1/14	1/28
CVB Financial (H)	CVB	5 for 4	12/17	1/14	1/31
Castle Energy	CECX	3 for 1	12/30	1/12	1/31
Globix Corp. (H)	GBIX	2 for 2	1/10	1/20	1/31
Universal Electronics	UEIC	2 for 1	1/04	1/10	1/31
CoreComm Ltd. (H)	COMM	3 for 2	1/18	1/28	2/02
NTL Inc. * (H)	NTLI	5 for 4	1/20	1/31	2/03
Asyst Technologies *	ASYT	2 for 1	1/03	1/07	2/04
FactSet Research Systems (H)	FDS	2 for 1	1/13	1/21	2/04
Sprint PCS Group*	PCS	2 for 1	12/14	1/4	2/04
Telefonos de Mexico ADRs *	TMX	2 for 1	1/20	1/31	2/04
Forrester Research	FORR	2 for 1	1/18	1/31	2/07
Microchip Technology * (H)	MCHP	3 for 2	1/03	1/18	2/07

FIGURE 5.3 The stock split calendar at The Online Investor gives the date of the announcement, the record date, and the pay date. The circled H links to the company's stock split history. *Source:* Reprinted with permission of The Online Investor, www.investhelp.com.

splits before they are announced by the company," along with a target date for the announcement.

✔ RightLine (www.rightline.net) offers a thrice-weekly e-mail report on trading stock splits. They use splits to define a universe of stocks, then teach short-term trading of the stocks. Subscription is $49.95/month or $399.95/year.

Trading IPOs

Initial public offerings, especially dot-com IPOs, are a favorite play for many day traders. In fact, day traders have been credited (blamed?) for the meteoric first-day rise of dozens of Internet IPOs. Trading IPOs is tricky, however. The best way is to get an allotment of shares at the offering price, virtually impossible on a hot IPO unless you have a six-figure account at an affiliated brokerage firm. If you don't, you'll have to be nimble and quick on the first day of trading.

Ordinary investors can get badly burned by the debut of a hot IPO, but day traders have some tools that give them a big advantage: direct access through electronic brokers, instantaneous executions, and SelectNet preferencing (limit orders are a must). With these tools, you stand a better chance than the average investor of getting in near the open and riding the spike (assuming it spikes). Further, no one will penalize you for *flipping*.

If you want to play the IPO game, however, you need to understand the IPO process.

The process of going public is a staged one. The major stages are: (1) the filing of a prospectus with the SEC, (2) establishing the offering price of the shares, (3) Day 1, when trading begins, (4) the quiet period, (5) the lockup period, and (6) performance in the aftermarket.

flipping
buying shares in an IPO at the offering price and selling soon after the shares start trading in order to cash in on an early profit. This practice is frowned upon by underwriters and brokers.

1. *The filing date.* The filing date is when the company files with the Securities and Exchange Commission its offering memorandum to go public. A calendar of filing dates lets you know which companies are in the pipeline.

2. *Pricing of the shares.* A range of offering prices is established well before the IPO is actually priced

(Figure 5.4). The range may be changed several times during the last few days before trading starts. On the day before the company goes public, the actual price at which shares will be offered to the public is established and announced. In a hot IPO, the offering price is usually at the high end of the range.

3. *Going public.* This is Day 1, the day on which the company's shares begin trading in the public market. The hottest IPOs will usually be followed closely by the financial media.

4. *The quiet period.* From the initial filing with the SEC until 25 days after the stock starts trading, the IPO company cannot do or say anything that could be interpreted as hyping its stock. This is a loosely interpreted restriction, however, as it is common practice for the CEO of a high-profile IPO to be interviewed on CNBC on the day of the offering.

5. *Lockup period.* Insiders cannot sell their shares in a new IPO until 180 days after the start of trading. When this lockup period is over, the stock price often takes a big hit as insiders start cashing in.

6. *Aftermarket performance.* Many IPO sites track the *aftermarket performance* of the IPO in the weeks and months after it starts trading, comparing the current price with the offering price.

Trading IPOs is risky, but if you decide to do it, pick your targets carefully and don't be greedy. It's better to get out a few points shy of the high than to get caught in the stampede when the day's euphoria starts to fade.

IPO Terms of Endearment. IPOs have inspired a whole glossary of colorful jargon. Three terms of special importance are: offering price, opening price, and flipping.

The *offering price* is the price paid by those who are allocated shares by the *underwriter*. In theory, this is the

aftermarket performance
The trading performance of a stock after it has gone public.

offering price
the price at which an IPO is priced by the underwriter and the price paid by those who are allocated shares in an IPO. On a hot IPO, the offering price may be significantly lower than the opening price.

ipoinfo calendar

Week of February 14, 2000				
Company (Symbol) Lead Manager	Date	Shares (in millions)	Offering Price	Est. Offering Amount
APROPOS TECHNOLOGY, INC. (APRS) Chase H&Q	Week of Feb. 14	3.20	$13.00 - $15.00	$44,800,000
CHOICE ONE COMMUNICATIONS INC. (CWON) Morgan Stanley Dean Witter	2/15/00	7.15	$15.00 - $17.00	$114,320,000
CHORDIANT SOFTWARE, INC. (CHRD) Robertson Stephens	2/14/00	4.50	$14.00 - $16.00	$67,500,000
DIVERSA CORPORATION (DVSA) Bear, Stearns & Co. Inc.	Week of Feb. 14	7	$20.00 - $22.00	$147,000,000
ELOQUENT, INC. (ELOQ) U.S. Bancorp Piper Jaffray Inc.	2/16/00	4.50	$10.00 - $12.00	$49,500,000
eSAFETYWORLD, INC. (SFTY) Kashner Davidson Securities Corporation	2/16/00	1	$7.00	$7,000,000
GIGAMEDIA (GIGM) Goldman, Sachs & Co.	2/17/00	8.83	$13.00 - $15.00	$123,620,000
INFORTE CORP. (INFT) Goldman, Sachs & Co.	2/17/00	2	$23.00 - $25.00	$48,000,000
JEREMY'S MICROBATCH ICE CREAMS, INC. (JMIC) First Montauk Securities Corp.	Week of Feb. 14	1.20	$6.00 - $7.00	$7,800,000
LENDINGTREE, INC. (TREE) Merrill Lynch & Co.	2/15/00	3.65	$10.00 - $12.00	$40,150,000
SAVVIS COMMUNICATIONS CORPORATION (SVVS) Merrill Lynch & Co.	2/14/00	17	$22.00 - $25.00	$399,500,000

FIGURE 5.4 The IPO.com calendar shows the range of the expected offering price of each IPO, along with the total amount of the offering, in shares and dollars to be raised. The name of the lead underwriter appears below the company's name. *Source:* Reprinted with permission of IPO.com, www.ipo.com.

price at which shares will be offered to the public. But the *opening price*—the price at which the new stock starts trading on the first day—is frequently much higher than the offering price. A hot IPO can gap up 20, 30, 40 points or more at the open.

Investors who receive the offering price in a IPO and then sell the stock shortly after it starts trading are guilty of flipping the stock. Flipping is frowned upon by the un-

underwriter
an investment banking firm that takes a company public by buying the securities from the company and reselling the shares to the public. The primary firm is the lead manager; the other firms assisting in the underwriting are the comanagers or counderwriters.

derwriters and brokerage firms, and some brokers penalize customers who flip shares by barring them from future offerings for 30 to 60 days, or longer.

Where to Find IPOs. Here are some places on the Web to learn about and track IPOs:

- ✔ CBS MarketWatch (www.cbs.marketwatch.com) has an excellent primer on IPOs. It's under Market Data → Research → IPO Basics.
- ✔ IPO.com (www.ipo.com) has a calendar of scheduled pricings, list of recent filings, and news on IPOs.
- ✔ Alert-IPO (www.alertipo.com) lets you track up to 20 IPOs of your choice through their various stages.
- ✔ For news on the hottest IPOs, go to Internetnews.com, CBS MarketWatch, and TheStreet.com.
- ✔ CNBC.com offers follow-ups of on-air broadcasts.

opening price
the price at which shares in an IPO start trading.

STOCKS ON THE MOVE

What if you're a scalper who just wants to find stocks on the move—those with lots of momentum and high volume? What if you want to find the day's technical breakouts or a small group of fundamentally sound stocks? Out of the 10,000 stocks on the Nasdaq and the NYSE, how do you narrow the choices down to a tradable few?

The first place to start is with your trading software. After that, there is the World Wide Web.

Finding Stocks with Your Trading Software

Most of the high-end trading systems incorporate simple selective screens that run in dynamic real-time tickers. They scan all NYSE and Nasdaq stocks for those that match the screening criteria. The most common screens are top 10 gainers, top 10 losers, and top 10 stocks with highest volume. Some systems offer screens for intraday highs and lows or stocks reaching or nearing their 52-week highs or lows. These lists, like the top 10s, are displayed in a dynamic ticker window and updated on a real-time basis.

One system—GROTrader at www.grotrader.com—incorporates a sophisticated screening program from Telescan, Inc., called ProSearch. ProSearch Alerts allow you to search for stocks based on the technical or fundamental criteria of your choice. The stocks that meet the screening criteria are displayed in a dynamically updating window.

Web-Based Screening Programs

Web-based screening programs are inadequate for scalpers and fast-moving markets because they use delayed rather than real-time data, but they can be used to find stocks for swing trading or position trading. Some sites offer predefined screens; some offer custom screens.

Predefined Screens. Predefined screens are those created by the web sites. Some sites simply list the stocks from the screens that they run on a daily basis; others allow you to run the screens yourself on their proprietary databases. Here are several to check out:

✔ The Big Easy Investor (www.bigeasyinvestor.com). Technical screens. You have to download the screening software—which, at the moment, is free. The site also lists stocks from three daily screens.

✔ Equis International (www.equis.com). Stock lists from 14 technical screens (click Hot Stocks under Free Stuff).

✔ HardRightEdge.com (www.hardrightedge.com). Top five stocks from several screens based on different technical trading strategies. Free. There is also a good article on "Effective Stock Scanning" to help you set up your own technical screens.

What's Hot, What's Not

If your trading software doesn't track hot stocks of the day, you'll have to find your own lists on the Web. Some sites present hot stocks by market (Nasdaq, NYSE); others, by specific categories. Some sites layer their lists: first by sector, then by industry group, then by stocks within the industry. Here are some sites to check out:

Web Site	*Hot Stocks/Sectors*	*Markets*
America-iNvest.com www.americainvest.com	Big Gainers, Big Losers, Most Active	Nasdaq microcaps
BigCharts.com www.bigcharts.com	10 Best Performing Industries, 10 Best Performing Stocks in each industry	All markets
Market Guide Investor www.marketguide.com	What's Hot: Sectors & Industries, Stocks $2–$10, Stocks $10 and Up	All markets—plus top five performance leaders in NYSE, Nasdaq, and AMEX markets
Nasdaq www.nasdaq.com	10 Most Active, 10 Most Advanced, 10 Most Declined	Nasdaq
Quicken.com www.quicken.com	Top 10 Biggest Gainers, Biggest Losers, and Most Active	U.S. stocks, NYSE, Nasdaq, AMEX, Canadian
Wall Street City www.wallstreetcity.com	✔Stock of the Hour (one that exhibits strong technical patterns or recent breakouts, complete with analysis) ✔Top 25 Stocks with Unusual Volume Alert ✔GroupThink (weekly industry group analysis) ✔Best & Worst Industry Group Chart ✔Industry Group Searches	All markets

✔ INVESTools (www.investools.com). Mostly fundamental screens that you can run on the INVESTools database. Free.

✔ SiXer.cOm (www.sixer.com). Daily screens of trending stocks. Free.

Custom Screens. The best screening tools allow you to create your own custom screen. CNBC.com's free screening tool (based on Telescan's ProSearch) lets you select from 60 criteria to customize a search. (The full-blown ProSearch with 300 criteria is available at www.wallstreetcity.com.) For each criterion you can instruct the computer to find stocks either within minimum and maximum ranges or with the highest or lowest values for that indicator.

Using nine screening criteria, we found a list of high-volume, upward-trending stocks with high volatility. We restricted the search to Nasdaq stocks over $25 and requested stocks with the highest possible values for each indicator:

✔ A high beta and high daily price range assure that the stocks have high volatility. (*Beta* measures the volatility of the stock relative to the market.)

✔ 50-day and 200-day moving average breakouts, plus high one-day and one-week relative performance, find stocks that are trending upward.

 beta
a measurement of volatility. With regard to stocks, beta measures how much a stock fluctuates in price, over a specified period of time, compared with the market as a whole. A beta of 1, for example, means that the stock and market move in tandem. A beta higher than 1 indicates that the stock is more volatile than the market; lower than 1, that it is less volatile than the market.

Do Your Own Analysis

Never take a stock pick or screening result at face value. They are meant simply to provide leads. You'll need to do your own analysis as to the potential of the stock for your trading style. More important, be sure to check out any disclaimer that accompanies the picks or screens. Anyone who holds a position in stock he or she is recommending obviously has an agenda. Such schemes are often called "pump and dump." Avoid them, or you may end up the dumpee.

✔ High volume, high 30-day average volume, and high 1-to-30-day average volume ratio ensure heavy trading volume.

Figure 5.5 shows an intraday graph of the top stock from a search on January 3. As you can see, it would have provided an active trading day for a scalper or trend trader.

Both CNBC.com and Wall Street City have dozens of prebuilt screens, in addition to the custom screens. Other Web-based screening programs can be found at Hoover's (www.hoovers.com), Market Guide Investor (www.marketguide), Quicken.com (www.quicken.com), and Thomson Investors Network (www.thomsoninvest.com).

Hybrid Styles

The trading styles described in this chapter are not cast in concrete. Many traders borrow a little from this and a little from that to create a hybrid style that is unlike any

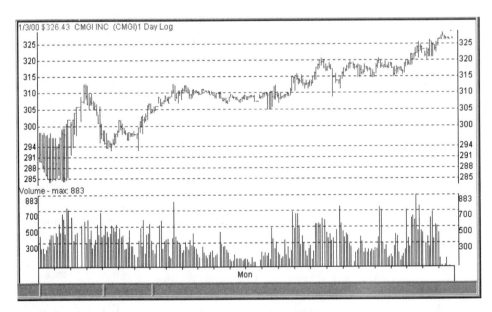

FIGURE 5.5 CMGI, Inc., shown in this one-day chart, was the top stock from a search made on January 3, 2000, for high-volume, high-volatility, upward-trending stocks. *Source:* Stock graph from TIP@Wallstreet, reprinted with permission of Telescan, Inc., www.telescan.com.

others. Two traders I met at the Online Trading Expo did just that.

Kevin, a scalper and ardent fan of Joe DiNapoli,[8] trades just two Nasdaq stocks, Microsoft and Dell Computer. A news event may be the impetus for a trade or he may simply trade the intraday trends, but he trades the

The Fallacy of Paper Trading

Paper trading allows you to test trading strategies and styles without risking any money. When you paper trade, you simply pick a point of entry on a stock and record it as a buy in a portfolio or a journal. When the stock reaches or fails to reach your target, you pick the exit point and record it as a sale.

The fallacy of paper trading is that the entry and exit points aren't necessarily the same as they'd be in actual trading. For example, in a fast-moving stock, you might not be able to buy the stock at the price reflected in your paper trade. By the time your order is executed, the stock could have ticked up a point or more. The reverse can happen when you're trying to get out of a stock.

The biggest fallacy of paper trading, though, is that there is no money behind your decision. Without your money at risk, fear and greed are not triggered, so your trades are made in an emotionless state (as they should be made in real life but rarely are!).

Paper trading is still worthwhile. Just recognize it for what it is, and don't think you're going to be a superstar based on your paper performance. One rule of thumb in judging paper trades is to cut your gains in half. If that leaves you in the black, then you may have found a good strategy or style.

The same caveats apply to *simulated trading*, which usually refers to using trading software in the demo mode. The major purpose of simulated trading is to become familiar with the software before trading for keeps.

 paper trading
picking entry and exit points on a stock as if you were actually making a trade and tracking the trades on paper. No money is involved in paper trading.

 simulated trading
using trading software to place mock buy and sell orders and track positions; similar to paper trading in that there is no actual money involved. The purpose is both to practice trading and to become familiar with the trading software.

two stocks throughout the day, using Fibonacci lines for timing signals. What would you call him? A news-event-driven Nasdaq-specialist technical scalper, perhaps?

Vince, an entrepreneur and a golfer, trades a small group of growth stocks, ones he would not mind owning on a long-term basis. He may make a trade in the morning, then head for the office or the golf course. If the trade goes against him while he's on the 18th hole, he really doesn't care; he just moves the stock to his investing portfolio and hangs on to it for a while. Is he a swing-trading fundamental specialist or an investor who dabbles in day trading?

Trading style is a personal matter. It should match your personality and behavior patterns, or else you'll not only be unsuccessful but miserable to boot. You probably know instinctively which styles you don't want. (For example, nothing about scalping or grinding appeals to me.) So start with a process of elimination. Borrow a little from different styles, if you wish. Paper trade the ones that interest you. Seek out a mentor in a style you like. It won't take long to discover whether you're a Bjorn Borg at heart or a John McEnroe.

COMING UP . . .

Some traders go their whole lives without knowing the first thing about technical analysis. One of the traders on the Million Dollar Panel flatly states that charts get in his way (because they're after the fact). Other traders use technical charts as their primary tool for trading. Before you make up your mind which way you'll go, take a look at the next chapter, which introduces you to technical analysis in its simplest and most user-friendly form.

Technical Analysis for the Technically Challenged

I f you want to know the price of a stock, just look at a stock quote. But all that tells you is what the stock is doing at the current time. To view the stock in any sort of context, you must look at a stock chart. A stock chart can show you a stock's history; its high and low for the day, week, month, or year; its current trading range; and whether it is in an uptrend, a downtrend, or trendless. Moreover, a chart can reveal where a stock is going, as well as where it's been.

Discerning the future direction of a stock is the goal of technical analysis.

If the mere words "technical analysis" make your eyes glaze over, think of it as visual analysis, as John J. Murphy calls it in his book, *The Visual Investor: How to Spot Stock Market Trends*.[1] A chart is a visual representation—a picture, really—of a stock's trading pattern. It presents in graphic form the relationship of today's price with that of a day, a week, a month, a year, or several years ago. To analyze a picture of the stock is to look for trends in its trading patterns. As John Murphy says, "If you can read a line on a chart and learn to tell *up* from *down*, you won't have any trouble grasping what visual analysis is all about."

I highly recommend *The Visual Investor*. It is straightforward and easy to understand, but if you haven't got a clue about charts and graphs and patterns and trends, this chapter will provide an introduction. At the end of this chapter, I'll point you to web sites where you can practice what you learn in this chapter and in any books that you read on the subject of technical analysis.

**linear
chart**
a chart that
shows the price
data on an arith-
metic scale, treat-
ing each price
increment
equally.

**logarithmic
chart**
a chart that
scales stock
prices by per-
centages.

START WITH A CHART

A price-and-volume chart plots the price of a stock and the number of shares traded over a given period of time. That said, you can count on the fact that every charting tool on the Web plots the same data a little differently. For example, most offer you a choice between *linear charts* and *logarithmic charts*, or they arbitrarily display one or the other. Here's the difference.

A linear chart shows the price data on an arithmetic scale, treating each price increment equally. Look at the linear chart of Qualcomm in Figure 6.1. All the lines are equally spaced. The price scale from $150 to $200 is

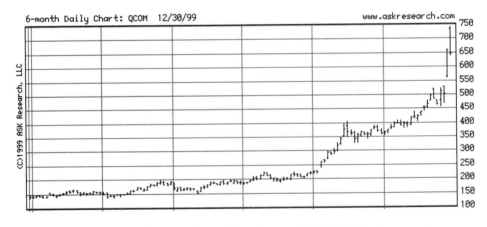

FIGURE 6. 1   This is a linear chart of Qualcomm (QCOM). Note the evenly spaced price increments. *Source:* Stock graph reprinted with permission of ASK Research, www.askresearch.com.

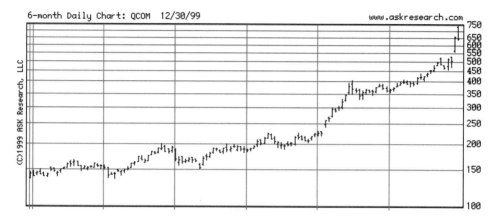

FIGURE 6.2   This chart of Qualcomm shows the same data as in Figure 6.1, but plotted on a logarithmetic scale. Note the decreasing price increments at the top of the chart, which represent smaller percentage gains. *Source:* Stock graph reprinted with permission of ASK Research, www.askresearch.com.

equal, graphically, to the price scale from $650 to $700— even though the former represents a 33 percent increase while the latter represents an 8 percent increase.

Now look at the same Qualcomm chart on a logarithmic price scale in Figure 6.2. The logarithmic chart is scaled by percentages. The lines are closer together at the top of the chart, making the 33 percent price move from $150 to $250 much more significant, graphically, than the 8 percent move from $650 to $700. Clearly, the logarithmic chart presents a more accurate picture of the price movement. Murphy suggests that linear charts are fine for the short-term picture but that logarithmic charts should be used for longer terms.

Time Span/Data Frequency

A stock chart may cover a time span as short as one or two minutes or as long as one or more decades. The time span dictates the frequency of the data plotted. On a one- or two-minute chart, the data is plotted tick-by-tick—every trade is a point on the chart. On longer intraday charts, prices might be plotted every minute, 5 minutes, 30 minutes, or hour. On longer time spans, say one month to one year, daily prices are usually plotted. On charts of more than two years, the data is compressed. For example, weekly prices might be plotted on 2-year chart, monthly prices on a 10-year chart.

Volume

A stock's trading volume is usually shown in vertical bars below the stock price chart, as in Figure 6.3. Each bar represents the cumulative number of shares traded during the period represented. For example, on the intraday graph in Figure 6.3, each bar represents 30 minutes' trading volume.

Volume offers a measure of the enthusiasm of the crowd in a rising market and the panic in a selling market.

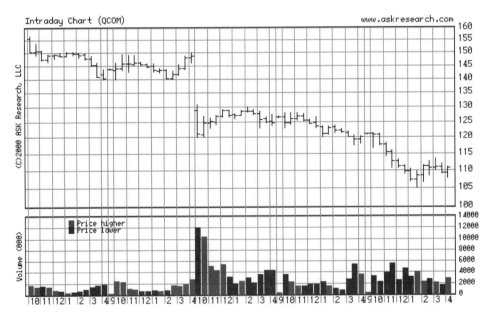

FIGURE 6.3 The cumulative volume for each time period is shown in the lower chart. (On the Web, the volume bars are color coded to reflect whether the closing price was higher or lower that the previous close.) *Source:* Stock graph reprinted with permission of ASK Research, www.askresearch.com.

It can also help you interpret the significance of a technical indicator. For instance, a technical breakout on high
volume is much more meaningful than a breakout on low
volume. Volume is especially significant to day traders
who like to trade stocks with a high daily average volume,
because it means the stock is more liquid.

There are many different ways to plot a chart. Let's look at
three common chart types: bar, line, and candlestick.

The Bar Chart

In a bar chart, each short vertical line—the bar—represents trading—the *open*, high, low, and *close*—within a
specified period. Figure 6.4 shows a one-month bar chart
with daily data.

- ✔ The top and bottom of the bar represents the
  range—the high and low—for the day.
- ✔ The tick mark on the left of the bar is the opening
  price of the stock.
- ✔ The tick mark on the right of the bar is the closing price of the stock.

open
the price at which
a stock first
traded during the
day.

close
the last price at
which a stock
traded during the
day.

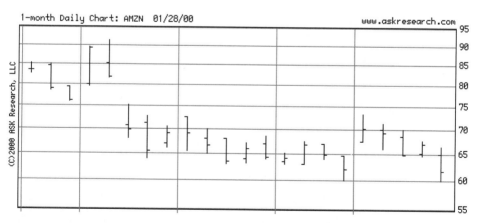

FIGURE 6.4 This one-month bar chart of Amazon.com clearly shows the open
(left tick) and close (right tick) on the daily bar. *Source:* Stock graph reprinted with
permission of ASK Research, www.askresearch.com.

Depending on the charting software, a bar chart may also be referred to as an OHLC (open high low close) chart, or an HLC (high low close) chart. The latter is plotted without the opening price tick.

The Line Chart

A line chart plots the most important price of the period—the closing price—and draws a line to connect the data. Figure 6.5 shows a one-month chart with daily data. Tick-by-tick intraday charts also are line charts.

The Candlestick Chart

The candlestick chart, shown in Figure 6.6, is the Japanese version of the bar chart. The same data—the open, high, low, and close—is represented, but in a more graphic way. An outlined or shaded area—called a candlestick—marks the open and close. If the close is higher than the open, the candlestick is white or clear; if the close is lower than the open, the candlestick is black. The thin line that creates the "wick" on the top and bottom of the candle marks the high and low or the trading range of the period.

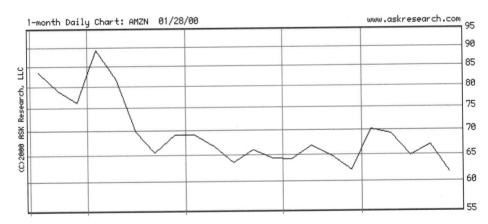

FIGURE 6.5 This chart uses the same data as Figure 6.4, with the closing prices plotted as a line chart. *Source:* Stock graph reprinted with permission of ASK Research, www.askresearch.com.

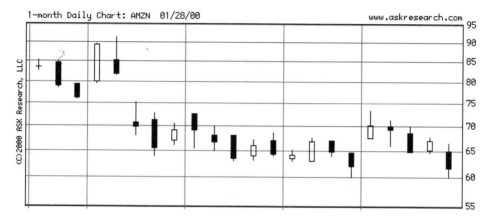

FIGURE 6.6 This candlestick chart plots the same data as the charts in Figures 6.4 and 6.5. The candlesticks provide a more graphical representation. For example, you can readily see that on the date of the graph (1/28/00) AMZN closed lower than it opened, because the candlestick is black. *Source:* Stock graph is reprinted with permission of ASK Research, www.askresearch.com.

At the simplest level (on a black-and-white chart) a white candle is bullish and a black candle is bearish; but interpreting candlestick patterns is an art, and a complicated one at that. Some traders like to use candlestick charts simply because they are more graphic than an ordinary bar chart. If you want to learn more about candlestick charts, read *Candlestick Charting* by Gregory L. Morris, which is available at www.murphymorris.com.

LOOKING FOR PATTERNS AND TRENDS

A stock never travels in a straight line on its upward journey. It moves up for a while, pulls back, catches its breath, starts up again, and repeats the pattern over and over as it reaches higher and higher highs and higher and higher lows. The trip down is a dance in reverse, with the stock making lower and lower highs and lower and lower lows.

These movements form short-term uptrends and downtrends within the long-term upward or downward trend. The force behind a short-term trend is often overreaction to rumors and news. The force behind a long-term trend is usually attributable to institutional money flowing into or out of the stock. Institutions such as pension funds or mutual funds represent billions of dollars, and when that money starts to flow into or out of a stock it can lift a stock to new heights or pull the rug out from under it.

The patterns produced by trends form the basis of technical analysis. The simplest form of technical analysis is trendlines, and the simplest form of trendline analysis is rising and falling trendlines.

Rising and Falling Trendlines

A rising trendline is drawn through stock bottoms to delineate an uptrend (Figure 6.7). The line defines the area of support created as the stock pulls back and surges forward in its climb toward higher and higher levels. The

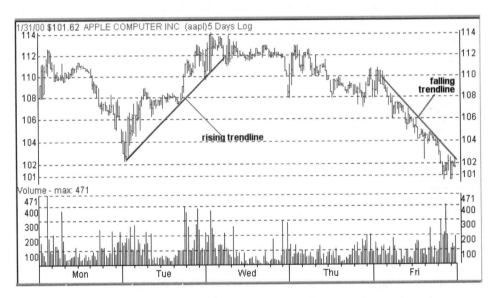

FIGURE 6.7 In this five-day graph for Apple Computer (AAPL) the intraday uptrend on Tuesday is marked with a rising trendline and the intraday downtrend on Friday, with a falling trendline. *Source:* Stock graph from TIP@Wallstreet, reprinted with permission of Telescan, Inc., www.telescan.com.

more bottoms the trendline touches, the more significant the uptrend.

When the stock price falls below a rising trendline, it is called a trend break. This is a sign of weakness, but whether it is significant depends on other technical signals. Few technical signals are used in isolation; most technicians have two or three favorite indicators that they use to gather a "preponderance of evidence."

A falling trendline creates a mirror image of the rising trendline (Figure 6.7). A falling trendline drawn through stock tops shows the area of resistance as the stock tries to pull out of its downward slide; each time the stock reverses, touches the trendline, and falls back, the trend is strengthened.

Thus, the more tops the trendline touches, the more valid the downtrend. When the stock penetrates the falling trendline, however, and moves above it, an upward trend break occurs. An upward trend break on high volume is a sign of strength, but again, it should not be relied on by itself.

Trends are sometimes referred to as primary (long-term) and secondary (short-term). Secondary trends occur within primary trends; the more short-term trends there are within a long-term trend, the greater the stock's volatility.

Intraday trends—those sharp spikes during the course of the trading day—are much loved by the trend trader, while short-term trends lasting a day to a week or two are favored by swing traders and those who trade news-driven events. Traders who restrict their trading to a

Analyzing Market Indexes

Most technical indicators can be used to analyze market indexes or industry groups. Some indicators, however, such as the advance/decline line, are designed especially as group indicators. For more on market analysis, see Chapter 7.

basket of fundamentally sound stocks may want to consider the stock's longer-term trend as well.

The LSQ Line

A unique kind of trendline is the LSQ line. This line is based on a mathematical formula called least squares, and it establishes the midpoint of the data by placing roughly half the price activity above the line and half below the line. An LSQ line (Figure 6.8) reveals the relationship of the current stock price with its historical price trend.

Drawing parallel lines through stock tops and bottoms on either side of the LSQ line will form a trading channel on the graph, as shown in Figure 6.8. This channel can help you assess the future trading range of the stock. The LSQ line can be applied to market indexes and industry groups as well as to stocks.

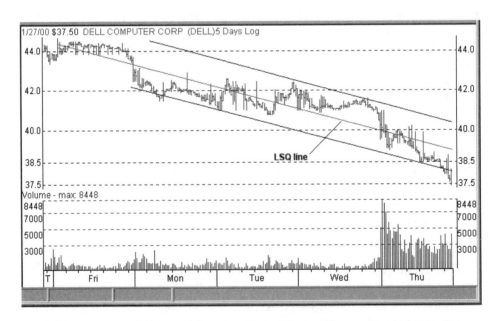

FIGURE 6.8 In this five-day graph, Dell is clearly oversold with regard to its short-term price trend as defined by its LSQ line. *Source:* Stock graph from TIP@Wallstreet, reprinted with permission of Telescan, Inc., www.telescan.com.

There is much more to trendline analysis than we've covered here. Keep in mind that the purpose of this chapter is to provide some basics for your further study.

Support and Resistance

An area of support or resistance occurs at a price level where a stock reverses its downward or upward trend. Resistance represents a ceiling—a price the stock seems to have trouble rising beyond; support represents a floor—a price level that catches and holds the stock when it tumbles from a high.

Long-term support and resistance areas are created to a large extent by institutional investors who target certain price levels as good entry or exit points for a stock and often base their targets on prior support and resistance levels. Thus, when the stock reaches a resistance level, sellers step in and start selling and the stock backs off. When the stock reaches a support level, buyers step in and start buying, and the stock stops falling.

Areas of support and resistance are delineated with horizontal lines. A support line is drawn horizontally through stock bottoms (Figure 6.9). It represents a price level at which the stock has reversed its downward trend again and again and again. The more bottoms the support line touches, the stronger the support at that level. And, the stronger the support, the more significant is the breaking of that support.

A resistance line is drawn horizontally through stock tops, representing a price level that the stock has trouble penetrating (Figure 6.10). Each time it reaches this level, it seems to lose heart and fall back. Again, the more tops the resistance line touches, the stronger the barrier to further increases. What the stock needs to push through the resistance and keep it moving is strong volume. Volume provides the momentum to keep a stock moving in the direction of the trend.

When a stock breaks through a resistance line or falls through a support line, it is called a trend break. Trend breaks offer good entry and exit points, given sufficient corroboration from other factors. They can also

 wash and rinse
refers to a situation that occurs when a stock drops just far enough to clear out your stop and then resumes its upward march. This happens when stops are set at obvious levels, such as support lines; market makers who realize this push the price down to take out the stops.

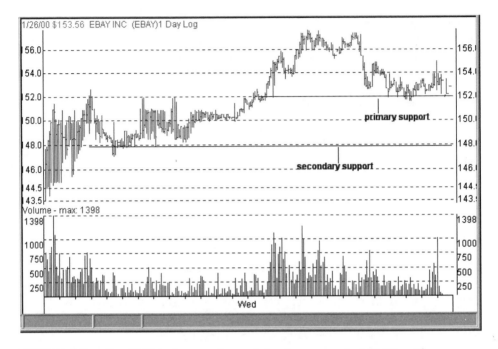

FIGURE 6.9   eBay (EBAY) shows primary intraday support at $152, with secondary support at about $148. *Source:* Stock graph from TIP@Wallstreet, reprinted with permission of Telescan, Inc., www.telescan.com.

be used as targets and stops, although it is not wise to set a stop too near a support level because you may get *washed and rinsed*—a practice of market makers who let a stock sink just low enough to take out the obvious stops.

When Resistance Becomes Support

You'll notice, after you've looked at many, many stock graphs, that an area of resistance often becomes an area of support, once the stock has moved beyond the resistance price. When the stock reverses its trend, it tends to fall back to the former level of resistance, which then becomes a new support level. The opposite is also true.

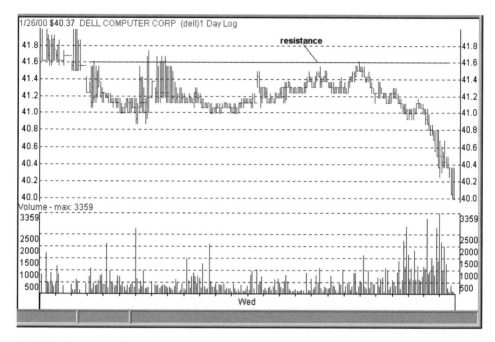

FIGURE 6.10   Dell Computer (DELL) shows an intraday resistance level of about $41⅝ on this one-day graph. *Source*: Stock graph from TIP@Wallstreet, reprinted with permission of Telescan, Inc., www.telescan.com.

Trendlines and support and resistance lines can be used to discern dozens of patterns in a stock chart. These patterns bear names like double tops, double bottoms, cups and handles, head and shoulders, and various kinds of triangles, but I will leave those to your further study (you can day trade forever without needing to know them). We will, however, talk about one pattern formed by support and resistance lines: *basing* periods.

Basing Period Breakouts

When support and resistance lines move close together, as they do in Figure 6.11, the stock may trade within a narrow price range for several hours, days, or weeks. During this time the stock is said to be in a basing period. Basing periods themselves are boring; it is when a stock breaks out of a basing period that you should pay attention.

basing
trading within a narrow range of prices. In effect, the resistance and support levels have moved close together and the stock is unable to break above resistance or below support.

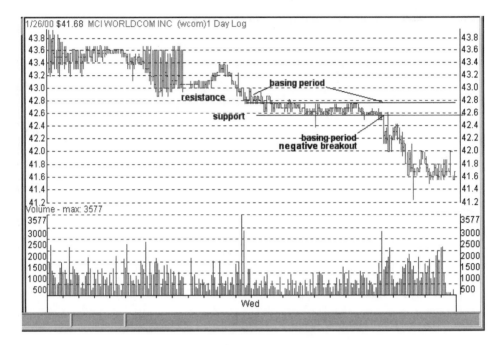

FIGURE 6.11 This graph shows a very narrow intraday basing period for MCI Worldcom (WCOM) and the subsequent breakdown (on high volume) in late afternoon. *Source:* Stock graph from TIP@Wallstreet, reprinted with permission of Telescan, Inc., www.telescan.com.

A positive breakout occurs when the stock moves above the line of resistance, fueled by an infusion of buyers. A negative breakout (or breakdown) occurs when the stock moves below support, pressured by an abundance of sellers. Whether the breakout is significant depends on three things:

✔ *The tightness of the basing pattern.* A basing pattern is measured by time span and price range. In other words, how long has the stock been basing and between what prices? A stock that bases for an extended period within a narrow price range, as WCOM did in Figure 6.11, has a very tight basing pattern. A breakout of that pattern would be significant, depending on the magnitude of the breakout and the volume behind it.

✔ *The magnitude of the breakout.* A half-point breakout is more impressive than a quarter-point breakout; a full point is more exciting than a half point.

✔ *The volume behind the breakout.* Strong volume helps sustain the upward or downward thrust of the stock. If a breakout is on weak volume, the stock may drift right back into the basing pattern.

A significant basing pattern breakout, then, would be a move of one-half to one point from a tight basing pattern, accompanied by strong volume.

Moving Averages

A moving average is another way to assess the trend of a stock. John Murphy calls a moving average a curving trendline. I call it a flowing trendline, because it moves through the peaks and valleys of the stock chart and smooths out the trend. Whatever you call it, a moving average indicates a directional trend and delineates yet an area of support and resistance.

A simple moving average is plotted by totaling the daily closing stock prices over a specific time span and di-

Variations on a Theme

In a simple moving average, each day's price carries the same weight, which tends to create a lot of whipsaws (reversals between buy and sell signals). A weighted moving average gives additional weight to the more recent stock prices and less to more distant prices, thus smoothing out the line. An exponential moving average is a weighted moving average based on a specific mathematical formula. Most charting programs offer a choice of simple or exponential averages.

viding that total by the number of periods in the time span. To make it "move," the average is recalculated each period to incorporate the current price and drop the most distant price.

A moving average can be of any length; some popular ones are 20-day, 30-day, 50-day, and 200-day averages—each indicating a successively longer trend. (Day traders who use intraday charts would use minutes, rather than days, but the principle is the same.) Moving averages with the shorter time spans are more sensitive and hug the stock price more closely (a short moving average is said to be "faster" than a longer one). Figure 6.12 shows a fast moving average (60-minute) and a slow moving average (180-minute) for Dell Computer.

Here are several ways to interpret moving averages.

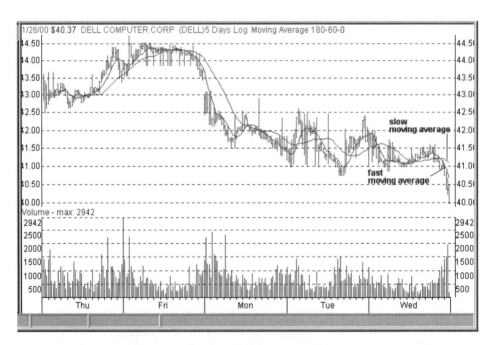

FIGURE 6.12 The crossovers of the fast and slow moving averages on this Dell Computer (DELL) graph pinpoint trend reversals and possible entry and exit points. (On the actual graph, the two moving averages are shown in different colors.) *Source:* Stock graph from TIP@Wallstreet, reprinted with permission of Telescan, Inc., www.telescan.com.

Keep in mind that these guidelines are very general and should not be used in isolation.

✔ When the stock price crosses over a moving average, a trend reversal may be imminent.

✔ Two moving averages can be used to determine the continuation of a trend. For example, if the stock is above its long-term moving average when it moves above a short-term average, it is likely to keep going because it has long-term support beneath it.

✔ The crossover of two moving averages might be used for a buy or sell signal. When the faster average crosses over the slower average, upward, it can be a buy signal. If the movement were downward, it would be a sell signal.

Bear in mind that the best technical signals are those that are confirmed by other technical indicators.

Envelopes and Bands

Stocks trade within a predictable area around their moving averages. To help you visualize this trading range, you can draw an "envelope" around the average.

The most common envelope is formed by plotting lines a fixed percentage above and below the moving average, as shown in Figure 6.13. These trading bands encompass the high and low trading range of the stock; the moving average forms an area of support, when the stock is above the average, or resistance, when it is below the average.

Trading bands help you judge how far a stock might go in the direction it is heading and when a trend reversal is likely to occur. They are best used to confirm other signals. Here are some positive confirmations:

✔ The stock makes a significant new penetration of the top band. (When this happens the stock may "climb the band" for a while as the band itself moves up.)

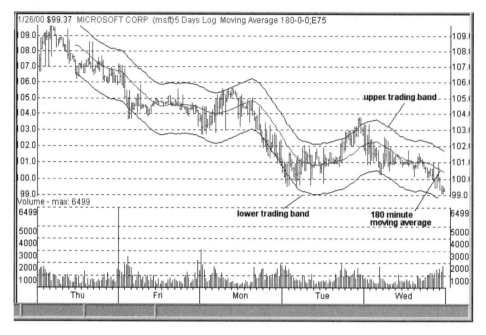

FIGURE 6.13 The trading bands in this graph describe the trading range of Microsoft (MSFT) during a five-day period. *Source:* Stock graph from TIP@Wallstreet, reprinted with permission of Telescan, Inc., www.telescan.com.

✔ The stock touches but doesn't penetrate the bottom band (called a failure swing) and heads back toward the moving average.

✔ After a penetration of the top band, the stock bounces off the moving average and heads back up.

A variation on the trading band theory is Bollinger bands, developed by technical guru John Bollinger. Rather than employing a fixed percentage, Bollinger bands let the market set the trading range by plotting the trading envelope two standard deviations above and below the moving average (Figure 6.14). In this way, the bands monitor a stock's volatility by expanding and contracting with extremes in the trading range: The bands widen in a volatile market and narrow in a calm market.

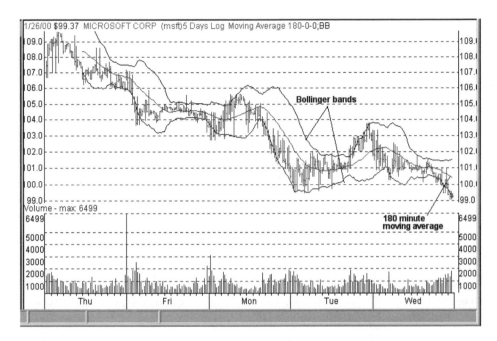

1/26/00 $99.37 MICROSOFT CORP (msft)5 Days Log Moving Average 180-0-0;BB

FIGURE 6.14 This figure shows the same graph as Figure 6.13, but with Bollinger bands. The narrowing of the bands may foretell a significant price movement. *Source:* Stock graph from TIP@Wallstreet, reprinted with permission of Telescan, Inc., www.telescan.com.

An excellent free tutorial on Bollinger bands can be found at www.bollingerbands.com. There's also a $295 video seminar taught by John Bollinger on *How to Trade with Bollinger Bands.*

OSCILLATORS: THE LEADING INDICATORS

So far, the indicators we've discussed are *lagging indicators.* They tell you where a stock has been. You can use them to discern trends, and support and resistance, and from this—since the past is indicative of the future—you can infer possible trend reversals. But for a true *leading indicator,* you'll need to look at oscillators.

An oscillator provides a graphic picture of *overbought*

lagging indicators
technical indicators that confirm the trend of a stock, based on its past trading patterns.

leading indicators
technical indicators that reveal market extremes (overbought or oversold conditions) and anticipate trend reversals.

overbought
a term used in technical analysis that refers to a stock or market having reached a high extreme (a preponderance of buyers) and due for a correction.

oversold
a term used in technical analysis that refers to a stock or market having reached a low extreme (a preponderance of sellers) and due for a reversal.

and *oversold* conditions. Overbought refers to a condition where a stock (or market index) has an overabundance of buyers and is at an extreme high and due for a correction. In an oversold condition, the sellers are in charge and have driven the stock or index to an extreme low. As with any extreme condition, a reversal toward the norm is likely.

According to market experts, one way to predict a reversal is to study the divergence of two trending lines, such as moving averages of different lengths, that normally go in the same direction. An oscillator incorporates this kind of divergence, so it can present both the overbought or oversold condition *and* an indication of when a reversal is likely to occur.

We'll look at two of the most popular oscillators, and then wrap up the discussion with what I called in a technical study several years ago "an indicator for all seasons."

Stochastics

The stochastics index is an oscillator based on a theory by George C. Lane that an upwardly trending stock tends to close around its highs for the trading range, and a downwardly trending stock tends to close around its lows for the trading range. And, as the trend matures, the stock will begin to close further and further away from its high (or low), signaling an imminent reversal.

In essence, the stochastics index uses a ratio of the stock's highs and lows within a given range. There are two numbers involved: One number is for the range of the simple stochastics—the ratio of those highs and lows—and the other is for a moving average of the simple stochastics. The most common stochastics index is based on a 14–5 period—14 periods for the range and 5 periods for the moving average.

You'll find that stochastics are plotted differently by different web sites and charting programs. Some use two lines, some three, and some, like the Intel graph from TIP@Wallstreet (Figure 6.15), use one line with solid overbought/oversold areas, which makes the chart easy to read.

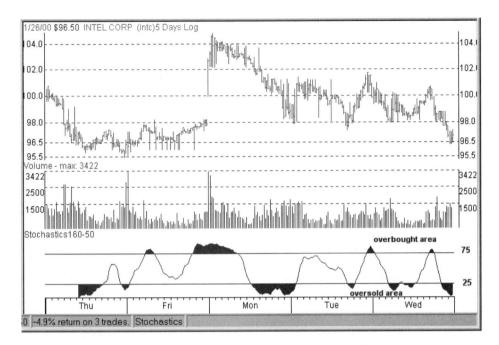

FIGURE 6.15 A five-day stochastics chart for Intel (INTC) shows that it is clearly oversold at the end of Wednesday, January 26. *Source:* Stock graph from TIP@Wallstreet, reprinted with permission of Telescan, Inc., www.telescan.com.

There are also different interpretations of the overbought/oversold areas. Some mark the areas at 80 and 20 percent. TIP@Wallstreet uses 75 and 25 percent: If the stochastics index is above 75, the stock is overbought; if it is below 25, the stock is oversold. On the chart in Figure 6.15, a buy signal is given when the index crosses the 25 line upward; a sell signal is generated when the index crosses the 75 line downward.

In *The Visual Investor*, Murphy uses two stochastics lines—a fast one and a slow one—and 80/20 for the overbought/oversold areas, as shown in Figure 6.16. A buy signal is given when the faster line crosses *above* the slower line in the oversold (below 20) area; a sell signal is given when the faster line crosses *below* the slower line in the overbought (above 80) area.

If you're dying to learn more about stochastics, buy the 90-minute video of the father of stochastics himself

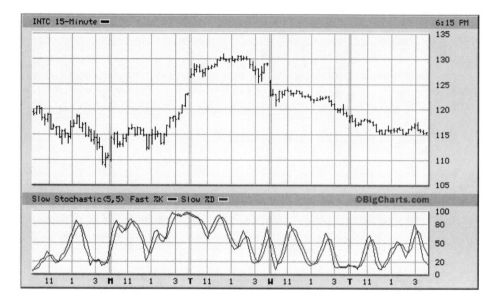

FIGURE 6.16 The lower chart shows a two-line stochastics chart for Intel (INTC). A signal is given when the fast stochastic crosses the slow stochastic. *Source:* Reprinted with permission of BigCharts, Inc., www.bigcharts.com.

(George Lane) discussing the theory, structure, and practical application of stochastics. It's available for $99.95 at www.lanestochastics.com.

The Welles Wilder RSI

The Welles Wilder relative strength index (RSI) was developed by J. Welles Wilder in 1978.[2] It compares a stock's highest highs and lowest lows over a specified period to measure the rate of directional price movement. (The most common periods for the RSI are 14 and 5.)

The RSI, like all of the best oscillators, has clearly delineated areas of overbought and oversold conditions (Figure 6.17). The vertical matrix is scaled from 0 to 100 percent: If the RSI line is over 70, the stock is overbought; if the RSI line is below 30, the stock is oversold. There is a way to pinpoint a divergence by comparing trendlines drawn on the RSI chart and the stock chart,

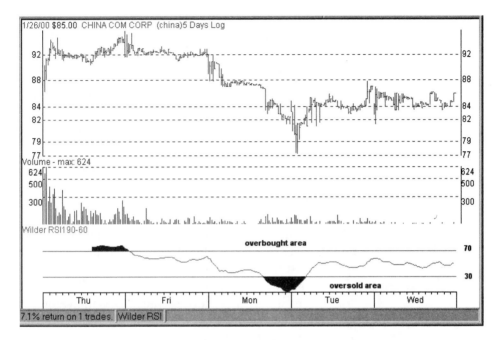

FIGURE 6.17 On this five-day graph, the Welles Wilder relative strength index (RSI) shows China.com (CHINA) in overbought territory late Thursday and moving to oversold by late Monday. *Source:* Stock graph from TIP@Wallstreet, reprinted with permission of Telescan, Inc., www.telescan.com.

but that requires a more detailed RSI than the one shown here. Some traders use the RSI crossing of the 70 line downward as a sell signal and the crossing of the 30 line upward as a buy signal.

The RSI indicator is much more complex than this simple description. You can read more about it in J. Welles Wilder's book, although the material in *The Visual Investor* and at Equity Analytics (www.e-analytics.com) is easier for the beginner.

The MACD: The Indicator for All Seasons

The moving average convergence/divergence indicator— the MACD—is a sort of super–moving average based on a theory developed by Gerald Appel. It is said to measure the intensity and direction of market sentiment and to provide early clues of a trend reversal.

John Murphy calls the MACD the "best of both worlds" because it is a trend-following system, like moving averages, and an oscillator, like the stochastics index. It determines overbought and oversold trends and also generates signals for trend reversals. In a study that I did on the MACD in 1988, I called it "an indicator for all seasons" because it is effective in both a trending *and* a trendless market.[3]

Three exponential moving averages are used to plot the MACD. The most popular lengths are 8/17/9 and 12/25/9—the numbers representing the length of the moving averages. The difference between first two averages is used to plot the MACD line. The third moving average forms the signal line.

There are two ways to view the MACD indicator, as a graph or a histogram. Figure 6.18 shows both the graph and histogram below the main chart.

The MACD Graph. On the MACD graph in Figure 6.18, the MACD line is formed by the vertical bars, and the signal line is the solid line curving through the graph. The convergence and divergence of the MACD line and the signal line provide the buy and sell signals.

✔ A buy signal is given when the MACD line crosses above the signal line.

✔ A sell signal is given when the MACD line crosses below the signal line.

Equally important, however, are the overbought/oversold areas, which are separated by a zero line. Above the zero line is the overbought area; below the zero line is the oversold area. The best buy signals occur in the oversold area, the best sell signals in the overbought area.

The MACD Histogram. The MACD histogram plots the difference between the MACD line and the signal line as solid areas that fluctuate above and below a zero line.

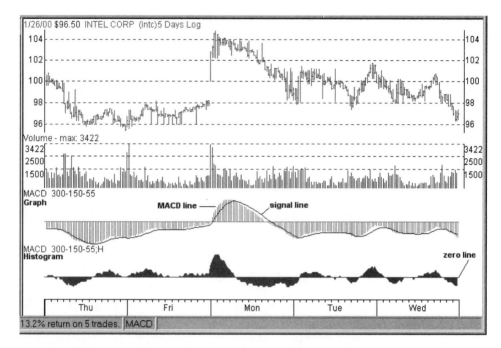

FIGURE 6.18 The first graph below the main Intel (INTC) chart is an MACD graph; the second is an MACD histogram. Both support the stochastics reading in Figure 6.16 which shows the stock as oversold. *Source:* Stock graph from TIP@Wallstreet, reprinted with permission of Telescan, Inc., www.telescan.com.

✔ A histogram above the zero line is bullish; below the zero line it is bearish.

✔ The direction of the histogram tells us whether the trend is gaining or losing momentum: Momentum is increasing if the histogram is moving away from the zero line; momentum is slowing if the histogram is moving toward the zero line.

✔ When the MACD histogram crosses the zero line upward, a buy signal is generated. When the histogram crosses the zero line downward, a sell signal is given.

Murphy says the MACD histogram provides an earlier warning of a potential trend change than the MACD graph. The buy and sell signals are also easier to read.

These few paragraphs barely scratch the surface of the MACD indicator. Murphy's book gives the most lucid explanation I've seen, along with good, clear charts. But if you want to go to the original source, order Gerald Appel's 90-minute MACD video seminar at www.signalert.com. It costs $195 and comes with a 36-page manual.

TECHNICAL ANALYSIS U

There are many web sites that offer educational material for the technical trader. Among them are:

Big Easy Investor

The Traders Playbook at Big Easy Investor (www.bigeasyinvestor.com) offers free slide presentations on several technical plays, including breakout plays, moving average plays, MACD plays, and price-and-volume tandem move plays. The main product, however, is a Windows-based software program that offers charting, analysis, and screening. You can download the software at the site. It is currently free (as of May 2000), but the planned fee schedule is $19.99/month or $199.99/year.

Decision Point

Decision Point (www.decisionpoint.com) offers a technical analysis short course and glossary. $10/month (includes access to daily charts).

Hard Right Edge

Hard Right Edge (www.hardrightedge.com) has a Trading Tactics section that offers free mini-lessons on trend reversals, tops and bottoms, breakouts, corrections, and technical indicators such as Bollinger bands and the mysterious Fibonacci numbers. It also has an interactive course called "Mastering the Trade" that concentrates on charting and technical analysis. It takes you "step-by-step through locating and trading profitable short-term price moves." The course includes RealAudio lectures, interactive charts, and mentoring. The cost depends on which materials you use, but you can get 60-day access to all materials for $99.95. Hard Right Edge is not affiliated with any software, broker, or system.

Mark Seleznov's "Market Call"

The CEO of Trend Trader, Mark Seleznov, writes a daily syndicated column called "Market Call." This is a mini-tutorial on a different technical indicator each day, along with a chart that shows a practical application. It's an excellent learning tool for newbie technicians and can be found at several web sites, including www.market mavens.com, www.investorlinks.com, www.hardrightedge. com, and www.daytradersusa.com.

MurphyMorris.com

John Murphy offers analysis and commentary on "charts of interest" at his web site (www.murphymorris.com). A subscription costs $79.95 a year, which includes a daily market recap and market commentary. You can also order a CD-ROM or VHS videotape of the *John Murphy Explains Market Analysis* series. For $49.95 Murphy walks you step-by-step through dozens of charts and trends.

Stock Cam

Stock Cam (www.thestockcam.com) offers an *Advanced Technical Charting Manual* for $199.

TradingMarkets.com

This trading supersite (www.tradingmarkets.com) offers dozens of technical articles that can help you get a handle on technical analysis. For the beginner, there is Stock Trading 101, with articles on basic chart analysis, short-term chart patterns, moving averages, and an introduction to volatility. For the advanced trader, there are more than two dozen articles on advanced trading strategies. The cost is $10/month or $95/year, with a three-day free trial.

Traders Magazines

Traders magazines offer excellent educational articles on technical analysis. Traders.com (www.traders.com), home of *Technical Analysis of Stocks & Commodities*, offers an online subscription for $14.95/year and the printed monthly magazine for $49.95/year. *Traders World* (www.tradersworld.com) costs $29.95 for an online subscription, $15 for the quarterly printed magazine.

Technical Bookstores

Most of the books mentioned in this section can be found at Amazon.com. But there are two bookstores that cater to the trader: Traders Library (www.traderslibrary.com) and TradersPressBookstore.com (www.traderspressbookstore.com).

Web Charting Tools

There are many places on the Web to do charting and simple technical analysis, but online charts don't have the sophistication needed for true technical analysis. Although your trading software will have some charting capability, you may want to look into a Windows-based program such as TIP@Wallstreet, MetaStock, AIQ, or SuperCharts, described on the next page.

If you want to experiment with technical indicators before spending a lot of money, check out the following web sites, many of which also offer educational material on technical analysis.

ASK Research	www.askresearch.com
BigCharts.com	www.bigcharts.com
ClearStation	www.clearstation.com
Equis.com	www.equis.com
ProphetFinance.com	www.prophetfinance.com
Silicon Investor	www.siliconinvestor.com
Wall Street City	www.wallstreetcity.com
WindowOnWallStreet	www.windowonwallstreet.com

Sophisticated Charting and Analysis Programs

True technicians require more sophisticated charting and analysis tools than those offered by investing web sites. These Windows-based products are also more expensive, but if you continue with technical analysis, you may wish to check out some of the following software, all of which offer free trials. In addition to the monthly data charge, some of the providers require a cable or satellite connection, which may carry an additional charge.

✔ *TIP@Wallstreet (www.telescan.com):* This product, which was used to create the graphs in this chapter, interfaces its charting and analysis program with the Wall Street City web site. It costs $299 for Wall Street City users and includes the ProSearch screening program. Delayed data, supplied by Telescan, is $53/month; real-time data is $99/month.

✔ *MetaStock Professional (www.equis.com):* $1,295. Real-time data from eSignal (www.dbc.com) starts at $79/month.

✔ *AIQ Trading Expert Pro (www.aiq.com):* $49, plus shipping. Data from MyTrack (www.mytrack.com) ranges from $59/month (delayed) to $160/month (real-time).

✔ *SuperCharts 4 (www.omegaresearch.com):* $395 (end-of-day data), $1,199 (real-time data). Data supplied by eSignal or BMI.

COMING UP . . .

Technical analysis can be applied to market indexes, as well as stocks. The next chapter shows you how.

When Greenspan Speaks, the Markets Listen

A s a day trader you will be more concerned with intraday and short-term market trends than the market's long-term performance. Nevertheless, short-term trends don't exist in a vacuum, and it is important to be aware of the long-term bullish or bearish trend. This chapter will discuss ways to monitor the markets, both long-term and short-term.

The 800-pound gorilla that can send the market into orbit or a tailspin is Alan Greenspan, head of the Federal Reserve Board. Greenspan-watching has become the great American pasttime of market pundits, and when he heads for the microphone, they not only listen, they anticipate, worry, twitter, fret, agonize, and speculate upon the outcome for days and weeks before the man utters a single word.

Inflation is Greenspan's big bugaboo. If inflation is on the rise, he will try to nip it in the bud by raising interest rates. If inflation is in check, he'll let things roll along until one of the government's economic reports raises the red inflation flag. If he even hints of an interest rate hike, the market clutches its throat and drops as if it has been shot. But if he backs away from an anticipated hike, the market reacts like Mighty Mouse and roars into orbit.

inflation
the rate of the general level of price increases for goods and services; high inflation erodes the purchasing power of the dollar.

In reality, the Fed doesn't actually raise interest rates; it tightens the money supply by raising the target for the federal funds rate and selling Treasury bonds to shrink bank reserves. When this happens, higher interest rates follow. (To learn more about the inner workings of the Fed, read "Greenspan 101" at SmartMoney University.)

As a trader, the only thing you can do about the Greenspan effect is to stay tuned and stay flexible.

WATCHING THE ECONOMY

Close behind Greenspan in the ability to rock the market are economic statistics released by various government agencies on a weekly, monthly, or quarterly basis. As a day trader, it is important to monitor these reports and take advantage of the market's reaction to them.

Some of the most important economic indicators are those on unemployment, consumer price index, producer price index, consumer confidence, personal income and consumption, retail sales, and gross domestic product. The Federal Reserve's *Beige Book* is also closely watched. Here's a brief rundown on these indicators.

✔ *Employment report.* The employment report measures the growth in available jobs and the percentage of the workforce that is employed. As a gauge of the strength of the U.S. labor market, it is the biggest indicator of the level of inflation. It is released the first Friday of every month by the Bureau of Labor Statistics (stats.bls.gov).

✔ *Price indexes.* The producer price index (PPI) measures the change in the price of goods at the wholesale level. The consumer price index (CPI) measures the change in the price of goods at the retail level (by measuring prices of a fixed basket of goods purchased by a consumer); it is also known as the cost-of-living index. Both are released monthly by the Bureau of Labor Statistics.

PPI: stats.bls.gov/ppihome.htm

CPI: stats.bls.gov/cpihome.htm

✔ *Consumer confidence.* The consumer confidence report is a measure of consumers' willingness to spend, based on their view of current economic conditions. It is issued monthly by the Conference Board at www.conference-board.org.

✔ *Personal income.* The personal income and consumption report measures the level of wages and consumer spending. It is released monthly by the Commerce Department's Bureau of Economic Analysis (www.bea.doc.gov).

✔ *Retail Sales.* The retail sales report measures the strength of the economy by reporting retail purchases during the prior month. Released monthly by the Bureau of the Census (www.census.gov).

✔ **Gross Domestic Product.** Gross domestic product (GDP) measures the nation's total output of goods and services. It is considered a primary indicator of the health of the economy and how fast it is growing. (This was formerly referred to as GNP—gross national product.) The GDP report is released quarterly (third week of the first month of the quarter) by the Bureau of Economic Analysis (www.bea.doc.gov).

✔ *The Beige Book.* This publication from the Federal Reserve (www.federalreserve.gov) contains qualitative summaries on various business sectors. Scott Gerlach, bonds editor of CNBC.com, suggests that it reflects the Fed's thinking and that "reading between the lines" you may get clues about the Fed's intentions.[1] Which can give you a jump on the market if you can correctly second-guess Alan Greenspan's next remarks. It is released every six to eight weeks.

There are several web sites that will provide more information on these and other government economic reports:

✔ Economy Watch at www.smartmoney.com (under Tools) explains the various economic reports, and offers interactive charts of current and historical data. SmartMoney also has a calendar of release dates for the reports.

✔ Economy Track (in the Money section) at USA Today (www.usatoday.com) analyzes new releases.

✔ The Conference Board's Business Cycle Indicators at www.tcb-indicators.org offers information on the leading economic indicators and consumer confidence reports.

✔ CNBC.com offers a "behind the report" explanation of the purpose and significance of many of the reports, as well as an analysis of current reports as they are released. Click Markets at www.cnbc.com.

WATCHING THE MARKETS

If you're new to market watching, a mini-lesson on market indexes may be in order. The main ones tracked by CNBC, Bloomberg, and investing web sites are the Dow Jones Industrial Average, the Nasdaq Composite Index, the S&P 500, and the 30-year bond.

The Dow

The Dow Jones Industrial Average (the Dow) is the most common barometer of market activity and has been in use since 1896. It measures market performance by tracking 30 *blue chip* stocks selected to represent the U.S. economy.

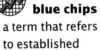
blue chips
a term that refers to established companies with large capitalization and a history of good earnings.

The index changes from time to time to maintain a representative mix. The most recent change was made in November 1999 when Home Depot, Intel, Microsoft, and SBC Communications Inc. replaced Chevron, Goodyear, Sears, and Union Carbide. This marked the first time that Nasdaq stocks (Microsoft and Intel) were included in the Dow. You can see a list of all 30 Dow stocks (and track their individual performance) at Bloomberg (www.bloomberg.com) under Stocks.

The unweighted Dow is calculated by adding the current prices of the 30 stocks and dividing the sum by a figure that is adjusted from time to time to compensate for stock splits and other distributions. The current divisor is printed daily in the *Wall Street Journal*; as of May 18, 2000, it was 0.18238596.

When David Brown and I wrote the first CyberInvesting book in early 1995, the Dow had just broken the 4,000 barrier. At the end of 1999, the Dow was 11,497. In just five years, it has gained more than 7,000 points, which is remarkable when you realize that it took almost 10 years to move from 2,000 to 4,000. A 12,000 Dow has been predicted, although as of May 2000 it was hovering around 10,500.

The S&P 500 and S&P 100

The S&P 500 (SPX) was designed by Standard & Poor's to measure the performance of the domestic economy. It is a weighted index of 500 large-cap stocks in leading industries, selected to represent the U.S. stock market. The S&P 500 closed above 1,500 for the first time in March 2000, but has since dropped back to the high 1,300s.

You can see a list of the best- and worst-performing S&P 500 stocks at the www.bloomberg.com site. For a list of all 500, along with company descriptions and ticker symbols, go to the Standard & Poor's site at www.spglobal.com. The FAQ at that site provides additional information.

The S&P 100 (OEX) is a weighted index comprised of 100 major blue chip stocks representing a diverse group of industries.

The Nasdaq Composite Index

The index generally quoted as "Nasdaq" on various market tickers is the Nasdaq Composite Index (ticker symbol

Weighted Indexes

In a weighted index, each stock in the index affects the index in proportion to its market value or market capitalization. Thus, a move in Yahoo!'s stock price would affect the S&P 500 more than a similar move in, say, AutoZone, Inc. (Market cap is measured by multiplying the most recent stock price by the total shares outstanding.) In an unweighted index, the performance of each stock affects the index equally.

NASD). It is a broad-based, weighted index that measures the performance of all stocks listed on the Nasdaq Stock Market. Because it is a weighted index, a change in the price of a Nasdaq stock affects the index in proportion to its market value. The Nasdaq is heavily concentrated in technology stocks, including Internet stocks. As such, it represents the so-called New Economy while the Dow and the S&P are more representative of the older, more established companies of the Old Economy. You can see a list of stocks that make up the Nasdaq Composite at www.nasdaqamex.com/reference/IndexDescriptions.stm.

Starting in the fall of 1999, the Nasdaq went on a tear, breaking one record after another. Having traded below 3,000 since its beginning, it broke that barrier in October 1999 and by year-end had passed the 4,000 mark. The index took a brief respite in January, then proceeded to charge above 5,000. The correction that began in late March brought the Nasdaq to its knees, and it reached a low of 3,300 from which it is now recovering.

The 30-Year Bond

The bond market as a whole is a barometer for inflation, and the 30-year Treasury bond yield is the bellwether of the bond market. It rises and falls in inverse relationship to interest rates. On the off chance you want to learn more about investing in bonds, go to the Bond Market Association (www.investinginbonds.com) or SmartMoney University (www.university.smartmoney.com).

Other Market Indexes

There are hundreds of other indexes, created to track various segments of the domestic and global markets. Here's where you can learn more about them online, if you're so inclined.

- ✔ The NYSE Composite Index is a weighted index of the 3,000+ common stocks listed on the New York Stock Exchange. It measures the changes in aggregate market value of all NYSE stocks. To see how the index is calculated, refer to the glossary at www.nyse.com.

- ✔ The AMEX Composite Index includes all the common stocks on the American Stock Exchange (www.amex.com).

- ✔ The Russell 2000 includes 2,000 small-cap companies (with a mean market cap of $428 million). There are more than a dozen domestic Russell indexes, which you can learn about at www.russell.com.

- ✔ The Wilshire 5000 is a weighted index made up of approximately 7,100 stocks traded on the NYSE, the AMEX, and the Nasdaq. All stocks in the index are headquartered in the United States, and it is said to be the best representation of the U.S. stock market. For more information, go to www.wilshire.com.

- ✔ More S&P indexes: In addition to the S&P 500 and 100, S&P has global, U.S., and Canadian indexes, which you can read about at www.spglobal.com.

- ✔ More Nasdaq indexes: The Nasdaq 100 is comprised of 100 of the largest nonfinancial growth companies in the Nasdaq National Market. In addition, Nasdaq has 10 subindexes described at www.marketdata.nasdaq.com/mr4a.html.

QQQ
the index track-ing stock for the Nasdaq 100, which is traded on the American Stock Exchange.

Spiders, Diamonds, Webs, and Qs

One successful day trader trades a stock you may have never heard of. It is a tracking stock based on the Nasdaq 100 Index (QQQ). QQQ is one of the new investment vehicles called index shares, which act like an index fund, but trade like a stock. Other index shares include SPDRs, WEBS, and DIAMONDS:

✔ *SPDRs.* Called "spiders," these are Standard & Poor's Depositary Receipts based on the S&P 500. Ticker symbol: SPY.

✔ *WEBS.* WEBS (World Equity Benchmark Shares) are index shares for a portfolio of foreign stocks in a specific country. There are 17 WEBS, repre-senting Australia, Austria, Belgium, Canada, France, Germany, Hong Kong, Italy, Japan, Malaysia, Mexico, Netherlands, Singapore, Spain, Sweden, Switzerland, and the United Kingdom.

✔ *DIAMONDS.* DIAMONDS are index shares that represent the 30 stocks in the Dow Jones Indus-trial Average. Ticker symbol: DIA.

Index shares trade on the American Stock Exchange. You can learn more about them at www.amex.com.

Internet Indexes

The newest market indexes are those created for Inter-net stocks. Internet.com tracks 13 different Internet stock groups, including ISDEX, the original Internet in-dex of 50 top Internet stocks. Stock lists and perfor-mance figures can be found at Wall Street Research Net (www.wsrn.com/apps/internetstocks).

TheStreet.com has created its own Internet sector index (DOT), which tracks the average value of a basket of 20 Internet stocks. The index trades on the Philadel-phia Stock Exchange. TheStreet.com also has an eCom-merce index (ICX) that tracks a basket of 18 electronic commerce stocks and an eFinance group (XEF) that tracks 14 online banking, brokerage, and transaction companies. Lists of stocks in these indexes can be found at www.thestreet.com under Investing Basics.

Global Indexes

While we are sleeping, the rest of the world is trading, and what happens overseas often impacts the markets in the United States. Staying in tune with major global markets can offer clues as to what might happen in today's U.S. market. You can track the world indexes online at www.bloomberg.com (Figure 7.1).

North/Latin America

Index	Value	Chg	Pct Chg	Date
DOW JONES INDUS. AVG (INDU)	11497.12	44.26	0.39%	12/31
S&P 500 INDEX (SPX)	1469.25	4.78	0.33%	12/31
NASDAQ COMB COMPOSITE IX (CCMP)	4069.31	32.44	0.80%	12/31
TSE 300 Index (TS300)	8413.75	7.68	0.09%	12/31
MEXICO BOLSA INDEX (MEXBOL)	7129.88	8.09	0.11%	12/30
BRAZIL BOVESPA STOCK IDX (IBOV)	17091.60	318.64	1.90%	12/30

Europe/Africa

Index	Value	Chg	Pct Chg	Date
BLOOMBERG EUROPEAN 500 (EURO500)	273.18	3.65	1.35%	12/30
FT-SE 100 Index (UKX)	6930.20	94.30	1.38%	12/30
CAC 40 INDEX (CAC)	5958.32	120.57	2.07%	12/30
DAX INDEX (DAX)	6958.14	98.56	1.44%	12/30
IBEX 35 INDEX (IBEX)	11641.40	60.00	0.52%	12/30
MILAN MIB30 INDEX (MIB30)	42991.00	189.00	0.44%	12/30
BEL20 INDEX (BEL20)	3340.43	37.66	1.14%	12/30
AMSTERDAM EXCHANGES INDX (AEX)	671.41	8.96	1.35%	12/30
SWISS MARKET INDEX (SMI)	7570.10	81.40	1.09%	12/30

Asia/Pacific

Index	Value	Chg	Pct Chg	Date
NIKKEI 225 INDEX (NKY)	18934.34	123.76	0.66%	12/30
HANG SENG STOCK INDEX (HSI)	17255.93	293.83	1.73%	21:02
ASX ALL ORDINARIES INDX (AS30)	3152.50	11.40	0.36%	12/30
SING: STRAITS TIMES INDU (STI)	2528.25	48.67	1.96%	21:01

FIGURE 7.1 Bloomberg.com tracks the world's major indexes: *Source:* Reprinted with permission of Bloomberg.com.

S&P Futures

Major indexes like the Dow, S&P 500, and Nasdaq simply tell you where the market is right now. To find out where it is likely to go, short-term, most trading experts suggest that you follow the S&P 500 futures.

S&P futures refers to futures contracts on the S&P 500. During premarket hours, CNBC displays (on the "bug" in the corner of the screen) the change in the S&P futures from the close of the previous session. But what you're concerned with in gauging the market is the difference between the S&P futures and the S&P 500 index—the spread or the premium. When the spread is at *fair value*—a mathematically derived relationship of what the spread *should be*—there is no advantage to owning futures over the stocks.

> **fair value**
> a mathematically derived relationship of the difference between the S&P futures and the S&P 500 index.

Mark Haines, one of the anchors at CNBC, has written a lucid explanation of the fair value concept (click Markets at www.cnbc.com). As he says, the subject is "as easy as you want to make it, or as complex as you can imagine." If you want to get a grip on fair value, read his article.

If you're watching the S&P futures in the premarket, don't assume that the market will open positive if the figure is positive, or vice versa. That figure has to be related to fair value, which continues to change as the futures trade. What you need to do is listen for comments by TV anchors with regard to how this figure relates to fair value.

The predictive ability of the S&P futures is very short-lived. It generally reflects how the market will open but not where it will be 30 minutes or an hour later.

For more on S&P futures and fair value, see David Nassar's and Marc Friedfertig's books.[2]

WATCHING TECHNICAL TRENDS

Another way to discern market trends is to analyze a broad market index, such as the S&P 500 or the Nasdaq Composite, with a few technical analysis tools. Most technical indicators can be plotted on a market index or in-

> ### *Market Index Graphs*
>
> StockCharts.com (www.stockcharts.com) analyzes
> the market six ways from Sunday! Each week it fea-
> tures a dozen or more index graphs overlaid with
> different technical indicators, along with market
> commentary.

dustry group graph and interpreted exactly the same way
as on a stock graph. Trendlines, support and resistance
lines, stochastics, the MACD, the LSQ line—all are well
suited for market analysis. In addition, there are indicators such as the advance/decline line that were created
specifically for analyzing groups of stocks (market indexes or industry groups). We will look at two indicators
to give you a taste of technical analysis of the market. If
you care to pursue the subject, there's no better place to
start than with John J. Murphy's book, *The Visual Investor*,
mentioned in Chapter 6.

The LSQ Line

The LSQ line is particularly good for revealing when a
market index is overextended and due for a correction. If
you had any doubt that the Nasdaq was due for a correction at the end of 1999—having set record after record
during November and December—an LSQ reading of the
Nasdaq Composite Index would have confirmed it (Figure 7.2). That correction came shortly after the first of
the year.

The Advance/Decline Line

The advance/decline line is a group indicator that reveals
the direction and strength of the market by plotting the
ratio of advancing to declining issues. Figure 7.3 shows an
advance/decline line for the NYSE index.

In this graph, the A/D line was moving down from
September through October, indicating that a majority of

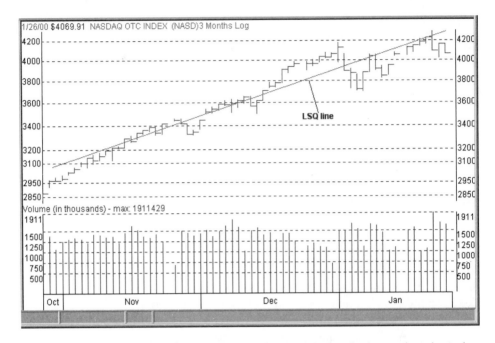

FIGURE 7.2   The LSQ line on this Nasdaq Composite graph shows that the index was very extended at the end of December. The correction at the beginning of January should have surprised no one. *Source:* Stock graph from TIP@Wallstreet, reprinted with permission of Telescan, Inc., www.telescan.com.

the issues were declining; then it moved sideways through the first part of November, indicating a more or less equal number of advancing and declining issues. The important feature, though, is the wide divergence between the index and the A/D line. When a weighted index moves to a new high and the A/D line is going in the other direction, it signals a top.

WATCHING THE MARKET ON TV

CNBC and Bloomberg Television provide continuous streams of market news and updates. At the current time, CNBC has a greater nationwide presence and is a favorite with day traders. For remote traders, it is a life-

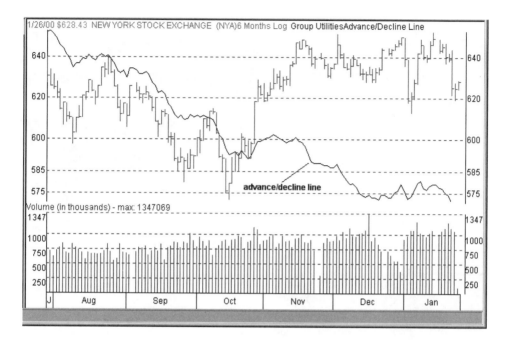

FIGURE 7.3 The wide divergence between the advance/decline (A/D) line and the NYSE index in December suggests that the market was topping, which, as it turned out, was correct. *Source:* Stock graph from TIP@Wallstreet, reprinted with permission of Telescan, Inc., www.telescan.com.

line to the markets, as well as a connection to the world at large.

And what you miss on cable you can pick up on the Web. At CNBC.com's home page (Figure 7.4), click CNBC TV, then CNBC 101 where you'll find a guide to the on-air ticker, an article that tells you all about the term *curbs in* (which refers to *trading curbs* to prevent *program trading*), and a definition of ticker symbols and key market indicators used by CNBC.

Bloomberg Television is available 24 hours a day via satellite through DIRECTV and during early morning hours on cable's USA Network. If you live in the New York/New Jersey area, you can catch it all day long on WMBC-TV.

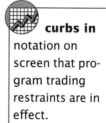

curbs in
notation on screen that program trading restraints are in effect.

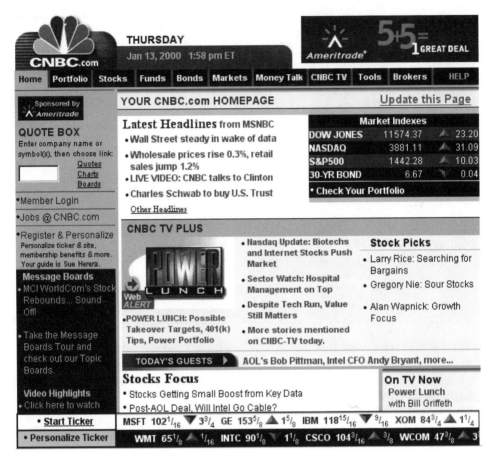

FIGURE 7.4 CNBC.com is a robust site that supplements and expands on the features broadcast by CNBC-TV. *Source:* ©2000 National Broadcasting Company, Inc. Used by permission. All rights reserved.

WATCHING THE MARKET ON THE NET

Market commentary is a staple of investing web sites. Many of the sites offer e-mail newsletters that sum up the day's activity and predict the next move of the market. In addition to CNBC.com and Bloomberg.com, some of the most popular are:

Barron's Online	www.barrons.com
CBS MarketWatch	www.cbs.marketwatch.com

InternetNews.com	www.internetnews.com
Raging Bull	www.ragingbull.com
Red Herring	www.redherring.com
TheStreet.com	www.thestreet.com
Wall Street City	www.wallstreetcity.com
Wall Street Journal Interactive Edition	www.wsj.com

All are free except for the Wall Street Journal and Barron's; a combined online subscription costs $59/year.

Several day trading sites also offer premarket commentary and postmarket analysis, both on-site and via e-mail. Most are pricey, but they usually have a free trial period so that you can check them out before you make a commitment. Here are some you might want to look at:

- ✔ CareerDayTrader.com has a free "Tradeometer" and premarket analysis (www.careerdaytrader.com).

- ✔ MTrader's real-time trading chat room and swing trading chat room (www.mtrader.com) offer daily market commentary. $200/month.

- ✔ TradingMarkets.com (www.tradingmarkets.com) has extensive commentary from market experts. $12/month or $120/year.

- ✔ Hard Right Edge's Morning Trader is free at www.hardrightedge.com.

- ✔ The Underground Trader (www.underground trader.com) offers market commentary in its trading pit. $250/month.

- ✔ WinningDayTraders.com (www.winningdaytrader.com) has market commentary in its trading pit. $295/month; daily and quarterly subscriptions available.

As an equity day trader, you won't really care whether the market is going up or down as long as you can correctly call a few of the intraday and short-term trends on your particular stocks. The tools described in

 trading curbs
restraints initiated by the New York Stock Exchange to prevent program trading if the Dow moves 2 percent in either direction from the previous trading day's closing price. The notation is shown on CNBC as "curbs in."

 program trading
trades executed automatically by computer programs (used by money managers and other professional traders).

this section can help you, but you'll discover others as you continue your investigation into day trading. Study them carefully and track their success rates; then concentrate on the one or two that work best for you.

COMING UP . . .

Knowledge, technique, timing, tools . . . they're all worthless unless you have—or can develop—the mind of a trader. Virtually every successful trader agrees that trading is mostly psychological, that it doesn't matter what kind of system or tools you use as long as you have psychological control. The next chapter explores this important subject.

Chapter

The Right Stuff

I t has been said that 80 percent of day traders fail during the first six months of trading. That figure has prompted everyone from the head of the SEC to the smallest online broker to issue warnings about the risks of day trading and the need for more education. But have you ever wondered *why* the percentage of failures is so high, much higher than virtually any other profession?

It's not just a lack of education. Day trading seminars are filled with people seeking knowledge about day trading; books about day trading often become best-sellers because of the apparently insatiable desire of the investing public to learn how to day trade. Although some may jump into the fray without sufficient training, day traders in general are pretty knowledgeable about the mechanics of trading.

So why is there such a high failure rate?

To find answers to that question, I talked with traders about what it takes to become a successful trader. I also read many books on the subject. The books (and the traders) fall into two categories.

The first relates experiences of their own or others' success, such as Jack Schwager's *Market Wizards* and *The New Market Wizards*.[1] These books are helpful (and entertaining) in the way that studying the habits of any successful person is helpful: You can glean nuggets of wisdom from someone else's successful journey. That wisdom usually boils down to trading rules such as, plan your trade and trade your plan, always use stops, cut your losses short, let your profits run, and so on. But few writers talk about what it really takes to live by those rules.

The second type of book explores the psychology behind the rules. These books delve into the psychological barriers that exist in trading, and some offer readers practical exercises and methods to change and control their trading behavior.

Trading actually tends to attract people who are ill suited to the task—those who are enamored with making lots of money; people who are willing to take high risks; individuals who seek excitement or who react to the world with emotional intensity.
Charles Faulker, as quoted in
The New Market Wizards

Two of the best of this genre are *The Disciplined Trader: Developing Winning Attitudes* by Mark Douglas[2] and *Trade Your Way to Financial Freedom* by Dr. Van K. Tharp.[3]

Douglas believes that successful trading is 80 percent psychology and 20 percent methodology. Tharp goes even further and says it's 100 percent psychological, because the system or methodology we use as traders is based on our psychological biases. Both authors, particularly Douglas, call for nothing less than a complete psychological transformation in order to succeed as a trader, and both books offer specific ways to achieve this transformation.

Somebody asked me today 'what should I study before I get into trading,' and I said, 'psychology.'
Paul RT Johnson Jr., as quoted in
The Mind of a Trader

As good as they are, however, the books are not easy reading. My goal in this chapter is to profile a successful trader—drawn from these and other books and conversations with traders—so that when you read the Douglas and Tharp books and others, you'll have a frame of reference in which to place them. Granted, you will also need practical knowledge of the markets and a well-developed trading plan to become a successful trader, but the psychological demands of trading should be explored before you make any commitment to a career in day trading. The Douglas and Tharp books are good places to start.

I started out by worrying about the system I was going to use to trade. The second factor I worked on was risk management and volatility control. The third area I focused on was the psychology of trading. If I had it to do over again, I would reverse the process completely. I think investment psychology is by far the most important element, followed by risk control, with the least important consideration being the question of where you buy and sell.

Tom Basso, as quoted in
The New Market Wizards

FEAR, GREED, AND THE MARKET

The psychological challenges facing the trader, according to Douglas, are rooted in the nature of the market. But what exactly is the market? It's not the Dow or the S&P 500. It's not the Nasdaq or the NYSE or regional exchanges or any of the hundreds of indexes that attempt to measure the temperature of the market. These are physical and metrical representations of the market, but when we think of the market we're thinking about invisible collective forces that drive stock prices.

Worth a Read

Linda Bradford Raschke, one of the New Market Wizards, has a few words to say on "The Mental Aspect of Trading." Free, at www.mrci.com/lbr.

Those forces—and thus the market—are the psychological perceptions of millions of investors and traders. Those forces—and thus the market—are what Robert Deel calls "an invisible amalgamation of a global mind."[4] It is a global mind based on fear and greed.

Fear and greed are at work on every trade, as Douglas points out in *The Disciplined Trader*. For every single trade there are two opposing views: a buyer who hopes to make a profit because he or she believes the stock is going to go up and a seller who fears a loss because he or she believes the same stock is going to go down. This creates an emotionally driven, irrational market that is in perpetual motion, one that soars on optimism to register a 200-point gain, then gives it all back and then some should Alan Greenspan start to frown.

To be successful, a day trader must have the discipline of a machine, the instincts of a fox, the emotions of a rock, the skills of a surgeon, and the patience of a saint (and a little luck wouldn't hurt either).
          Jack Swensen, Day Traders USA Tutorials

At a seminar taught by Dr. Van Tharp, I participated in a game designed to illustrate the fear and greed that drives the market. Each player started off with $100,000 on paper and was required to wager at least $10 on every trade. Fifty trades were to be made during the course of the game; the result of each trade was to be determined by the color of the marble drawn from a paper bag by one of the players. The bag held 20 marbles. Eleven, or 55 percent, were white, signifying a win; seven, or 35 percent, were black, signifying a loss. To make things interesting, the bag contained one yellow marble and one green marble, each representing 5 percent of the total. When the yellow marble was drawn, we won 10 times what we risked on the trade. When the green marble was drawn, we lost five times what we risked. The chance of an exceptional win or an exceptional loss was the same: 5 percent.

The results of our game were typical, according to Tharp. Out of about 30 players, two ended up bankrupt and two turned the initial $100,000 into more than $4 million. The rest of us fell somewhere in between. What I found most fascinating about the game was the emotion I felt during each trade. I wanted to win, but more important, I didn't want to lose all that "money." So I started off with smallish trades—$3,000 to $5,000—but after several wins and losses, I realized I would have to risk more if I wanted to win big. As I slowly edged up to five-figure trades, I could feel the tug of fear and greed with every trade, even though this was a game without real money at stake. Each win made me bolder, while each loss gave me butterflies and made me hover over my remaining capital like a threatened mother hen.

On the 20th trade, I made my first big win. I risked $20,000 and made $200,000 when the yellow marble was drawn. In an unusual display of odds, the yellow marble was drawn twice over the next five trades and my winnings soared to $1.5 million. I was flying! Then I plummeted to earth when I lost two-thirds of my total capital in the next several trades. I ended the game with more than $500,000 imaginary dollars, but the overriding emotion was the fear of losing and the greedy elation of every win. I could only imagine what it would feel like if I were playing with real money.

The game gave the players (me, at least) the emotional experience of trading, but the point of the game was to illustrate the importance of what Dr. Tharp calls position sizing—the amount of money risked on each trade. This was the only variable among the 30 players. We all started out with the same amount of investment capital; we all won or lost on the same trades. Yet some went bankrupt while others became millionaires. Why? Because the amount each of us was willing to risk on a trade—our position size—was determined by our deep-seated and mostly irrational attitudes toward money, attitudes that were driven by fear and greed.

The frame of mind of the average trader is one notch away from unrestrained terror.
Mark Douglas, *The Disciplined Trader*

Coming to terms with your fears about money and about loss is part of the psychological transformation that Douglas talks about in his book. It is part of the self-awareness that Tharp talks about in his. But it is clear that much of our fear comes from operating in the unstructured environment that Douglas evokes so eloquently in his book.

Do You Have the Mind of a Trader?

There is a way to find out before you quit your day job. Go to Van Tharp's web site at www.iitm.com and take his free "mini-evaluation." It is a simple questionnaire that will help pinpoint your trading biases.

A more extensive "Investment Psychology Inventory" is recommended but only if you have been investing (or trading) for over six months. This profile evaluates your strengths and weaknesses as a trader and then ranks your psychological characteristics, decision-making skills, and management and discipline characteristics. It also includes a 10-minute phone consultation with Dr. Tharp.

The cost of the inventory is $195. If you purchase the Peak Performance Home Study Course for $595 (to help you correct any weaknesses you find on the inventory), the inventory is $125.

THE DAY TRADER'S BIGGEST CHALLENGE

The biggest challenge facing day traders, according to Douglas, is the market's unstructured environment. After reading his book and others on the subject, after talking with successful and unsuccessful traders, I'd have to agree.

Think about it. As a trader, you go to work every day in an environment that holds the potential either to fulfill your financial dreams or to create your worst nightmare. Every decision you make, every trade you place, has a possibility of giving you more and more profits or losing more and more of your hard-earned money, depending on when you enter and exit the trade. And, there are no rules and regulations that say, for sure, that if you do X, Y will follow.

The speculator's chief enemies are always boring from within. . . . [W]hen the market goes against you, you hope that every day will be the last day—and you lose more than you should had you not listened to hope. . . . And when the market goes your way you become fearful that the next day will take away your profit, and you get out— too soon. . . . The successful trader has to fight these two deep-seated instincts. . . . He must fear that his loss may develop into a much bigger loss, and hope that his profit may become a big profit.
Jesse Livermore, in Edwin LeFèvre's
Reminiscences of a Stock Operator

In the market, every day is like a minefield littered with gold bullion, but there is no map to lead you safely to the gold. What's worse, if you managed to grab a piece of the gold yesterday without stepping on a mine, the tactics used to get it may not work today because, while you slept, somebody rearranged all the mines and the gold.

Not only is there open-ended potential for gain and loss in such an unstructured market, but there are endless possibilities of entry and exit points, each related to the potential for gain or loss. You have to decide how much money to risk on each trade. You have to decide when to get in, how long to stay in, and, most important, when to get out. And the most critical aspect related to this no-beginning/no-ending marketplace, according to Douglas, is that it allows you to be a passive loser. No one tells you when the game is over. *You* have to decide when enough loss is enough. And as every trader I talked with agreed: Learning to cut your losses short is one of the hardest lessons for new traders.

Most of us are not used to working in this kind of unstructured environment. We have spent our lives erecting structures to guide us from one life experience to another. From preschool to college, from first job to second marriage, from parenthood to grandparenthood, from the cradle to the urn, we have had beginnings, endings, rules, rituals, logic, structure. The thought of escaping from a structured environment can be as intoxicating as champagne in the beginning—there's no boss hovering over your shoulder, no set working hours, no one to tell you what to do or how to do it—but unless you impose your own structure on the market, you will never become a successful trader.

The structure Douglas offers is a "thinking methodology" which he says is a "means of interfacing a trading system with the mind's psychological structure."[5] In other words, you have to establish rules to guide your behavior. Tharp offers a guide to developing a trading system that includes discovering and overcoming your biases, setting your objectives, and developing a system for money management and for entry and exit strategies.

In essence, both writers are talking about creating a trading plan. A trading plan imposes structure on an unstructured environment, and every successful trader has one. But before we talk about trading plans, let's take a brief look at what Douglas, Tharp, and others describe as the most important mental traits you'll need to become a successful trader.

WHAT *IS* THE RIGHT STUFF?

When asked, What does it take to become a successful trader? Most experts come up with lists that include self-discipline; control of the ego and the ability to accept loss; a flexible, agile mind; patience; and a passion for the market. These traits won't guarantee your success as a trader, but without them, you will never become a successful trader. (The psychological underpinnings of these traits are what trading coaches like Douglas and Tharp help you work on.) Let's take a brief look at each.

Self-Discipline

In all my research, the one trait mentioned by traders and writers alike as being the single most essential ingredient of trading was self-discipline.

Although writers often call it by different names—Tharp calls it internal control[6]—discipline was the one common trait exhibited by every trader interviewed by Jack Schwager for his *Market Wizard* books. It is the refrain of every tutorial or seminar you will take, every day trading book you will read: discipline, discipline, discipline.

> *I discovered you can't train people how to trade by just imparting knowledge. The key to trading success is emotional discipline.*
>
> Victor Sperandeo, as quoted in
> *The New Market Wizards*

What exactly is self-discipline? My Random House dictionary defines discipline as "training to act in accordance with rules" and "a regimen that develops or improves a skill." In trading, you must first discipline yourself to learn everything you need to know about trading and the markets; then you must discipline yourself to create your own rules and trading plan; and on a daily basis, you must discipline yourself to follow your rules as set forth in your plan.

Self-discipline is not a talent, thankfully. It can be learned. Mark Douglas calls it a process of learning how to take conscious control of your actions, of operating outside your belief system in order to change a belief that may be standing between you and your goal. In a sense, self-discipline is like a muscle: The more you use it, the stronger it gets. Learning self-discipline should be the number one goal on your journey to becoming a trader.

The successful trader must be able to recognize and control his greed. If you get a buzz from profits and depressed by losses, you belong in Las Vegas, not the markets.

> Mark Ritchie, as quoted in
> *The New Market Wizards*

Control of Ego

Your ego can be your biggest enemy when it comes to trading. Why? Because it can prevent you from taking responsibility for a losing trade. Most of us don't like to admit it when we are wrong, and with an oversized ego, we will go to great lengths to keep from admitting that we were wrong. (Psychologists call this narcissistic behavior.) And yet being wrong is part of the trading game. Even successful traders are wrong 50, 60, 70, even 80 percent of the time. They can be wrong most of the time and still be successful because they keep their losses small and let their profits run.

But in order to do this you must be able to control your ego and take responsibility for your trades. When a trade turns bad, you can't blame it on the market; the market is neutral. You can't blame it on the company whose stock you bought; the company has no direct control over stock prices. You can't blame it on the head trader or mentor whose advice you took. If you let someone else call the shots, you're responsible for handing over your control. You and you alone are responsible for your trades.

Are You Addicted to Trading?

"It's gambling, pure and simple," a friend said, when I told him I was writing a book about day trading. I argued with him, backing up my words with everything I had read about speculation versus gambling: that speculation had to do with probabilities and controlled risk while gambling dealt with thrills and the rush of the action; that a speculator was cool, controlled, and disciplined while a gambler was emotional, compulsive, and often out of control. Of course, not all gamblers are compulsive. Many have a high degree of self-control and operate within a very disciplined structure. But a person who is addicted to gambling—or to trading—gets his or her primary gratification from the action, not from winning and losing. (In some cases, losing can be what is being sought after unconsciously!)

If you're wondering whether you might be at risk for addiction to trading, take the following quiz, which has been reprinted with the permission of the Council on Compulsive Gambling of New Jersey, Inc.

1. Are you trading in the stock market with money you may need during the next year?
2. Are you risking more money than you intended to?
3. Have you ever lied to someone regarding your online trading?
4. Are you risking retirement savings to try to get back your losses?
5. Has anyone ever told you that you spend too much time online?
6. Is the way you are investing affecting other areas of your life (relationships, vocation pursuits, etc.)?
7. If you lost most of your money trading in the market would it materially change your life?
8. Are you investing frequently (day trading) for the excitement and the way it makes you feel?
9. Are you becoming secretive about your online trading?
10. Do you feel sad or depressed when you are not trading in the market?

The more yes answers you have, the more likely you are to become addicted to trading. For more information on gambling and compulsive behavior, go to 1-800-Gambler at www.800gambler.org.

Taking responsibility for successful trades is not difficult. But a bad trade? No way! It goes against our grain to admit we were wrong. But to keep a small loss from turning into a big loss, you have to be able to admit you were wrong, and cutting your losses short is one of the hallmarks of successful traders.

The typical trader will do most anything to avoid creating definition and rules because he does not want to take responsibility for the results of his trading.

Mark Douglas, *The Disciplined Trader*

When you read Douglas, you'll understand why it is so hard for us to admit we are wrong, why it goes against our grain to cut our losses quickly and without remorse. It has to do with the market's endless potential for gain. If our stock is down a point or two, there is always the possibility that it will not only reverse its direction and recover those points but that it will also increase beyond our break-even point and turn our loss into a profit.

It could happen.

So we become H&P traders—hoping and praying that the trade will turn around and make us whole. Which is why it is so hard to admit we were wrong and to cut our losses.

What we need to realize is that there will be other opportunities. And as long as you hang on to that loss— hoping and praying it'll turn around—your money is unavailable for other trading opportunities.

Don't try to make a profit on a bad trade, just try to find the best place to get out.

Linda Bradford Raschke, as quoted in
The New Market Wizards

Winning can also be dangerous if you listen to your ego. How many times have you heard someone say, "All she really needs is a couple of successes under her belt and she'll be okay"—meaning that winning begets winning. One success builds on another. That's what we've all been taught. But in trading, that's not necessarily true.

A big win can give you a false sense of power over the market, a feeling of omnipotence. It can make you cocky. It can make you feel as if you beat the market, which puts you in an adversarial frame of mind, so that winning again—being right again—becomes the goal. But remember, no matter how successful you become, it is very likely that you will be making more losing trades than winning trades.

Whenever you think 'I'm going to make a killing,' watch out!

Joe DiNapoli

Controlling your ego is probably one of the hardest things you will ever have to do, but to become a successful trader you must do it. One way to control your ego is to learn to be flexible and let the market lead the way.

An Open Mind

An open mind—mental flexibility—is a common trait of successful traders. To illustrate this, let's look at two traders.

Trader A has an open, flexible mind. She approaches the market each day free of expectations. She observes various market indicators to get a feel for what the market *might* do today. She keeps abreast of the news and tunes in to any speech that Alan Greenspan might be making, but her whole attitude is to wait and see what the market does. And when the market leads the way, she follows. If the market heads down, and the stock she is trading trends down, she goes short. If the stock trends up, she goes long. If she can discern no trend at all, she stays on the sidelines and waits for a trend to appear. When she makes a trade, she sets her stops and lets her profits run. If the stock reverses and triggers a stop, she exits the trade without remorse and waits for the next setup.

> *The less I cared about whether or not I was wrong, the clearer things became, making it much easier to move in and out of positions, cutting my losses short to make myself mentally available to take the next opportunity.*
> Mark Douglas, *The Disciplined Trader*

Trader B has a closed, rigid mind with opinions about the market engraved in stone. This trader has decided that Greenspan's speech will have a negative effect on the market, so he sits on the sidelines. He remains on the sidelines as the market climbs (because it has already discounted Greenspan's negative comments in a minor correction the day before). When he finally decides to jump on the band-wagon of his favorite stock, which is trending unmistakably upward, he sells on a minor *downtick* after a one-point gain because he still believes the market is headed for a fall and so misses the subsequent five-point rise in the stock. When the stock tops out and heads down on an intraday swing, he doesn't even think of shorting it because he believes that the only way to trade is to go long. And what does he do on a losing trade? You guessed it. He hangs on to it while his losses mount because he *knows* the stock will recover and give him back all his losses and more.

downtick
a quote that is lower than the preceding quote; a trade executed at a price that is lower than the preceding trade.

> *Your spouse will never ask you how many times you were right; they'll just ask you how much money you made.*
> Mark Seleznov, CEO, Trend Trader LLC

Mental flexibility allows you to see the market clearly and go where it takes you. It keeps you from trying to control the market (you can't) or second-guess it (you can't do that, either). Mental flexibility comes from a thorough understanding of the markets, which you get only after study and practice, and from letting go of your assumptions and beliefs about the market and go where the market takes you.

It's not easy, however, to let go. As Tharp says:

> Typically we trade our beliefs about the market, and once we've made up our minds about those beliefs, we're not likely to change them. And when we play the markets, we assume that we are considering all the available information. Instead, we may have already eliminated the most useful information by our selective perception.[7]

Tharp calls our assumptions and beliefs judgmental heuristics or biases, and in his book he describes 13 different biases that can prevent you from developing and using a successful trading system. (Tharp uses the term trading system to describe the methodology used to put on your trades, not the trading software.) Getting rid of your biases and letting go of your assumptions and beliefs are two important steps on the road to successful trading.

Mental Agility

An agile mind is a kissing cousin to an open, flexible mind, but it's not the same thing. You may be open and flexible but still require a lot of pondering and thoughtful reflection to arrive at a decision. This kind of person may be an astute investor but a terrible day trader. A day trader must be able to absorb and quickly analyze a lot of rapidly changing data.

> *You have to be able to think clearly and act decisively in a panic market. The markets that go wild are the ones with the best opportunity.*
> Mark Ritchie, as quoted in
> *The New Market Wizards*

Demo one of the trading platforms described in Chapter 4 to understand the mental agility needed to analyze data in perpetual motion. On each trade you will be watching the constantly changing Level 2 quote montage, the Time & Sales screen, and one or more technical charts, trying to interpret data that changes second by second. You'll be monitoring a news ticker for stories of interest and a watch list of a dozen or more stocks to see which might be coming into play. You must monitor and analyze the relative importance of all this data and then make split-second decisions about when and if to enter a stock and when to exit.

And remember, all of this takes place in a highly volatile, emotional setting that offers that endless possibility of gain and loss.

Can a person develop mental agility? I would say no, you either have it or you don't. The best traders, I've been told, come from careers that reward quick, flexible minds. They are people who are used to thinking on their feet and responding quickly to the conditions in which they find themselves, such as pilots or salespeople. Doctors, according to one professional trader, make the worst traders. Although a doctor must have an open mind to let the patient's symptoms lead the way, doctors are so accustomed to being right that they find it difficult to admit to being wrong.

The Virtue of Patience

Patience is one of the less heralded qualities of a successful trader. It is the ability to wait for a good setup before you pull the trigger. It is the ability to refrain from overtrading. It is the ability to emulate Jim Rogers, one of the original *Market Wizards*, who said, "I just wait until there is money lying in the corner, and all I have to do is go over there and pick it up. I do nothing in the meantime."

The key to building wealth is to preserve capital and wait patiently for the right opportunity to make the extraordinary gains.

Victor Sperandeo, as quoted in
The New Market Wizards

Patience is not a quality that is easy to develop. But it is not necessarily a case of you either have it or you don't. A well-thought-out trading plan—and the discipline to follow it—are the prerequisites for developing patience.

A Passion for the Market

A passion for the market—a love of the game itself—seems to be an essential ingredient of a successful trader. Virtually every trader profiled in Schwager's and Patel's books talks about his or her passion for the market. Every successful trader I talked to told me he loves what he does and can't imagine doing anything else.

Passion might appear to be in direct conflict with self-discipline. But passion is the fuel that will drive you to learn the market inside and out. It is the energy you will draw on to effect the mental changes necessary to become a supertrader. It is the resilience you'll need to recover from losses and, more importantly, to learn from them.

Many traders, including Mark Douglas and Jesse Livermore, were mauled by the market. At one point they lost everything they owned—sometimes more than once—but they picked themselves up, learned from their mistakes, and started over. It took self-discipline to do that, but it took passion to *want* to do it.

A truly successful trader has got to be involved and into the trading; the money is the side issue.
Bill Lipschutz, as quoted in
The New Market Wizards

You may have a passion for the market going in; maybe that's what has led you to consider day trading. You may develop a passion as you begin to learn about the market. But if you don't have or develop a true passion for the market, if all you are trying to do is to make money, you had best hang on to your day job because you probably won't make it as a trader.

To be a successful trader, you will need practical knowledge of the markets and a well-thought-out trading plan, but the psychological demands of trading should be explored before you make any commitment to a career in day trading. Preparing yourself for these psychological challenges is the most important thing you can do. It should take precedence over trading styles, market savvy, finding stocks, or memorizing trading rules.

Trading rules, in fact, are simply clichés unless you have a grasp of the psychology behind them. Transforming your mental environment can be done concurrently with studying the nuts and bolts of trading. Just don't neglect it or you may end up in the 80 percent losing section of failed traders. I urge you to read both the Douglas and the Tharp books—and as many others as you need to *get it*—and to do the exercises. Because you will never become a successful trader until you develop the right mental stuff.

THE TRADING COACHES

As more and more investors turn to day trading, the need for trading coaches—the shrinks of the trading room—grows. A trading coach works with traders on a one-on-one basis to help them manage their emotions and develop self-discipline. Coaches are not cheap, charging upwards of $175 an hour, but some also offer less expensive group classes online and off.

Money spent on one-on-one coaching seems to me a better use of your educational dollars than a rah-rah training seminar that teaches only the nuts and bolts of Level 2. The nuts and bolts you can and should learn on your own before consulting a trading coach.

Here are several coaches to check out. See the individual web sites for pricing.

Robin Dayne

A trader and coach for five and one-half years, Robin Dayne (www.robindayne.com) bases her coaching on neurolinguistics, the study of how humans think and experience the world. Dayne can help novice traders develop discipline and good trading habits, and she can help advanced traders get back on track. With regard to the latter, she is quoted by TheStreet.com (11/9/99) as saying her neurolinguistic process "literally breaks the connection between the event and the emotion. . . . [I]t works 10 years of therapy in 10 minutes." (To which my psychologist friend muttered, "Yeah! Right!") She offers one-on-one coaching by phone, private face-to-face instruction, and instruction via chat rooms.

Stephen Boren

Stephen Boren is the consulting psychologist at Train to Day Trade (www.traintodaytrade.com). A clinical psychologist and a day trader, Dr. Boren develops psychological tests for assessing and coaching traders. Take a free online test at the web site to see if you have what it takes.

Mark Douglas

Mark Douglas is an author, lecturer, and trading coach. He offers workshops, personal consultations, and two books—*The Disciplined Trader*, which we've talked about in this chapter, and a new book to be published in 2000, called *Trading in the Zone: How to Create a State of Mind That Eliminates the Fear, Stress, and Anxiety from Your Trading*. You can reach him at his web site at www.mark-douglas.com.

Van Tharp

Dr. Tharp is one of those featured in Jack Schwager's original *Market Wizards* book. He holds a Ph.D. in psychology and is an expert in the use of neurolinguistic programming. In addition to writing books, such as *Trade Your Way to Financial Freedom*, Dr. Tharp teaches seminars, offers audiotapes and home study courses, and provides one-on-one coaching. You can take a free mini-evaluation at his web site (www.iitm.com) to discover which of your psychological biases will affect your trading. There is also a free market simulation game at the site.

BOOKS ON A TRADER'S PSYCHOLOGY

Here are some of the best books I've found on a trader's psychology:

Robert Deel. *Trading the Plan*. New York: John Wiley & Sons, 1997.

Mark Douglas. *The Disciplined Trader: Developing Winning Attitudes*. New York: New York Institute of Finance, 1990.

Alexander Elder. *Trading for a Living*. New York: John Wiley & Sons, 1993.

Robert Koppel and Howard Abell. *The Inner Game of Trading*. New York: Irwin Professional Publishing, 1997.

Edwin LeFèvre. *Reminiscences of a Stock Operator*. New York: John Wiley & Sons, 1994 (originally published in 1923).

Alpesh B. Patel. *The Mind of a Trader: Lessons in Trading Strategy from the World's Leading Traders*. London: Financial Times, 1997.

Jack D. Schwager. *The New Market Wizards*. New York: HarperBusiness, 1992.

Van K. Tharp. *Trade Your Way to Financial Freedom*. New York: McGraw-Hill, 1999.

COMING UP . . .

The structure that you must impose on the unstructured market environment is your trading plan. It details the where, when, what, why, and how of your trading. It sets forth the rules that you will abide by each trading day of your life. As you will see in the next chapter, we will go beyond a simple trading plan and show you how to create a master plan for your day trading career.

Chapter 9

The Master Plan

I f you were thinking about becoming a pilot, you wouldn't read just one book, quit your job, file a flight plan, climb into the cockpit of a Learjet, and start taxiing down the runway. You'd have to take a battery of tests to see if you have what it takes physically and mentally to fly a plane; then you'd have to master many different areas of knowledge and skills before you ever set foot in the cockpit. Finally, you'd have to log hundreds of hours with an instructor before you could take the plane up by yourself.

A career in day trading should be approached in a similar manner.

I think the single most important element [to being successful in the markets] is having a plan. First, a plan forces discipline, which is an essential ingredient to successful trading. Second, a plan gives you a benchmark against which you can measure your performance.

Howard Seidler, as quoted in
The New Market Wizards

The Trading Plan

A trading plan is your written plan for making each trade. It is your trading system. To be specific, this system describes the particulars of an actual trade: the conditions for the setup, the time span for charts, the technical indicators, the entry signal, the stop level, and the exit strategy. A trading plan distills the essence of your trading style, your strategies, your approach to the market. It is the structure that gives order, direction, and consistency to your life as a trader.

You must determine if you have "the right stuff" to be a day trader; you must educate yourself about all the facets of trading and the market; and you must log hundreds of hours—about six months' worth—practicing your trading skills with real dollars in a live market arena. What you need is a master plan to help you crystallize the path from point A—a person who wants to be a day trader—to point B—a practicing and successful trader.

A master plan is much broader than a trading plan. It is more of a business plan that details every aspect of your new business as a day trader, with the trading plan just one of its many components. Here is what it includes:

✔ *Mission statement.* A business plan has one, and so should your master plan. A mission statement summarizes what it is you are trying to accomplish in your new career.

✔ *Study plan.* This section outlines the areas you intend to study and the tools available to you, both online and offline.

✔ *Risk management plan.* This section helps you assess your tolerance for risk and determine how to manage it on a daily basis.

- ✔ *Trading plan.* This is the trading system that details the conditions for making a trade.
- ✔ *Daily routine.* This section addresses your daily premarket and postmarket routines.
- ✔ *Trading journal.* This is a daily record of every trade.
- ✔ *Getting started plan.* This is where you'll work out the details of getting started: choosing a broker, setting up your office, installing and learning the software, and all the little administrative tasks of setting up a new business.

For each of these sections, I suggest you make a list of specific objectives and a time frame for accomplishing them. (Some areas can be worked on simultaneously, even though they are discussed here in a linear fashion.) I strongly recommend that you commit your entire master plan to writing. Unwritten goals have a way of evaporating or changing to meet present circumstances. Written goals are much more binding.

Keep this in mind: Once you commit to becoming a day trader, you'll have many decisions to make before you can actually start trading. These decisions may be made in a very different order than they are listed here. But in this chapter, we're just talking about writing your business plan. Its written goals and objectives will help you sort out the various options discussed in this and other books.

THE MISSION STATEMENT

Start your master plan with a mission statement to help you focus on your overall goals. A mission statement looks at the forest, while the rest of the master plan examines the trees. A mission statement should include the following:

- ✔ The amount you plan to use as risk capital. Remember: no retirement funds, no second mortgage money, no children's college funds. In the event you ignore this advice, write down where the money came from in your mission statement . . . just as a reminder.

✔ The amount you are willing to invest (i.e., lose) during the learning process. This money should be considered as tuition in the school of day trading. Looking at it as money spent to learn new skills puts the inevitable losses in proper perspective. And writing it down makes it part of your plan.

✔ The date you expect to be profitable. This is the goal at which everything else is directed. Be realistic. Two weeks is dreaming. Six months might be doable.

THE STUDY PLAN:
THE COLLEGE OF DAY TRADING

In the beginning, education should be your top priority. As a novice day trader, you should be like a sponge, absorbing everything in sight that has anything to do with the markets and trading. You have made a start by reading this book, but there are miles to go before you trade. Here are some points to consider.

Educate Yourself Online

Make a study plan of the tutorials, courses, classes, and seminars you plan to take, using as your curriculum the no-cost and low-cost online educational resources described in Chapter 11.

No trading plan! This is the basic feature that separates losing traders from winning traders. Lack of confidence disappears in direct relation to the validity of a back-tested trading plan.

Robert Krauz, as quoted in
The New Market Wizards

Your initial objectives should be to learn everything you can about the markets, Level 2 quotes, trading styles, and trading strategies. What you're trying to do in this first stage is to discover the possibilities and build a foundation of basic knowledge about trading and the markets.

If there are free or low-cost introductory day trading seminars in your city, by all means sign up, but first steep yourself in the markets, Level 2, and a variety of trading styles. Laying a foundation before you attend a day trading seminar or training class will help you get more out of it.

Start a Day Trading Library

Make a list of books that you plan to read (see the Suggested Reading list, Appendix 2.) A good place to start is Michael Turner's *Day Trading into the Millennium*.[1] Consider it an appetizer before the heavy meals offered by Friedfertig, Nassar, and Farrell.

I highly recommend that you buy the books and start your own day trading library, rather than borrowing them from a library. You may want to read the books more than once, and you'll certainly want to use them as a reference. The books on trading strategies make a lot more sense if you first ground yourself in the basics of the NYSE, Nasdaq, and Level 2.

Explore Your Mental Environment

We talked about the psychology of trading in the previous chapter, but that was just an introduction. To see the mind of the trader at work, read the classic *Reminiscences of a Stock Operator* by Edwin LeFèvre and the two *Market Wizards* books of Jack Schwager. LeFèvre takes you into the mind of the best-known stock speculator of all times, Jesse Livermore, while Schwager interviews two dozen super-traders to reveal the mental traits that led to their success.

Reading these books won't give you the mind of a trader. But they're a good place to start. To develop the mind of a trader, you may have to undergo the psychological transformation that Mark Douglas talks about. Read his *The Disciplined Trader* and do the exercises; then read

Van Tharp's *Trade Your Way to Financial Freedom* and follow the plan he outlines.

Learn about Technical Analysis

Some traders say you can't day trade without using technical analysis. Others say all you need is a Level 2 quote screen. Both are right—for themselves. You'll have to make your own decision. You should at least have a passing knowledge of technical analysis, which is what you got in Chapter 6. How much further you want to go is up to you.

If you want to pursue technical analysis, start with John Murphy's book *The Visual Investor*. Then use some of the online technical tools mentioned in Chapter 6 to practice using technical indicators and interpreting buy and sell signals. Test your favorite signals by paper trading (be sure to read "The Fallacy of Paper Trading" in Chapter 5). You'll learn very quickly whether you want to pursue the subject. If you do, it may well become a lifetime of study.

Online News Sites

Keyword searches at the major news sites will keep you abreast of the latest articles related to market and day trading issues. Best news sites:

CBS MarketWatch (www.cbs.marketwatch.com). Free.

CNBC.com (www.cnbc.com). Free.

InternetNews.com (www.internetnews.com). Free.

New York Times (www.nytimes.com). Free.

SmartMoney.com (www.smartmoney.com). Free.

TheStreet.com (www.thestreet.com). Free. TheStreet. com is launching a network of sites for market commentary, including RealMoney.com as a showcase for its market experts. The cost will be $200/year.

Wall Street Journal Interactive Edition (www.wsj. com). $59/year includes Barron's Online.

Keep Up with Day Trading News

The markets are in a state of flux and will likely remain that way indefinitely. The only way to keep up is to keep up. Check out the major online news sites (see previous page) and search for articles related to day trading, ECNs, the Nasdaq, and the NYSE. You may find, as I did, that your newly sensitized trading antennae will instantly flag any news remotely related to trading and the markets.

THE RISK MANAGEMENT PLAN: HOW WILL YOU MANAGE YOUR MONEY?

A trading plan is based on risk management, which is another term for money management. The risks created by the market's unstructured environment should be understood and dealt with, but it is also important to deal with risk on a practical level.

Assess Your Tolerance for Risk

The first step in managing risk is to figure out your tolerance for risk. You probably know at the gut level whether

---

Risk Tolerance Tests

Several web sites feature free interactive tests that help you assess your tolerance for taking financial risks. These are fairly superficial, but they're fun to take and if you answer the questions honestly you might learn something about yourself.

✔ Ameristock Mutual Fund: www.ameristock.com.

✔ KCET Public Television: www.kcet.org/education/funding.

✔ Microsoft's MoneyCentral Investor: www.money-central.msn/investor (click Insight, then Step-by-Step Guides).

you are basically conservative or an aggressive risk taker. If you don't, take a risk tolerance test (see box). Regardless of your score, if you intend to become a day trader you must learn to manage risk, because trading is a high-risk profession.

The number one money management rule is to preserve your capital so that you can stay in the game. Remember this as you go through the process of developing your risk management plan.

Use Discretionary Trading Capital

An important aspect of risk management is your attitude about the money with which you're trading. People feel differently about hard-earned money—savings painstakingly deposited in a bank account over the years—than they do about easy money, that which is inherited or won at a casino table.

Unless you have money that you can afford to lose and still sleep at night, you don't belong in the market.

Mark Ritchie, as quoted in
The New Market Wizards

Why? Because trading with precious funds increases the fear element in trading decisions. If you're trading with capital that you can't afford to lose—or that you've worked long and hard for—your fear will turn every loss into a bigger loss. Fear will make you cautious when you should be bold; it will make you foolhardy when you should be cool; it will turn you into an H&P investor—holding on to a losing trade and hoping and praying it will turn around—which will in all likelihood increase the loss.

Everything you will read about day trading will stress this point: Trade only with money you can afford to lose. Some electronic brokers require proof of income and net worth to open a day trading account. This may put their minds at ease, but only you know whether the funds with which you're trading really is money you can afford to lose.

Establish Realistic Income Goals

If you're planning to make your living as a trader—as opposed to dabbling in it as a hobby—you need to establish realistic income goals. Let's say you want to make at least $150,000 a year. That breaks down to $2,900 a week, or almost $600 a day. What do you think you'd most likely have to gross each day as to make that much? Almost $2,000.

Here's a sample breakdown, using 20 1,000-share trades (*round trips*) a day, with half of them gaining 3/16 of a point ($187.50) and half losing a teenie ($62.50):

10 winning trades @ $187.50 each	$ 1,875.00
10 losing trades @ 62.50 each	– 625.00
Commissions @ $30/round trip	– 600.00
Profit before taxes and fixed costs	$ 650.00

Fixed costs, such as data feeds, software, computer lease, telephone line, and connection charges can add $50 to $200 a week to your expenses. So in reality, you'd have to up the number of trades or increase your profits on each trade to cover your fixed costs—or to increase your income.

round trip the entering and exiting of a single position (i.e., a buy order followed by a sell order for the same stock). Some commissions and other fees are quoted on round trips, rather than on a single trade.

I view the objectives in trading as a three-tiered hierarchy. First and foremost is the preservation of capital. When I first look at a trade, I don't ask "What is the potential profit I can realize?" but rather, "What is the potential loss I could suffer?" Second, I strive for consistent profitability by balancing my risk relative to the accumulated profits or losses. Consistency is far more important than making lots of money. Third, insofar as I'm successful in the first two goals, I attempt to achieve superior returns. I do this by

*increasing my bid size after, and only after, peri-
ods of high profitability.*

Victor Sperandeo, as quoted in
The New Market Wizards

As you begin to trade you'll see whether your income goals are realistic, and you can adjust your plan ac-
cordingly. It is important, however, to quantify your goals
in the beginning on a daily or weekly basis—either as a
dollar profit figure or as a number of winning trades—and
write them down. You can fine-tune them as you go along,
but if you don't write down your income goals and your
results, you'll gloss over the losses and inflate the wins
and end up with a totally distorted view of your progress.

Determine Your Trade Size and Drawdown

The size of your trades is a critical element in risk management. If you wager too much money on a trade, you
run the risk of a large *drawdown* on your account—which
increases the amount you need to gain just to get even
again. But if you risk too little on each trade, it'll take forever to build up capital.

 drawdown
a method of cal-
culating cash
flow in an ac-
count.

Dr. Van Tharp calls the decision of how much to risk
on each trade position sizing and says it is the most important aspect of trading, aside from psychology.[2]

If you'll recall the marble game in Chapter 8, position sizing was the only difference between those who
went bankrupt and those who turned $100,000 into $4
million. Those players who ended up with $4 million did
so by increasing the size of their trades when in winning
streaks. This is the classic anti-martingale strategy.[3]

*Controlling position size is indispensable to suc-
cess. Of all the traits necessary to trade success-
fully, this factor is the most undervalued.*

Mark Ritchie, as quoted in
The New Market Wizards

Tharp talks extensively about position sizing in his book, *Trade Your Way to Financial Freedom*, and offers four different models for determining position size. Each model assesses risk differently to arrive at a position size. Tharp explains each model in detail and compares the advantages and disadvantages of each. Whether or not you use his models, the chapter is helpful in understanding how position size affects your success as a trader.

Not every trader sees risk management the same way, however. In fact, read 10 different books on the subject and you'll probably get 10 different views. In his book *Trading the Plan*, Robert Deel creates an equation that takes into account your trading ability and methodology.[4] He calls it the DDRL equation for direction, discipline, risk, and leverage, and shows you how to arrive at a DDRL score to determine how much of your total available capital should be risked on each trade.

With regard to drawdown calculations, Deel suggests you start with your first losing trade. Whatever that loss is, add every positive and losing trade to that figure to calculate your ongoing drawdown. If the figure should reach zero or go positive, the drawdown remains at zero until the next losing trade. Then the calculation starts over again.

It doesn't really matter whether you follow a Tharp strategy or a Deel strategy or one you find in another book or seminar. It doesn't matter if you create one of your own. What matters is that you become aware of how the size of your trades affects your performance as a trader.

Keep in mind that during the learning curve, when you are first starting out, you should keep your trade size small. The objective during this period is to learn the trading game, not to make money. Keeping trades small in the beginning will help you preserve your capital so that you can suffer the inevitable losses and still live to trade another day.

Decide How Much You Can Lose on a Single Trade

How much are you willing to lose on one trade? The answer to this question determines where you set your stops.

Always understand the risk/reward of the trade as it now stands, not as it existed when you put the position on.

Bill Lipschutz, as quoted in
The New Market Wizards

One rule of thumb is to risk no more than 1 to 1.5 percent of your risk capital on each trade. Let's say your available capital is $50,000, and you're willing to risk 1 percent on each trade. Your stop should be set at a point that represents a $500 loss. With a 100-share trade, the stock price can drop 5 points and you're still within your risk objectives. With a 1,000-share trade, the price can drop only half a point and remain within your risk objectives.

But there is another consideration. The number of trades you have on at any given time multiplies your risk. If you have three positions and each loses 1 percent, your total losses for the day are $1,500. If you lose five trades in one day, your loss is $2,500. And what about gaps? A stock can gap down several points on bad news, plummeting past your stop and magnifying your losses beyond your worst nightmare. You could find yourself in the red by several thousand dollars, with or 10 to 15 percent of your risk capital gone.

You have to decide how much you're willing to lose in a single day as well as on a single trade. The number one goal is to preserve your capital so that you can stay in the trading game.

Both Tharp and Deel address this subject—in different ways—in their chapters on money management. Read them both, and others, and then work out your own system.

THE TRADING PLAN: PLAN YOUR TRADES, TRADE YOUR PLAN

Your trading plan is a specific system for putting on a trade. It details your methodology for setting up the trade, and for the entry trigger, exit strategy, and stop levels. Some systems are sophisticated, back-tested computer models; others are simple statements scribbled on a sheet of paper. Whichever you use, you won't be able to create a trading plan until you've settled on a trading style (discussed in Chapter 5). Once you've done that, you can address the following questions to help you develop your own unique plan.

- ✔ *What kind of charts will you use, if any?* Specify the time span of the chart and the frequency of the data. Example: I will use three-minute charts with tick-by-tick data.
- ✔ *What kind of technical indicators will you use, if any?* Example: Moving average crossovers.
- ✔ *What is the setup?* A setup describes the conditions that must be in place before you enter the stock. Example: The fast moving average is below the slow moving average and both are moving up.
- ✔ *What is the trigger?* A trigger is an event that alerts you to enter a position. For example, with moving average crossovers, your trigger to buy may be when the fast moving average crosses above the slow moving average.

If your system isn't any good, you're still going to lose money no matter how effective your money management rules are. But if you have an approach that makes money, then money management can make the difference between success and failure.

Monroe Trout, as quoted in
The New Market Wizards

- ✔ *What is your exit strategy?* At what point will you close out a trade? Tharp says that you do not have a trading system until you know—before you enter a trade—exactly when you will get out of it, regardless of which way it goes. You need a worst-case scenario and an exit strategy to cut your losses, which has to do with setting protective stops. You should also have a plan for taking your profits if the trade goes well, which has to do with risk-reward ratio and managing your stops. Tharp devotes a chapter to each of these subjects, which I suggest you study.

Once your trading plan is written, post it on your bulletin board or near your computer so that you can see it as you trade.

THE DAILY PLAN: PREMARKET AND POSTMARKET ROUTINES

The hours you trade and your actions before the market opens and after it closes are closely related to risk management. Ritualizing your premarket and postmarket activities can help give your day form and structure. As we discussed in Chapter 8, this is vitally important in an unstructured market environment. Here are some things to consider.

When Will You Trade?

By the time you read this, the market will be well on its way to a 12-hour trading day. Chances are, you won't want to be glued to your computer for 12 straight hours, even if you could take the tension and stress! If you're a part-time trader, your trading hours are pretty much dictated by your primary job, but other than that, no one is going to tell you when you can trade. It is up to you to erect a structure of specific trading hours on this unstructured environment.

Some periods carry more risk than others. At the current time, trading before or after market hours is more risky because low liquidity creates wider spreads and more volatility. This most likely will improve after Nasdaq and the NYSE extend their trading hours.

But there are other periods of high risk during regular market hours. The market is usually at its most volatile the first two hours or so after the open and the last hour before the close. For experienced traders, these hours are prime time. But for the inexperienced trader, the volatility during these hours increases the risk, which is why many experts advise beginners to stay on the sidelines during early morning and later afternoon hours.

Like so much else in day trading, this is something you'll have to work out for yourself.

What Is Your Premarket Routine?

What do you do to get ready to trade? Read the *Wall Street Journal* or *Investor's Business Daily*? Watch the premarket shows on CNBC or Bloomberg? Surf the news sites on the Web? One trader starts his day off with 20 minutes of meditation to focus his mind; another wouldn't dream of starting off without her three-mile run.

It doesn't matter what you do to get ready for your trading day, but it is helpful to structure the premarket hours and to condition your mind for a positive trading experience. It is also helpful to review your goals and trading rules.

What Is Your Postmarket Routine?

When the market closes, it is a good idea to go over the day's activity while events are still fresh in your mind. Look at your net position for the day. Did you meet your daily goals? If not, why not? Go over your trading journal (more about this later) and analyze each trade. See if you can determine exactly why a trade went bad or why a small loss turned into a large one.

Don't concentrate just on losses, though. Learn from your winners as well. Look at the notes you made about your mental state when you placed the trade and when you exited it. These notes may well reveal the real reasons behind your failures and your successes.

Part of your postmarket routine may be to look for

stocks to trade the next day. Depending on your style, you might watch the news for earnings releases or study charts for technical breakouts. The more you can formalize your after-hours activities, the better prepared you will be for the next trading day.

THE TRADING JOURNAL: RECORDING YOUR TRADES

A trading journal is a record of your trading day. It details every trade you made, when and why you made it, when and why you got out of it, whether it was a winner or a loser, how you felt about it afterward, how much money you made or lost, and so on. Like any good journal, the more you write about your feelings before, during, and after the trade, the more valuable the journal will be when you review it.

A journal can take any form, from handwritten notes to an Excel spreadsheet. Whatever the form, you should use it religiously, with the objective of studying why your winners won and why your losers lost. (It can also provide a good backup at tax time.)

A web site called The Security Blanket has a free form that makes an excellent trading journal (click Growth Chart at www.thesecurityblanket.com). The form can be downloaded into an Excel chart spreadsheet. For the super-industrious, David Nassar suggests using a database program such as Microsoft Access so that you can look for trading patterns and repeat the successful ones and eliminate the unsuccessful ones.

Checklist for a Trading Journal

The following list is adapted from the "purchase log" in *CyberInvesting*.[5] I've expanded it to include actions specific to trading, drawn from my research and conversations with traders and investors.

> ✔ *Stock symbol and sector.* The stock itself doesn't mean much to scalpers who trade anything that

moves, but if you trade a small group of stocks or concentrate on specific sectors, it is important to record this, so you can review your success rate with each stock or sector.

✔ *Date and time of your entry and exit.* The duration of the trade will be helpful in assessing a trading pattern. Make a note if the trade was made during extended-hours trading.

✔ *Number of shares.* If the share size varied from your standard trade size, make a note. Did you increase it or decrease it because of a winning streak or a losing streak? Because of a gut feeling about the market?

✔ *State of the market.* What was the market like when you made the trade? You can state this as simply as the Dow was up X, Nasdaq was down X; or you might be more specific about what was going on in the market at the time—a bull rally, a correction, a jittery market awaiting a Greenspan speech, and so on.

✔ *Type of order and how it was executed.* Indicate whether it was a limit order or market order and whether it was routed through SOES, SelectNet, or an ECN.

✔ *Type of trade.* Indicate the type if it varied from your written trading system, or if your system includes a variety of plays. For example, a swing trader might specify an earnings play, a stock split, an IPO, or a technical trade.

✔ *Long or short.* Indicate whether the trade was long or short.

✔ *Gain or loss.* Record both points and percentage.

✔ *Exit strategy.* Did you follow your preplanned exit strategy—you did have one, didn't you? Or did you exit for another reason? If so, what was the reason?

✔ *State of mind.* What were your expectations at the time you made the trade? How did you feel while you were watching the trade? What was your motivation to exit?

The last point is the most important. Your state of mind will reveal how much you were being driven by fear or greed. Your goal is to eliminate these emotions, and the first step toward eliminating them is to become aware of them. But unless you write down your feelings about each trade, I promise you won't remember exactly what you felt about it tomorrow or next week or next month.

If you record your emotions and your state of mind about each and every trade, your journal can become a first-class learning tool. And if you decide to hire a trading coach, your trading journal will be invaluable in pinpointing the areas of concern.

THE GETTING STARTED PLAN: SETTING UP SHOP

It's difficult to write a "getting started" plan since everything in the master plan—in fact, everything in this book—is about getting started. Nevertheless, once you make the commitment actually to start day trading, there are 10 specific steps you'll need to take. This section is presented simply as a checklist because everything is discussed in other sections of this book.

1. Define your trading style. Almost everything else flows from this decision.
2. Create a master plan.
3. Decide on remote versus on-site trading.
4. Demo various kinds of software and evaluate brokers.
5. Open and fund a brokerage account.
6. Set up your trading station, if you're trading from a remote office.
7. Do simulated trading to learn the software.
8. Take a training seminar or find a mentor.
9. Start trading.
10. Continue to study and learn about trading.

Creating a master plan forces you to think through the many steps you will need to take to become a day trader. It can transform a rather vague goal into discrete chunks of achievable tasks. By putting the plan into writing, you both strengthen your commitment to trading and give yourself a benchmark by which to measure your progress.

Beginner's Rules

These are virtually universal rules for the beginner trader, from traders who've been there, done that.

1. Start with small trades of 100 or 200 shares.

2. Avoid highly volatile stocks during the learning process.

3. Don't have too many positions at once. In fact, make one trade at a time until you build your confidence in your software and your trading style.

4. Focus on a small group of stocks.

5. Don't *chase a stock*. If your limit order misses it, let it go. There will be other days, other trades.

6. When a trade is open, let everything else wait.

7. Set tight stops and get out of a losing trade quickly.

8. Don't *down-average*.

9. Don't hold a losing trade overnight.

10. Pyramid your profits. As a stock moves up, take partial profits—and use trailing stops to protect your profits.

11. Know when you're going to get out—before you get in.

12. Don't worry about a missed trade. Another opportunity will come along. And another. And another. And another.

13. Don't trade when you're emotionally or physically stressed out.

14. Take responsibility for your trades.

 chasing a stock
continuing to up your bid in order to get an execution on a fast-moving stock. Not a good thing to do.

 down-average
to buy additional shares of a declining stock in order to lower your average cost per share.

15. Keep your journal and review your trades at the end of the day.

16. Learn from your mistakes and create your own rules!

COMING UP . . .

If you plan to be a remote trader, you'll need to set up your office, install the trading software, and practice simulated trading until you become familiar with your system. We'll talk about this in the next chapter.

Chapter 10

The Home Office: Setting Up Shop

If you plan to trade on-site at a day trading shop, you can skip this chapter. But if you're going to trade from a home office—becoming one of the thousands of remote day traders—this chapter will steer you toward the resources you'll need to set up a remote office. If you haven't made up your mind yet, this chapter may help you decide.

Day trading shops attract traders who don't like working alone or who want to earn their trading wings without a large setup cost. Some brokers charge a monthly fee; others act as mentors and teach their trading style for a percentage of the trader's profits. Either way, the initial cost of on-site trading is less than setting up an equivalent home office.

There are benefits to on-site trading. It erects an immediate structure on your activities, which can be reassuring to a new trader. The presence of the head trader offers a sense of comfort and authority—at least one of us knows what we're doing!—and there is the ritual of going to an office, interacting with coworkers, and being part of a group. But the camaraderie of fellow traders is a two-edged sword. Traders frequently comment on their trades and it is easy to get caught up in the emotional atmosphere of the shop. That can make it difficult to concentrate on your own trades, which can adversely affect your trading.

The remote trader, on the other hand, works alone. On the plus side, there is zero commute time with a home office and a very relaxed dress code—some traders been known to trade in their underwear. On the minus side are the isolation and the cost. There are ways to deal with the isolation (online trading pits and chat rooms, for example), but the cost can't be avoided. You have to supply everything—hardware, software, high-speed Internet connection, data feeds—all of which can run several thousand dollars for traders who want high-end systems.

Which brings up a whole range of questions. What kind of system will you need? What kind of computer? What kind of monitor? Will a 56K modem do or must you get a high-speed connection like cable, ISDN, or DSL? And exactly what are these, anyway? And what about real-time news and stock quotes? Do they come with the trading system or do you have to order them separately?

The answers to these questions depend on, yes, your trading style. If you plan to make a dozen or so trades a month, you can probably get by with a Web-based broker and an Internet browser. But if you plan to make a dozen trades a week (a low-end trader) or 50 to 100 trades a day (a high-end trader), you'll need the whole enchilada.

This chapter will tell you what goes into the enchilada. How big it needs to be depends on the kind of trading you expect to do.

A Gallery of Trade Stations

If you want to take a look at some actual home trading stations, go to Phactor.com's Gallery of Stations at www.phactor.com. There's also a handy fraction converter that you can print out.

SET UP YOUR TRADING STATION

A remote trading station can be simple or elaborate. The primary considerations are your trading style and the depth of your pockets. If you already have a computer, maybe all you need to do is upgrade it, but you'll want the fastest possible processor, a capacious hard drive, more memory than you think you'll need, and an Internet connection at the speed of light! Table 10.1 gives three levels of hardware specifications.

Hardware Considerations

Here are some points to consider about the hardware requirements:

- ✔ Some low-end systems can use Windows 95 or 98 as the operating system, but they are less reliable than Windows NT. Windows 2000 should solve many of the reliability problems of Windows 95 and 98.
- ✔ Memory is cheap. More is better than less.
- ✔ Some trading software will not work with Apple Macintosh even with a virtual platform (which normally allows the Mac to work with PC software).
- ✔ To view multiple charts, windows, and spreadsheets, you'll need multiple monitors, which could increase your system requirements. Be sure to consult the video card manufacturer for specific requirements. Appian Graphics (www.appian graphics.com) is the premier provider of video cards.

Software Considerations

If you use an electronic broker, your trading software is supplied by the broker (Chapter 4). In addition, you'll need some or all of the following:

TABLE 10.1 Technical Specifications

The following specifications are for the RealTick™ system, courtesy of Townsend Analytics, Ltd. (www.taltrade.com). Be sure to check the specific requirements of the trading software that you select.

System

	Min.	*Rec.*	*Best*
Processor	Pentium	Pentium II 200 MHz	Pentium II 400 MHz or +
RAM	64 MB	64 MB	128 MB or +
Hard Drive	2 GB	4 GB or +	4 GB or +
Operating System System	Windows 95 or 98	Windows NT Workstation 4.0 w/Service Pack 3	Windows NT Workstation 4.0 w/Service Pack 3
Other Software	Internet Explorer 4.0, Email	Adobe Acrobat Reader	Microsoft Office
Peripherals	Standard	Graphical Printer	Color Printer

Display

	Min.	*Rec.*	*Best*
Screen Size	15 in.	17 in.	19 in. +
Video Card RAM	512 KB	2 MB	4 MB +
Resolution	640 × 480	800 × 600	1024 × 768
Refresh Rate	60 Hz	72 Hz	85 Hz
Color Depth/Palette	4-bit/16 Colors	8-bit/256 Colors	16-bit/65,536 Colors
# of Monitors	1	1	Multiple[1]

[1]Multiple monitors may require additional system resources.
Source: RealTick™ © 1986–2000. All rights reserved. Used with permission of Townsend Analytics, Ltd.

✔ Web browser (the latest version of Internet Explorer or Netscape Navigator).

✔ E-mail program, such as Eudora.

✔ Adobe Acrobat Reader, which allows you to print documents in a wysiwyg (what you see is what

Computer Literacy

How much do you have to know about computers to be a remote trader? The more, the better. If you're comfortable surfing the Net and if you know how to install a Windows-based program, you probably won't have any trouble with a low-end system. But trading software that requires multiple monitors and elaborate customization may be beyond your skills. Check out the technical support offered by your broker, but be prepared to hire a technical consultant to set up the system for you.

you get) format. The Reader can be downloaded free at many web sites and at www.adobe.com.

✔ Microsoft Office, which includes Word, Excel, PowerPoint, and other programs. This is optional but you'll probably need some kind of word processing and spreadsheet programs.

✔ Charting software (Chapter 6). Unless you're a technician, your trading software may include all the technical analysis tools you'll need.

✔ PC Anywhere. This is a software package required for troubleshooting and help-desk support for remote traders using CyBerTrader, CyBerX, and other trading software. You can purchase it at any computer store or download it off the web for a free 30-day trial from the web site www.symantec.com. The cost is approximately $170.

GET A HIGH-SPEED CONNECTION

You can have the best trading software in the world, the most elaborate computer system, and enough software to start an e-commerce shop, and you'll miss half your trades if you have a slow Internet connection.

The keyword is bandwidth. Bandwidth refers to the maximum amount of data that a connection can transmit in a given period of time. It is measured in bits per second (bps); one Kbps or K is a thousand bits per second; one Mbps is a million bits per second.

The goal of anyone connected with the Internet is to get more and more bandwidth. At the moment, the choices are computer modems, ISDN lines, DSL lines— all of which connect through telephone lines—and cable modems, which connect over a cable television network.

Computer Modems

A modem is a device that allows your computer to communicate over a telephone line. It uses a dial-up connection via your local telephone company to your Internet service provider (ISP).

Computer modems are the cheapest connection to use and the easiest to install (although they are inadequate for the high-end user). The modem itself will cost about $100; the ISP monthly service is about $20.

What Is a Kbps?

K stands for Kbps: K means 1,000; bps means bits per second. Here's a comparison of data transmission speeds:[1]

28.8K modem	28,800 bps	(28.8 Kbps)
56K modem	56,000 bps	(56 Kbps)
ISDN line	128,000 bps	(128 Kbps)
DSL line	1.5 million bps	(1.5 Mbps)
Cable modem	2.8 million bps	(2.8 Mbps)

These are downstream speeds—the speeds at which data is received by your computer. Downstream data speeds are faster than upstream speeds—the speeds at which data can be sent from your computer.

Computer modems currently come in four speeds: 14.4, 28.8K, 33.6K, and 56K. These numbers, however, refer only to the maximum possible speed, not necessarily the actual speed. A 56K modem, for example, allows you to receive data (referred to as downstream speed) at speeds up to 56K, but the data you send (referred to as upstream speed) is transmitted at only 33.6K. Modems less than 56K are not practical for direct access trading.

Your ISP has a lot to do with the speed of your modem. Unless the ISP is equipped with the proper lines to handle the data transmission, actual speeds may be a lot lower. It is recommended that you use one of the major ISPs (or ask your broker which has a direct connection to its server). Small providers may not be able to transmit data at speeds exceeding 30K. Also, be aware that some phone lines do not support 56K connections at all. You'll have to check your local telephone company for this information. The major ISPs are:

Earthlink	www.earthlink.com
Sprint	www.sprint.com
MCI WorldCom	www.wcom.com
AT&T	www.worldnet.att.net

By the way, one software manufacturer suggests that you not install the software supplied by the ISP because it may not be compatible with your trading software. All that is necessary is that you enter your name, password, and the connection phone number into your Windows dial-up window. The best thing to do is to ask the opinion of the broker that supplies your trading software.

For more on computer modems, go to V90.com at www.v90.com.

ISDN Lines

ISDN stands for integrated services digital network. It is a dial-up connection that combines analog (for voice) and digital transmissions and can transmit data up to 128K. For comparison, a 56K modem may take 30 seconds to establish a connection with your ISP; an ISDN line can do it in two seconds.

An ISDN connection consists of the ISDN line and router, and an ISP. Cost for installing a residential ISDN line is approximately $150, plus a monthly charge of about $35 and usage charge. ISPs charge slightly more for an ISDN connection than for a computer modem connection. You will need to contact your local telephone company for the line installation and router, and your ISP for ISDN access. There may be a per-minute charge by the phone company for ISDN access, in addition to the charge made by the ISP. There's an excellent tutorial on ISDN lines at www.ralphb.net/ISDN.

DSL Lines

DSL stands for digital subscriber line. (It is also called ADSL for asymmetrical digital subscriber line.) It is a high-speed Internet connection available through some local telephone companies. Transmission rates vary, depending on how close you are to the phone company's central office and other factors, but are typically either 1.5+ Mbps downstream and 348 Kbps upstream, or 384+ Kbps downstream and 128 Kbps upstream.

DSL, as it is referred to, is not a dial-up connection; it is always on, and it allows you simultaneously to use a phone or fax. Costs vary, but the ballpark is about $40 to $130 a month, based on the speed, and about $150 for installation and equipment, with a one-year lease. ISP service is usually included.

For more about DSL and a list of providers, go to DLS Life at www.dsllife.com or call your local phone company.

Cable Modems

A cable modem is a device that allows you to access the Internet through your local cable TV company. (Yes, you can watch TV and use the cable modem at the same time.) It is a continuous connection, with speeds ranging from 500 Kbps to 10 Mbps. As with any connection, downstream speeds are faster than upstream speeds. The cable provider @Home offers downstream speeds up 2.8 Mbps and upstream speeds of 128 Kbps.

The cost for a cable modem is comparable to a DLS line—about $150 to install and about $40 to $50 a month; there is no ISP involved. The disadvantage is that a continuous connection is more susceptible to hackers. Cable modems are not available in every area. For more information and to check availability, go to @Home at www.home.com or RoadRunner at www.rr.com/rdrun. Or call your local cable company.

Be sure to check with the electronic broker you select to see if a cable modem presents a problem with its software.

THIRD-PARTY DATA FEEDS

Some data are supplied by the broker and incorporated into the trading system, such as Level 2 quotes. Some, such as the Dow Jones News Wire, must be ordered through the broker or data supplier. But there are some data that you may want to subscribe to on your own.

Real-time streaming quotes, for example, may be required if you plan to use sophisticated technical charting beyond the charting capabilities of your trading software. Or you may need a third-party source of quotes and news if you use a Web-based browser or one of the lower-end direct access systems that does not come with the data you want.

This section will introduce you to a number of data suppliers. But decide first on your broker and trading software, and find out what data is supplied by the broker. For proper integration into the trading software, you should use the data suppliers recommended by your broker. Check the web sites of the data suppliers to find out the brokers with which they are affiliated.

Most data suppliers offer free trials, but you'll have to pay the exchange fees during the trial. The prices quoted are for the basic services as of the date of writing. Current prices can be found on the company's web site. (These suppliers also have stand-alone products.)

A-T Financial

A-T Financial (www.atfi.com) offers three packages. The basic package, Attitude, has real-time streaming quotes, one-year historical charts, technical studies, tickers, fundamental data, and a link to Microsoft's Excel for $75 a month. Attitude Plus adds advanced customized charting, dynamic time and sales data, current intraday data, and three years of historical information for $150/month.

For $225/month, Major Attitude adds intraday data for five days, 15 years' historical information, options analytics, customized pages, portfolio, and Dow Jones Business News. Exchange fees are included. Nasdaq Level 2 quotes can be added to basic and Plus packages for $85/month and to Major Attitude for $70/month. See the web site for other add-ons. A-T Financial can be linked to PreferredTrade.

DTN.IQ

DTN.IQ (www.dtniq.com) offers real-time streaming quotes and news in a basic service for $89 a month, plus $6.25 in exchange fees and a setup fee. In addition to Level 1 quotes and news from 35 wire services, it includes free software that formats the data into charts, watch lists, time and sales data, tickers, and portfolios. For additional fees, you can add Nasdaq Level 2 quotes, 15 Most Active Issues, Dow Jones Newswire, or Associated Press Newswire. DTN.IQ can be linked to PreferredTrade or CyBerCorp's CyBerX.

eSignal

eSignal, from Data Broadcasting Corporation (www.esignal.com), is one of the oldest and largest data suppliers. It offers an equities-only package of real-time streaming quotes for $99/month or $948/year with no exchange fees. Nasdaq Level 2 quotes are free with a prepaid annual subscription.

The equities-only package includes quotes for market indexes, bulletin board stocks, Canadian stocks, forex (foreign exchange) rates, and bonds. It also includes portfolio alerts, time and sales, a stock screener, and intraday and interday charting and analysis. You can add on Dow Jones Business News for $30/month (headlines) or $40/month (full text) and real-time SEC filings for $20/month. eSignal can be integrated with trading systems from CyBerCorp, All-Tech, On-Site Trading, and PreferredTrade, among others, as well as with charting software such as MetaStock.

InterQuote

Interquote (www.interquote.com) offers real-time tick-by-tick quotes for stocks, options, and futures in a spreadsheet format. It comes with a charting package, alert service, and option tools. The cost is $69.95/month or $629.55/year. Many add-ons include Level 2 quotes, Dow Jones and Associated Press news wires, First Call earnings estimates, and theflyonthewall.com (news). InterQuote can be linked to PreferredTrade.

Quote.com

Qcharts from Quote.com (www.quote.com) provides real-time streaming quotes, charts, time and sales data, historical data, and hot stock lists. Qcharts can be linked to PreferredTrade and CyBerCorp. The cost is $79.95/month plus exchange fees. Add $20 if you want access to news stories, fundamental data, portfolio trackers, and research sources at the Quote.com web site.

PCQuote

PCQuote is a RealTick™ product, so it interfaces with the RealTick™ trading software, offered by many broker/dealers. PCQuote supplies streaming real-time quotes, Level 2 quotes, news, technical analysis, charting, tickers, and alarms. For costs (the schedule is complicated) go to www.pcquote.com.

THE WIRELESS CONNECTION

If you want to be plugged into Wall Street without being tethered to your desk, you might want to consider a wireless connection. With a wireless device, such as a pager, a cell phone, or a PDA (personal digital assistant), you can get stock quotes, receive price and news alerts, or monitor a portfolio of stocks. You can even—with an Internet-ready phone or PDA—tap into the Internet to place a stock trade.

When going wireless, your first decision will be to decide exactly what kind of data you want to receive. This is too exhaustive a subject to treat at length here, but consider these points:

1. If you want to be alerted to price changes and news on certain stocks, all you really need is a data provider and an alphanumeric pager. In most cases, you will enter your stock symbols at the provider's web site and set your alert triggers. When the price reaches a trigger or when there is news related to one of your stocks, you will receive an alert on your pager or other wireless device.

2. If you want stock quotes on demand, you'll need a data provider and a two-way wireless device, such as an alphanumeric pager, a digital cell phone, or a PDA. This will allow you to request a quote on any stock, as well as receive alerts and news on preselected stocks.

3. If you want to place a trade on the go, you'll need an Internet-ready cell phone or PDA, a wireless data network, and a broker who offers wireless trading.

The wireless Web is in its infancy. (One observer compared it with the stage of black-and-white television in the early 1950s.) It's crowded, confusing, and chaotic. If you want to read about it in depth, run a search at PC

As you investigate the wireless world, you'll find references to PCS (personal communication service) phones, smart phones, Web phones, Internet-ready phones. It's all very confusing. But before you buy a new one, check your current cell phone to see if it is Internet-ready. According to a recent study, some 26 percent of the 85 million wireless phones in the United States are Internet-ready, although only a small percent are being utilized for Web browsing.

World Magazine (www.pcworld.com) using the keywords *wireless web*. You'll find many informative articles, and PC World is a good place to keep up with the changes that will inevitably take place.

Meanwhile, here are some sources for wireless devices, data providers, Internet-ready phones, and wireless trading.

Wireless Hardware

Rather than list the sources for the dozens of wireless communications devices, I will refer you to a handy list of links at www.stockboss.com/pages.htm. You can click your way to manufacturers of one-way pagers, two-way pagers, and PCS phones. In addition, you might want to check out the Palm PDA products at www.palm.com and the wireless products at Phone.com (www.phone.com).

Wireless Data Providers

Here is a sampling of data providers for wireless quotes and alerts. In most cases, they offer real-time stock quotes and news headlines, although one offers alerts on technical breakouts and one comes with its own wireless device.

✔ *Datalink.net*. Datalink.net (www.datalink.net) offers a number of financial wireless data services. QuoteXpress offers real-time stock alerts over a pager or PCS phone. RelayXpress provides quotes and news on demand with Motorola's Timeport P930 and Pagewriter 2000/2000X and RIM's Inter@ctive 950. RumorXpress alerts you to Wall Street rumors via a pager. Net-2-GO lets you retrieve real-time information through a Web-enabled phone. See the web site for pricing.

✔ *eSignal.* If you subscribe to eSignal's real-time or Level 2 quotes for your desktop system (www. esignal.com), you can get the same quotes without additional charge for your laptop computer by subscribing to a wireless ISP service.

✔ *OmniAlert.* OmniAlert (www.omnialert.com) offers real-time price and news alerts for $29.95 a month. Quotes-on-demand are available if you have a wireless Internet browser on your cell phone or PDA. OmniAlert works with most wireless devices.

✔ *QuoTrek.* Data Broadcasting packages its wireless data in a proprietary handheld quote monitor called QuoTrek (www.dbc.com/products/quotrek). It offers real-time quotes, news, and price alerts from all major U.S. exchanges, including money market funds, mutual funds, forex rates, and bonds. The QuoTrek monitor is $295, or $20/month to lease it; the data costs $99/month.

✔ *Stock-Alerts.com.* Stock-Alerts.com (www.stock-alerts.com) provides stock alerts via e-mail free of charge and for a small fee will send the same alerts to your pager or cellular phone. (Data is 20 minutes delayed.) The U.S. markets, plus the United Kingdom, Germany, France, Italy, Australia, and Canada, are covered.

✔ *StockBoss.* StockBoss (www.stockboss.com) offers price and volume alerts for a one-way pager ($9.95/month) and quotes-on-demand with a two-way pager ($17.95/month). The latter is its

StockBoss Interactive service, which works with any wireless device.

✔ *Telescan Direct.* Telescan Direct (www.telescan direct.com) offers technical breakout alerts, price alerts, volume alerts, and news. The technical breakout alerts are available for 13 technical criteria, including moving averages, unusual volume, 52-week highs and lows, basing patterns, MACD, price gaps, and analyst rating changes. Telescan Direct works with any alphanumeric pager or PCS phone. Real-time data is $44.95/month; 20-minute delayed data starts at $19.95.

Wireless Trading

If you want to place a trade on a wireless device—rather than just receive price and news alerts—you must open an account with a broker that offers wireless trading. Your choice of broker will dictate the device and wireless data network you'll need. Costs can run from $50 for a two-way pager to $800 for a Web-enabled cell phone, plus $80 to $100 a month for the data network. Commissions are usually the same as for an online trade.

Each of the brokers listed in Table 10.2 has a de-

TABLE 10.2   Wireless Trading

Below are several Web-based brokers who offer wireless trading:

1800daytrade.com	www.1800daytrade.com
Ameritrade	www.ameritrade.com
Dreyfus Brokerage	www.edreyfus.com
DLJdirect	www.dljdirect.com
Fidelity Investments	www.fidelity.com
FirstTrade	www.firstrade.com
Morgan Stanley Dean Witter Online	www.msdwonline.com
MostActives.com	www.mostactives.com
SiebertNet	www.siebertnet.com
Wyse Securities	www.wyse-sec.com

tailed FAQ about wireless trading. By the way, none of the electronic brokers mentioned in Chapter 3 offer wireless trading at this writing.

That just about does it, as far as setting up a remote office is concerned—with one critical exception: taxes.

A WORD ABOUT TAXES

If you are a short-term trader engaged in trading on a regular, full-time basis, you might be considered a professional trader in the eyes of the Internal Revenue Service (IRS), which can mean substantial benefits to you at tax time. We won't even attempt to go into this in detail, but treatment as a professional trader could mean that you can deduct your expenses for a home office, including your trading station, which may qualify as capital equipment.

It is important to keep good records from Day 1. You must be able to figure your gain or loss on every single trade. Your trading software will probably do this for you, but it must be done. Another important thing to understand going in is the *wash sale rule*. A wash sale occurs if you trade a stock at a loss and within 30 days purchase the same stock again. In a wash sale, you can't deduct losses but gains are taxed as capital gains.

For more information, read the interview with CPA Paul S. Mann at CareerDayTrader.com. Other sources of tax guidance for day traders include:

 wash sale rule
an IRS rule that states you can't claim the loss if you sell shares at a loss and buy them back within 30 days.

- ✔ DayTraderTax.com (www.daytradertax.com) offers a day trader tax guide for $29 and a tax preparation and strategies package for $99. For $199 you can get all that, plus an hour of personal consultation.
- ✔ TradersAccounting.com (www.tradersaccounting.com) offers free advice in its the Trader Status Analysis and Q&A section. It also conducts seminars in various cities for $395.
- ✔ TheStreet.com (www.thestreet.com) has several articles on Taxes for Traders in its Investing Basics section.

Thinking about taxes is never pleasant. But it's a lot easier to set up your accounting system correctly in the beginning than to overhaul a patchwork system several months down the road.

COMING UP . . .

We've talked about education throughout this book. The next chapter will bring it all together in one place.

The College
of Day Trading

T he education of the day trader is the refrain that
has emerged from negative publicity that hit the
industry during 1999. After the summer shootings
in Atlanta turned the spotlight on day trading, the media
stepped up their reporting and began to focus on the pressure and tension of trading and on disillusioned traders
who had lost it all. Arthur Levitt, head of the Securities
and Exchange Commission, warned brokers to educate
their customers and warned traders that their dollars were
at risk. The NASD quickly proposed that day trading firms
be required to screen potential traders for their ability to
handle the stress and tension of the job. Brokerage firms
began to post notices to customers about trading in "fast,
volatile markets."

As a result, an atmosphere of caution has enveloped
the entire day trading industry. At the first annual Online
Trading Expo held in Ontario, California, in September
1999, virtually every speaker dwelled at length on the
risks of day trading and cautioned novice traders to educate themselves thoroughly before wading into the churn-
ing markets. New sites promising to educate the day
trader have popped up all over the Net, and established
sites have begun to beef up their educational offerings.

Everyone is trying to protect day traders from themselves, but the best protection must come from the day traders themselves.

If you choose to become a day trader, you should prepare for it as you would any new, highly skilled profession—with education, training, and practice. Accept the fact that you are an amateur entering a professional game—a high school quarterback trying to play with the pros. Even scarier, you might be the high school math whiz suiting up for the Super Bowl. Unless you want to end up a mass of bruises and broken bones, or worse, you'll learn how to play the game before you step onto the field.

To be a successful trader, you should learn everything you can about the markets, about trading, about strategies, about risk management. This book is a start, but it is basically a survey course to tell you what's out there. Now you need to learn more about each of the subjects we've touched upon, so that your knowledge will be deep as well as broad.

There is no free lunch. Some of your training may be expensive. But the Internet offers many free and low-cost ways to lay the foundation for your day trading career. Most day trading sites offer educational material, and firms that specialize in educating the trader are beginning to take advantage of the interactive nature of the Web.

Using these resources, it is possible to become a day trader without ever setting foot inside a $3,000 day trading seminar, but it takes discipline, initiative, and perseverance (three qualities, by the way, of a successful trader!). One approach is to learn everything you can on your own, then find a coach or a mentor to help you reach your full potential.

This chapter can be used as a starting point for your continuing education as a day trader.

STOCK MARKETS 101

As a trader you should become intimate with the market. You should learn its moods, its history, and its day-to-day

---

Economics 101

If you need a refresher course in economics, enroll in "Economics Essentials for Investors," an online course offered by Dow Jones University (www.dju.com). David Wessel of the *Wall Street Journal*'s Washington bureau teaches the interactive course, which takes 60 to 90 minutes and costs $49.

---

operations. The best place to start is the robust, informative sites offered by the New York Stock Exchange and Nasdaq.

Learn More about the NYSE

If your only view of the New York Stock Exchange has been the backdrop for CNBC reports, check out the NYSE at www.nyse.com. The Trading Floor section offers panoramic views of the main floor, trading posts, broker booths, the bell platform, and more. About the NYSE provides insight into how the exchange works. A particularly cool feature is the Time Line under Historical Perspective. There is also an excellent glossary of financial terms.

Learn More about Nasdaq

Information about Nasdaq is plentiful, but it is scattered over several NASD-related web sites. Here are some direct routes to the most pertinent material for day traders.

✔ *History and profile.* At www.nasd.com click the Profile link to go to background information on the NASD and Nasdaq. Links of interest on this page: History of the NASD, All about Nasdaq (under the Nasdaq Stock Market), and How It Works, which describes Nasdaq market makers. The Evolution of Nasdaq provides a time line of the Nasdaq Stock Market, and the FAQ describes such things as the Order Handling Rules and spreads, and provides another detailed write-up on market makers.

✔ *Market maker activity.* The Nasdaq Trader (www.nasdaqtrader.com) provides a lot of information on current market maker activity. In particular, you can learn the identity of market makers that you see on a Level 2 screen (click Symbol Directory at the home page). To find the dominant market maker on a particular stock, click Trading Data, then select Issue and enter a stock symbol. You can also download the entire list of the 500+ market makers.

✔ *SOES and SelectNet.* To obtain information about SOES and SelectNet services unfiltered through writers or the media, read the Nasdaq Trader Manual at www.nasdaqtrader.com. You can print the whole manual or just relevant sections. It's not as abstruse as you might expect a training manual to be, but it helps if you already have a basic understanding of the SOES and SelectNet.

✔ *New SEC rules affecting Nasdaq.* At the NASD Regulation site (www.nasdr.com) under Education, you can learn about new SEC rules which, if approved, will affect the day trading profession. Proposed changes to the SEC Order Handling Rules—which could put a few obstacles back onto the playing field—can be found in notices to NASD members. (They are reviewed briefly in Chapter 2.)

ONLINE AND OFFLINE COURSES

Take advantage of the free and low-cost tutorials, seminars, and online courses aimed at day traders. Some are fairly simplistic, but they serve as good introductions to the game. As day trading firms acquire the newest interactive technology, online training for day traders should get better and better.

Elite Trader

Elite Trader (www.elitetrader.com) offers a free Level 2 tutorial that should be the first stop on your learning tour. It also offers another fee-based online course that goes deeper into Level 2 and covers order routing strategies—the Advanced Day Trading Course. (It's really more intermediate than advanced.) It lays a good foundation for some of the popular day trading books that focus on trading strategies. The course has no interactive features, but once enrolled you have access to the material forever. (The material is updated as necessary.) The cost is $199, but the section on market maker games alone is worth the price.

MTrader University

MTrader's 21-unit "cyber trading" course (www.mtrader. com) is one of the more comprehensive online educational offerings (Figure 11.1). This course is designed for new traders, with sections on stock market basics,

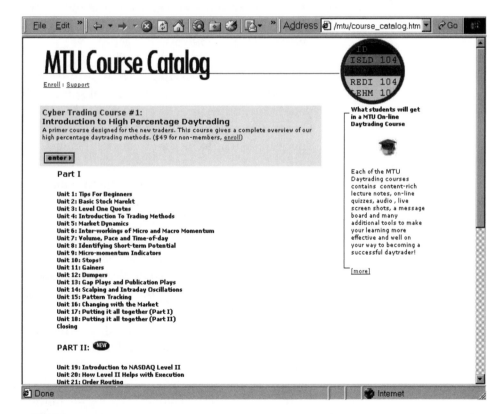

FIGURE 11.1 MTrader University has one of the best low-cost online courses for day traders. *Source:* Reprinted with permission of MTrader.com. www.mtrader.com.

Level 2 quotes, trading methods, market dynamics, momentum, stops, and an introduction to Ken Wolff's "high percentage day trading." (Wolff is the founder of MTrader.)

Wolff's high percentage plays include four pattern types, all based on news events and forms the basis for MTrader's real-time educational chat rooms (more about these later). The course includes lecture notes, online quizzes, and message boards for corresponding with the instructor. It costs $49 for a four-month membership, and it's free for chat room members.

DayTraders USA

DayTraders USA (www.daytradersusa.com) is one of the best bargains on the Web for day traders (Figure 11.2). For a membership fee of $39/year, you get:

✔ *Bimonthly chapter meetings.* These feature talks by market experts on a wide range of subjects. If you live in Southern California (they're located in Orange County) you can attend in person; if not, you can listen to audio webcasts (soon with video).

✔ *Home Sweet Trading Floor.* This trading manual, downloadable at the site, offers practical, real, everyday trading skills for the new trader. Updated regularly.

✔ *Trading tutorials.* Some of the case studies and tutorials from members come with explanations of the thought processes behind the trades and screen shots at the time of execution.

✔ *Monthly newsletter.* Offers trading strategies, training course evaluations, product reviews, broker evaluations, and member profiles.

The site also has a Day Trader Network for finding traders in your area, a news page designed for traders, and a classified section. A mentor program is in the works.

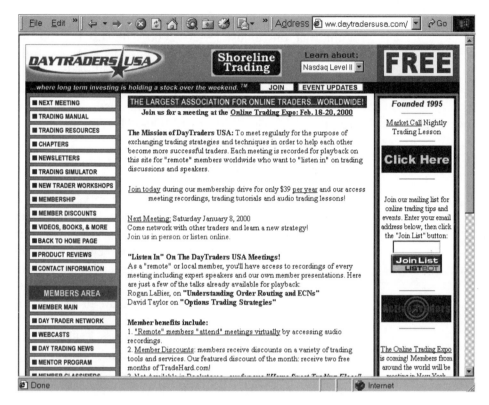

FIGURE 11.2 DayTraders USA offers many free features and low-cost membership to chat rooms, workshops, and tutorials. *Source:* Reprinted with permission of DayTraders USA, www.daytradersusa.com.

The Online Trading Expo

The first International Online Trading Expo was held in Ontario, California, in September 1999. It was a two-day affair packed with more than 50 tutorials taught by supertraders and market experts and attended by some 3,000 novice and experienced traders. Nearly 100 exhibitors displayed their wares in the exhibit hall—every name you've seen in this book and then some. It is an experience you shouldn't miss, but be forewarned: Don't go until you've steeped yourself in the basics of day trading. Otherwise, you may come away more confused than informed.

The next national Expo will be held again in Ontario, California, on August 18–20, 2000. The cost is $199. Regional Expos are held in different cities across the country. For schedules and details, go to www.daytradingexpo.com.

Should you miss the Expos, you can order tapes or CDs of all the sessions from www.the-resource-link.com (tapes, $10; CDs, $13) or call 800-241-7785.

The Pristine Day Trader

The Pristine Day Trader (www.pristine.com) has a lot of free educational material. There are more than a dozen articles written by Pristine CEO Oliver L. Velez. I recommend reading them all, but the least technical are the tutorials on Using Level 2, Playing Market Maker, and the Cardinal Rules of Trading. The Level 2 tutorial includes eight steps for assessing the market picture of a stock and determining where to sell.

Pristine also offers a Chart and Stock Play of the Week. The chart analyzes a stock or index chart in clear, easy-to-read callouts; the stock play discusses the trading strategy for a particular stock, along with a chart.

The Underground Trader

At The Underground Trader (www.undergroundtrader. com) you'll find a Level 2 tutorial worth the $90 price tag. It starts with the basics such as understanding a Level 2 screen, moves on to interpreting the sleights of hand and finesse tactics of market makers, and finishes off with trading techniques. At this time, it can be ordered only by check and snail mail.

Legend Trading Seminars

Legend Trading (www.tradingseminars.com) offers two-day introductory seminars in New York on day trading and swing trading. They are taught by one of the Market Wizards, Victor Sperandeo, and partner Warren Sulmasy.

Sperandeo is the author of *Trader Vic: Methods of a Wall Street Master*. The cost of a seminar is $3,000.

Online Trading Academy

The Online Trading Academy (www.onlinetradingacademy. com) is known for its one-week "boot camp" and "immersion" courses for training day traders. Each is $3,000 and the boot camp is a prerequisite for the immersion course. You would do well to try their 12-hour multimedia course first (available on the Web or on CD-ROM for $199). It is described as a simplified version of the boot camp course and includes a demo of CyBerCorp's CyBerTrader. Training videos are also under development, but as of April 2000 only the Introduction to Day Trading was available (for $19.95). In the works, they say, are videos on Charting in Depth, Trading with the Level 2 Screen, and Executions and Trading Disciplines. OTA also offers mentoring programs.

Tradingschool.com

Located in Duarte, California (near Los Angeles), Tradingschool.com (www.tradingschool.com) is the web site of trading expert Robert Deel. The school offers hands-on workshops (in L.A.), which range in cost from $49.95 for a one-day "No Fear" workshop to $2,500 for a four-day workshop on short-term trading.

The school is expanding to the Web with online courses that cost $225 to $375 for a year's membership. These courses are currently under development, but most appear to be audio reports that identify stocks for trading. The course to watch for is the year-long audio/e-mail class on technical analysis. If you're interested in expanding your technical skills, this might be a relatively painless and cheap ($295) way to do it.

TradersEdge.net

TradersEdge.net sponsors a week-long seminar on day trading featuring Marc Friedfertig and George West, coauthors of *The Electronic Day Trader*. The seminar costs

$1,695 and is held in New York. If it is out of your reach, try their training videos ($49.95 each). Tape 1, about discipline and how to control profits and losses, and Tape 2, interpreting market maker actions, are the most appropriate for the novice trader. Tape 3 is simply a panel discussion of TradersEdge students.

Phactor.com

This site is a potpourri of tutorials and tips, including ones on Level 2, setting up your trade station, and detailed instructions for using the RealTick™ trading software. The address is www.phactor.com.

TeachMeToTrade.com

TeachMeToTrade.com, which is located in Salt Lake City, teaches two-day group seminars in various U.S. cities. The seminars cost $1,000. An interactive training CD offers 12 hours of instruction on technical analysis, Level 2 quotes, and trading rules for $299. You can view a Power-Point demo of the contents at www.teachmetotrade.com.

TeachTrade.com

This site from Louis Borsellino, author of *The Day Trader: From the Pit to the PC*, offers a free psychological profile and a "personal trainer" for trading. The latter analyzes 20 trades and provides a written critique of your trading performance. There is a $100 setup fee and a $25 per month charge for online analysis. There is also a Q&A section called the Trade Doctor. The address is www.teachtrade.com.

Daytrading University

Daytrading University (www.trainingaloha.com) offers a four-month membership to a comprehensive online day trading course for $69. An advanced day trading video ($74.95) lets you "look over [the] head trader's shoulder" for live Nasdaq and swing trading examples.

ROOMS, BOARDS, AND PITS

Traders like to share their experiences in person, in chat rooms, and on message boards. All you have to do is ask them what they think about a certain product, stock, training seminar, or broker, and you'll get an earful. While this advice can be helpful in steering you away from something bad or toward something good, don't take just one (anonymous) person's word for it. Get a second and third opinion and then check it out for yourself.

If you've never been in a chat room or read a message board, here's the difference: A chat room is a live, real-time event where participants carry on virtual conversations with the group and with individuals in the group. You type in your question and see it posted instantaneously in the "room" where the chatters are gathered.

Message boards are online bulletin boards where you can read or post messages at your leisure, replying to a current topic or starting a new one. In most cases, the messages are "threaded"—the original topic and all related replies are linked together. Threaded messages give the boards a coherence you won't find in a live chat room.

Let's break this discussion down into four areas: social chats, moderated chats, message boards, and trading pits.

Social Chats

These chat rooms are the Starbucks of the Web, the place where you go to relax and swap stories with fellow chatters. They can be lively and chaotic places where it's hard to follow the conversational thread, but some traders love 'em. One of the best is #daytraders, which is a members-only 24-hour chat room that comes with a membership in DayTraders USA at www.daytradersusa.com. Membership costs just $39 a year, which gives you all the privileges mentioned earlier in the chapter, plus access to the chat room.

To use the chat room you must download and install mIRC software, which takes about five minutes at

Let the Trader Beware

Be particularly wary of anyone who is hyping or trashing a stock. With nicknames to hide behind, chatters don't have to reveal their true identity or hidden agendas, which makes chat rooms and message boards hotbeds for stock scams. The chatter may be planning to dump a stock that's being pumped.

www.mirc.com. By the way, once you've installed the mIRC software, you can chat on any of hundreds of chat rooms on virtually any subject.

Moderated Chats

Moderated chats are live chat rooms hosted, usually, by a well-known expert. The format is Q&A, with the chatters asking questions and the host answering them. Moderated charts provide an excellent opportunity to get that question that's been bugging you answered by an expert. Here's a short list:

✔ *DayTraders USA* (#daytraders—described in the previous section) also has a weekly session with a trading coach Robin Dayne, who discusses trading tactics and trader psychology.

✔ *TradingMarkets.com* (www.tradingmarkets.com) offers live trader forums hosted by various professional traders. These are webcast through Broadcast.com, which provides audio. You'll need RealPlayer to participate; it is downloadable at the site.

✔ *TradersEdge.net* (www.tradersedge.net) sponsors a weekly one-hour moderated chat (currently on Tuesdays, 5:00 to 6:00 P.M. eastern time) with different day traders. Marc Friedfertig and George West, co-authors of *The Electronic Day Trader*, are owners of TradersEdge.net and have appeared in the chat room.

✔ *MTrader* (www.mtrader.com) hosts The Learning Room, an educational chat room for beginners. Its purpose, according to the moderator, is to provide a slower, more relaxed and open forum for learning to trade real-time. Questions are encouraged, and there's a lot of supporting material that you can print and peruse at your leisure.

Moderated chats are growing in popularity, and there will likely be many more by the time you read this.

Message Boards

Message boards are not conducted in real time, which makes them more organized and less chaotic than chat rooms. Message boards are a good place to learn what other day traders think of hardware, software, brokers, and other tools of the trade, but again, beware of those hyping stocks. Try these on for size:

✔ *Elite Trader Forum.* At last count, the Elite Trader (www.elitetrader.com) had five message boards, some more popular than others, all free. Topics include general discussion, brokers, software, hardware, and day trading news.

✔ *The Motley Fool.* At the Motley Fool (www.fool.com), you'll find a lively, popular day trading board called The Devil's Den (click Discussion Boards, then Investor's RoundTable). It covers anything and everything about day trading. Free.

✔ *Raging Bull.* For the day trading board here, enter the symbol DAYTR on the home page.

✔ *Short-Term Trader Forums* at Silicon Investor (www.siliconinvestor.com) include dozens of day trading subjects. You can read the boards at Silicon Investor without charge, but only members can join in the discussions. Cost to join: $200/year.

Trading Pits

Remote day traders can enjoy an online version of the day trading shop, where they gather during market hours to trade with a leader or head trader who calls the plays. These virtual trading rooms are real-time chat rooms that mimic the camaraderie and give-and-take of the day trading shops. They can help a new trader learn the ropes, especially if the leaders actively teach as well as call the plays.

If you decide to go this route, pick one whose trading style matches your own and remember all the precautions about hyped stocks. Most trading pits are pricey, so take advantage of their free trials before you subscribe. If you join, paper trade for a month or so before you trade for real, keeping in mind "The Fallacy of Paper Trading" described in Chapter 5.

MTrader. MTrader (www.mtrader.com) offers an Advanced Trading Room that uses Ken Wolff's "high percentage day trading" style (see earlier in chapter) and a Swing Trading Room that focuses on stocks with the potential for sharp, rapid gains over one to five days. Both are a mixture of call alerts and instruction. The basic method and rules can be printed and studied.

An MTrader membership costs $250 for the first month and $200 per month thereafter, on a month-to-

---

The Chatter's Dictionary

Do you know what IMHO means? LOL? IRL? Do you know when to use :) instead of :(? If all this is gibberish to you, check out the acronym and emoticon listings at www.chatlist.com. (Answers: in my humble opinion, laugh out loud, in real life, smile, frown.)

month basis. Membership includes access to all chat rooms, including The Learning Room, mentioned earlier, and a workbook on momentum investing. Sign up for the five-day trial membership to see if you like it, but be sure to cancel within that period if it doesn't suit you.

The Underground Trader. The Underground Trading Pit (www.undergroundtrader.com) is manned by head trader Jay Yu, author of the *Underground Level 2 Day Traders Handbook*. Yu developed the one-minute intraday stochastics that is used in the Trading Pit to react to stock price fluctuations. UGT publishes a morning report and a nightly recap of the trading day.

Membership is $250/month, on a month-by-month basis, with a one-week free trial. Check out the sample log (Figure 11.3) at the site, which is a transcript of one hour of a trading day. If you like what you see, sign up for the free trial and lurk on the sidelines for a week. You'll know after few days whether it is your kind of pit.

Trading Places. This is the home of head trader "Merlin," who was credited by the *New York Times* as the force behind the Internet stock craze. Membership costs $495.95 a month, with monthly instruction, and includes a comprehensive study guide. The address is www.trading-places.net.

Precision Buy/Sell Points (PBSP). Precision Buy/Sell Points (www.feargreed.com) offers a live trading room based on trend trading for $49 a month or $249 a year. There's a five-day free trial. If you live in or near Phoenix, you can go in to the offices for a one-day trading seminar.

WinningDayTraders.com. WinningDaytraders.com (www.winningdaytraders.com) offers a trading auditorium that uses various technical strategies. $295/month or $34.95/day. One-week free trial.

The interactivity of the Web is ideal for education and training, as online companies are just realizing. As broadband capabilities improve and technology expands, we

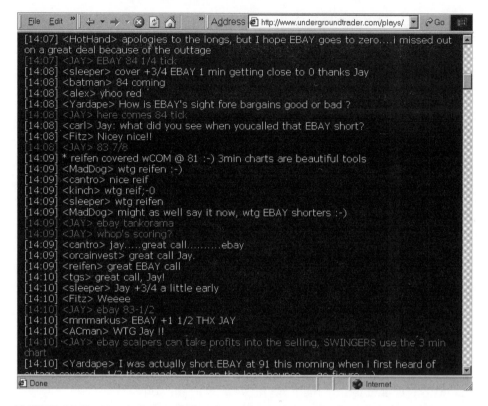

File   Edit   »   ⇦ ▾ ⇨ ▾ ⊗ 🗋 🏠   »   Address 🔘 http://www.undergroundtrader.com/plays/ ▾ ⟳ Go   🔳

```
[14:07] <HotHand> apologies to the longs, but I hope EBAY goes to zero....i missed out
on a great deal because of the outtage
[14:07] <JAY> EBAY 84 1/4 tick
[14:08] <sleeper> cover +3/4 EBAY 1 min getting close to 0 thanks Jay
[14:08] <batman> 84 coming
[14:08] <alex> yhoo red
[14:08] <Yardape> How is EBAY's sight fore bargains good or bad ?
[14:08] <JAY> here comes 84 tick
[14:08] <carl> Jay: what did you see when youcalled that EBAY short?
[14:08] <Fitz> Nicey nice!!
[14:08] <JAY> 83 7/8
[14:09] * reifen covered wCOM @ 81 :-) 3min charts are beautiful tools
[14:09] <MadDog> wtg reifen :-)
[14:09] <cantro> nice reif
[14:09] <kinch> wtg reif;-0
[14:09] <sleeper> wtg reifen
[14:09] <MadDog> might as well say it now, wtg EBAY shorters :-)
[14:09] <JAY> ebay tankorama
[14:09] <JAY> whop's scoring?
[14:09] <cantro> jay.....great call.........ebay
[14:09] <orcainvest> great call Jay.
[14:09] <reifen> great EBAY call
[14:10] <tgs> great call, Jay!
[14:10] <sleeper> Jay +3/4 a little early
[14:10] <Fitz> Weeee
[14:10] <JAY> ebay 83-1/2
[14:10] <mmmarkus> EBAY +1 1/2 THX JAY
[14:10] <ACman> WTG Jay !!
[14:10] <JAY> ebay scalpers can take profits into the selling, SWINGERS use the 3 min
chart
[14:10] <Yardape> I was actually short.EBAY at 91 this morning when i first heard of
outage covered   1/2 then made 2 1/2 on the long bounce   go figure :-)
```
🔘 Done   🌐 Internet

FIGURE 11.3   Here's a sample log from the real-time Underground Trader trading pit. ("WTG" in chat-room lingo means "Way to go!") *Source:* Reprinted with permission of The Underground Trader, www.undergroundtrader.com.

should begin to see an explosion of multimedia training programs aimed at day traders.

COMING UP . . .

During the writing of this book, the markets were changing on an almost daily basis. Where possible, I've mentioned the changes in the text, but the landscape is still shifting faster than the Sahara. A year from now it is likely to be totally altered. The next chapter will tell you what to look for as we move into the new century.

Chapter

The Future
of Day Trading

As the new century begins, the sound of change is rumbling in every corner of the markets, and traditions are falling right and left. The New York Stock Exchange, Nasdaq, and the ECNs are redefining themselves. Market hours are extending into the night. Decimalization will soon change the way we quote stock prices. A 24-hour electronic global market is peeking over the horizon. Barriers between professional and private investors, which have been crumbling for years, are continuing to fall. And everything is happening at Internet speed.

Whatever the outcome of these changes, the stock market of the twenty-first century promises to be very different from the stock market of the late 1900s. Here are some events that will shape the markets of tomorrow.

THE TRANSFORMATION
OF THE STOCK EXCHANGES

Two of the hottest IPOs to hit Wall Street in 2000 may be the New York Stock Exchange and Nasdaq. Right now, both markets are privately held. The NYSE is a corporation owned by member firms; Nasdaq is a subsidiary of the National Association of Security Dealers, an association supported by member fees. Going public would entail major changes in the way they do business.

In January Nasdaq announced that it will begin a restructuring that could lead to an IPO. The first phase is a private placement among NASD members and other market participants, scheduled for completion by May 2000, with a second-phase private placement in the fall of 2000. Nasdaq also plans to register as an exchange.

As public companies concerned with the bottom line, Nasdaq and the NYSE would be responsible to shareholders, not to member firms, and they would be under the myriad financial disclosure requirements that the SEC places on public companies. Then there is the issue of regulation. Both are self-regulatory entities, but as public companies that might not be acceptable to the SEC. One solution might be to combine their regulatory bodies, which Nasdaq and the NYSE have reportedly discussed.

Another issue as a public company is the susceptibility to being taken over by a larger entity. One pundit suggested the NYSE might end up as a financial trophy with "Trump" tacked in front of its name. However far-fetched that may be, Nasdaq has started down that road and the NYSE is right behind.

An equally intriguing notion is the ECN-ification of the New York Stock Exchange. Dick Grasso, head of the NYSE, announced in November 1999 that the NYSE will create an ECN-like network within the exchange that will allow traders to execute orders of less than 1,000 shares, much like orders are executed today over ECNs, without human intervention. Granted, the Super-Dot system is already in place, but orders routed through SuperDot are currently worked by the specialist. This "ECN within the NYSE" would circumvent the specialist.

Should this be taken to its logical conclusion, the entire NYSE could be electronically networked with Nasdaq and the ECNs.

THE TRANSFORMATION OF ECNS

The changes taking place at the NYSE and Nasdaq are directly attributable to ECNs, which have been shaking things up ever since they arrived in 1997. They currently function as order-handling entities under the aegis of the National Association of Security Dealers (NASD). Many are now moving into roles as major market players. Here are the changes to watch for in the next few months.

Island (ISLD) and Archipelago (ARCA) have applied with the SEC for full exchange status. (ARCA recently announced a merger with the Pacific Exchange.) The objective is to escape regulation by the NASD, whom ECNs rightly consider a competitor, and to obtain other benefits of exchange status, such as being able to accept listings of public companies. If approved, look for other ECNs to follow suit.

Another move toward the big league is going public. Three ECNs may beat Nasdaq and the NYSE to the punch. Officials at Island, ARCA, and Instinet have been quoted as "thinking about" an initial public offering, but as of April 2000 none has actually filed documents with the SEC.

Those ECNs not thinking about IPOs are thinking merger. BRUT and Strike merged in February 2000, and the pundits say they will not be the last match made in this fragmented and crowded field.

THE MOVE TOWARD GLOBALIZATION

The Internet has already shrunk the world to the size of a computer screen. It has reduced travel time to the nanosecond of a mouse-click. And it is fueling the globalization of the markets.

The markets are already interlinked in cause and effect. If the Dow goes to bed happy, the FT-SE wakes up smiling. If the Nikkei stubs its toe, the U.S. markets limp around for days. We can't day trade global stocks yet, but that day isn't far away. As James W. Brinkley, chairman of the Securities Industry Association, said, "[We operate] in a world where distinguishing between domestic and foreign markets will become increasingly difficult and eventually irrelevant."

The Instinet ECN already trades in over 40 global markets and Nasdaq is working hard on globalization.[1]

✔ Nasdaq and the Stock Exchange of Hong Kong (SEHK) are currently beta-testing a web site that will provide stock prices on SEHK and Nasdaq-AMEX stocks and maintain portfolios in either U.S. or Hong Kong dollars. You can view the site at www.porttracker.nasdaq-sehk.com.

✔ Nasdaq-Japan (www.nasdaq.co.jp) will be an electronic market in Japan for Nasdaq-listed U.S. stocks and high-growth Japanese companies.

✔ Nasdaq UK (www.nasdaq.co.uk) links the U.S. and the United Kingdom clearance systems to make it easier for U.K. investors to trade Nasdaq stocks.

✔ Nasdaq-Europe, scheduled for early 2001, will be the first pan-European market for IPOs and will offer European investors "seamless, low-cost trading across multiple international borders."

In Nasdaq's words: "We need and are working toward an Internet-age system for the global exchange of stock. . . . This next-generation market will provide investors instant stock quotations and executions, both day and night, anywhere on the globe. . . . [It] will allow investors to trade across borders and around the clock with an ease and economy we can only imagine today."[2]

THE ARRIVAL OF DECIMALIZATION

The entire securities industry is moving to decimalization—reporting all security prices in dollars and cents, rather than fractions. Why? Because the United States is the only market in the world that operates on a fraction system. We have to get in step with the rest of the world to be competitive and to pave the way for globalization of the markets.

The conversion to decimals is a massive process that has been under way since August 1998. All computer systems that have anything to do with securities pricing must be converted and tested; all written materials must be updated. The launch was scheduled for July 2000, but it has been postponed until March 2001 because of Nasdaq's inability to meet the July deadline. However, the Island ECN has announced that it will begin trading in decimals in July as scheduled. Trading systems will have to accommodate both decimal and fractional pricing during the phase-in period, but by the end of the first quarter 2001, fractional pricing will be a relic of the past.

What are the advantages for individual traders and investors? Officials say we'll be able to understand the numbers better (apparently they know how much trouble we had with fractions in school) and that spreads will narrow. Conceivably, they could narrow to a penny, which could have a negative effect on scalpers. Anything less than a nickel, according to one trader, would making the scalping style of trading unfeasible. Nevertheless, ready or not, decimalization is coming.

MORE LEVELING OF THE PLAYING FIELD

The Internet has opened up the floodgates to formerly privileged market information. Individual investors and traders can tap into real-time quotes and news, expert market commentary, research reports, earnings estimates and whisper numbers, SEC filings, insider trading data, and even rumors that circulate on Wall Street about impending stock splits, mergers, acquisitions, and other corporate events. In the past year, companies have even begun broadcasting their quarterly earnings conferences on the Web. Now, with a little prodding from the SEC, the doors to corporate boardrooms may swing open on analyst meetings as well.

These meetings have traditionally been closed to the public because management might make "forward looking statements" that could possibly be misinterpreted by the unwashed masses. Such statements usually have to do with the company's earnings potential. Since earnings are the fuel for stock price growth, this kind of selective disclosure has given the professionals yet another edge. Arthur Levitt, head of the SEC, has proposed a rule to prohibit this practice, specifically stating that it is unfair to the individual investor. Once this privileged bastion falls, the markets will be as level as a football field.

As we move into the twenty-first century, technology continues to improve and redefine the tools with which we access market information. High-speed data connections are becoming cheaper and more widespread. Artificial intelligence is making trading software easier to use. Wireless trading is freeing traders from the confines of their desks. Improvements in broadband technology is hastening the convergence of television and the Web; events webcast over the Internet will soon become indistinguishable from those broadcast over television.

Clearly, the market shaping up in the new millennium is not your father's market. And one of the beneficiaries of all these changes will be the day trader.

Where to Go for Help

Electronic Traders Association
1800 Bering, Suite 750
Houston, TX 77057
713-706-3300
www.electronic-traders.org

National Association of Securities Dealers, Inc.
Office of Individual Investor Services
1735 K Street, NW
Washington, DC 20006
202-728-6964
www.investor.nasd.com

NASD Regulation, Inc.
15201 Diamond Back Drive
Rockville, MD 20850
301-590-6500
www.nasdr.com
District offices: www.nasdr.com/2320.htm

New York Stock Exchange
11 Wall Street
New York, NY 10005
212-656-3000
www.nyse.com

North American Securities Administrators Association, Inc.
10 G Street, NE, Suite 710
Washington, D.C. 20002
202-737-0900
www.nasaa.org
E-mail: info@nasaa.org

Securities and Exchange Commission
450 Fifth Street, NW
Washington, DC 20549
Office of Investor Education and Assistance:
202-942-7040
www.sec.gov
E-mail: help@sec.gov

Appendix

Suggested Reading

These books are available online through Amazon.com (www.
amazon.com), Traders Library (www.traderslibrary.com), Traders
PressBookstore.com (www.traderspressbookstore.com). For more
books on day trading, run a search at Amazon.com under the keywords
"day trading" and/or "swing trading," and scan the readers' reviews.

Day Trade Online. Christopher A. Farrell. (New York: John Wiley & Sons,
1999).
If you want to trade listed stocks, this is the book to read. In-depth chapter on the role of the NYSE specialist.

Day Trading into the Millennium. Michael Turner. 1998.
One reader calls this "the definitive guide to day trading." Chapters are
short and to the point. Good chapter on the S&P futures. Book is listed
at $62.50 but you can get it at 40 percent off at TradersResource
(www.tradersresource.com).

The Disciplined Trader: Developing Winning Attitudes. Mark Douglas. (New
York: New York Institute of Finance, 1990).
This should be required reading for anyone who wants to be a day trader.

The Electronic Day Trader. Marc Friedfertig and George West. (New York:
McGraw-Hill, 1998).
Written by the founders of the Broadway Consulting Group, one of the major
providers of day trading seminars. Affiliated with Broadway Trading and
TradersEdge.net.

Exceptional Trading: The Mind Game. Ruth Roosevelt (Greenville, SC: Traders Press, 1999).
Outlines methods for developing the mental skills essential to high profit trading.

How to Get Started in Electronic Day Trading. David S. Nassar. (New York: McGraw-Hill, 1999).
Good graphics on trading stock splits, earnings plays, and news-driven events.

How Wall Street Works: The Basics and Beyond. Second Edition. David L. Scott. (New York: McGraw-Hill, 1999).
This is more for investors than day traders, but it has basic information on how the markets work. Written in question-and-answer format.

The Inner Game of Trading. Robert Koppel and Howard Abell. (New York: Irwin Professional Publishing, 1997).
Another book on the psychology of trading.

The Mind of a Trader: Lessons in Trading Strategy from the World's Leading Traders. Alpesh B. Patel (London: Financial Times, 1997).
Patel interviews 10 men he credits with significantly improving his own trading. Each chapter has a helpful content list of trading topics at the beginning and a summary of trading tactics at the end.

New Concepts in Technical Trading Systems. J. Welles Wilder. (Trend Research, 1978).
If you want to learn about the Welles Wilder RSI theory, this is the place to go. But it's not for beginners.

The New Market Wizards. Jack D. Schwager. (New York: HarperBusiness, 1992).
Schwager interviews some of the world's top traders. They are a diverse group who trade stocks, options, futures, and currencies, but the psychology behind the trading is the same, and their trading rules are timeless and universal. Schwager condenses all this market wisdom into 42 trading rules that he calls "Market Wiz(ar)dom." If you like this book, try its predecessor, the original *Market Wizards*.

Reminiscences of a Stock Operator. Edwin LeFèvre. (New York: John Wiley & Sons, 1994).
Another book that should be required reading for day traders. It is a classic about the self-education of a stock speculator named Jesse Livermore. It was first published in 1923, but the lessons are as current as today's market commentary.

Secrets of the SOES Bandits. Harvey Houtkin (with David Waldman). (New York: McGraw-Hill, 1999).
Houtkin, who gained fame as one of the original "SOES bandits," is the founder of All-Tech Trading and the Attain ECN. The book is strictly for Nasdaq traders.

Trade Your Way to Financial Freedom. Van K. Tharp. (New York: McGraw-Hill, 1999).
Great book to help you develop your trading system and manage risk, from the guru of position sizing. (Tharp suggests that you read the book at least three times!)

Trading for a Living. Dr. Alexander Elder. (New York: John Wiley & Sons, 1993).
Psychology, trading tactics, money management. Comes with a study guide.

Trading the Plan. Robert Deel. (New York: John Wiley & Sons, 1997).
Good book for developing a trading plan.

Trading with DiNapoli Levels. Joe DiNapoli. (DiNapoli, 1997).
Highly technical, but DiNapoli fans swear by his system.

Understanding Wall Street. Jeffrey B. Little and Lucien Rhodes. (New York: McGraw-Hill, 1991).
This book is recognized as the leading primer on the stock market. It was originally written in 1978 and updated in 1991.

The Visual Investor: How to Spot Stock Market Trends. John J. Murphy. (New York: John Wiley & Sons, 1996).
The best beginner's book on technical analysis.

Market Maker and ECN IDs

MMID	Market Maker
BEST	Bear Stearns & Co.
CANT	Cantor Fitzgerald
COWN	S. G. Cowen Securities
DEAN	Dean Witter Reynolds Inc.
DLJP	Donaldson, Lufkin & Jenrette
FBCO	Credit Suisse First Boston
FIFI	Fidelity Financial Group
GRUN	Gruntal & Co.
GSCO	Goldman Sachs
HMQT	Hambrecht & Quist
HRZG	Herzog, Heine, Geduld
JBOC	J. B. Oxford
JPMS	J. P. Morgan
LEHM	Lehman Brothers
MASH	Mayer & Schweitzer
MHMY	M. H. Meyerson
MLCO	Merrill Lynch
MONT	Banc of America Securities/Montgomery
MSCO	Morgan Stanley Dean Witter & Co.

NEED	Needham & Co.
NFSC	National Financial Services
NITE	Knight Securities
POPP	Oppenheimer & Close
PERT	Pershing Trading Company
PIPR	U.S. Bancorp Piper Jaffray
PRUS	Prudential Securities
PWJC	PaineWebber
RSSF	BancBoston Robertson Stephens
SBSH	Salomon Smith Barney
SHON	Schonfeld Securities
SHWD	Sherwood Securities
SLKC	Spear, Leeds & Kellogg
SNDV	Soundview Technology Group
SWCO	Schroder Wertheim & Co.
USTC	U.S. Trading Corp.

MMID	**ECN**
ARCA	Archipelago
ATTN	Attain
BRUT	Brut
BTRD	TradeBook
INCA	Instinet
ISLD	Island
MKXT	MarketXT
NTRD	NexTrade
OPTI	OptiMark
REDI	REDIBook

Note: On some systems, the entire limit order book for Island or Archipelago is merged with the Level 2 quotes. The inside quote from Island is identified as ISLD, but the rest of the Island book is identified as ISLAND; the inside quote from Archipelago is identified as ARCA, the rest of the Archipelago book, as ARCHIP.

Web Site Addresses by Chapter

Introduction

CyberInvest.com	www.cyberinvest.com
Securities and Exchange Commission	www.sec.gov
Trend Trader LLC	www.trendtrader.com

Chapter 1

American Stock Exchange (AMEX)	www.amex.com
Archipelago ECN	www.tradearca.com
Arizona Stock Exchange (AZX)	www.azx.com
Attain ECN	www.attain.com
Boston Stock Exchange (BSE)	www.bostonstock.com
Chicago Stock Exchange (CHX)	www.chicagostockex.com
Cincinnati Stock Exchange (CSE)	www.cincinnatistock.com
Dreyfus Brokerage	www.edreyfus.com
Instinet ECN	www.instinet.com
Island ECN	www.island.com
MarketXT	www.marketxt.com
MatchBookFX	www.matchbookfx.com
Morgan Stanley Dean Witter Online	www.msdwonline.com

Mydiscountbroker.com	www.mydiscountbroker.com
Nasdaq Stock Market	www.nasdaq.com
Nasdaq Trader	www.nasdaqtrader.com
National Association of Security Dealers	www.nasd.com
National Quotation Bureau	www.nqb.com
New York Stock Exchange	www.nyse.com
NexTrade ECN	www.nextrade1.com
OptiMark	www.optimark.com
OTC Bulletin Board	www.otcbb.com
Pacific Exchange (PCX)	www.pacificex.com
Philadelphia Stock Exchange (PHLX)	www.phlx.com
REDIBook ECN	www.redi.com
Salomon Smith Barney	www.salomonsmithbarney.com
TradeBook ECN	www.bloomberg.com/products/trdbk.html

Chapter 2

Island ECN	www.island.com
MTrader.com	www.mtrader.com
Nasdaq Trader.com	www.nasdaqtrader.com
National Association of Security Dealers	www.nasd.com
Pristine Day Trader	www.pristine.com
Securities and Exchange Commission	www.sec.gov
A. B. Watley	www.abwatley.com

Chapter 3

Adobe Systems, Inc.	www.adobe.com
All-Tech Direct, Inc.	www.attain.com
Broadway Trading	www.broadwaytrading.com
CareerDayTrader.com	www.careerdaytrader.com

Castle Online	www.castleonline.com
CyBerCorp.com	www.cybercorp.com
CyberInvest.com	www.cyberinvest.com
Datek	www.datek.com
E*Trade	www.etrade.com
Fidelity Investments	www.fidelity.com
EdgeTrade.com	www.edgetrade.com
The Executioner	www.executioner.com
GRO Corporation	www.grocorp.com
Island ECN	www.island.com
MarketXT	www.marketxt.com
MaxTrade Financial Services	www.maxtrading.com
MBTrading	www.mbtrading.com
NASD Regulation	www.nasdr.com
On-Site Trading	www.onsitetrading.com
PreferredTrade.com	www.preferredtrade.com
QuarterMove Securities	www.quartermove.com
RML Trading	www.rmltrading.com
Charles Schwab & Co.	www.schwab.com
Securities and Exchange Commission	www.sec.gov
TerraNova Trading	www.terranovatrading.com
TradeCast Securities	www.tradecast.com
Tradescape.com	www.tradescape.com
Trend Trader LLC	www.trendtrader.com
A. B. Watley	www.abwatley.com

Chapter 4

Broadway Trading	www.broadwaytrading.com
CyBerCorp.com	www.cybercorp.com
GRO Corporation	www.grotrader.com
Symantec.com	www.symantec.com
Townsend Analytics (RealTick™)	www.taltrade.com
TradeCast Securities	www.tradecast.com
Trend Trader LLC	www.trendtrader.com

Chapter 5

Alert-IPO	www.altertipo.com
America-iNvest.com	www.americainvest.com
BestCalls.com	www.bestcalls.com
BigCharts.com	www.bigcharts.com
Big Easy Investor	www.bigeasyinvestor.com
CBS MarketWatch	www.cbs.marketwatch.com
CNBC.com	www.cnbc.com
Equis International	www.equis.com
First Call	www.firstcall.com
Fly on the Wall	www.theflyonthewall.com
GRO Trader	www.grotrader.com
HardRightEdge	www.hardrightedge.com
Hoover's Online	www.hoovers.com
IndividualInvestor.com	www.individualinvestor.com
InternetNews.com	www.internetnews.com
InvestmentHouse.com	www.investmenthouse.com
INVESTools.com	www.investools.com
Investor's Business Daily	www.investors.com
IPO.com	www.ipo.com
JagNotes	www.jagnotes.com
Linda Bradford Raschke	www.mrci.com/lbr/index.htm
Market Guide Investor	www.marketguide.com
MTrader.com	www.mtrader.com
Nasdaq Stock Market	www.nasdaq.com
NewsTraders.com	www.newstraders.com
Online Investor	www.investhelp.com
PersonalWealth.com	www.personalwealth.com
Quicken.com	www.quicken.com
RightLine	www.rightline.net
SiXer.cOm	www.sixer.com
SmartMoney.com	www.smartmoney.com
SwingTrader	www.swingtrader.net
TheStreet.com	www.thestreet.com
Thomson Investors Network	www.thomsoninvest.com

TradersPressBookstore.com	www.traderspressbookstore.com
TradingMarkets.com	www.tradingmarkets.com
Wall Street City	www.wallstreetcity.com
WhisperNumber.com	www.whispernumber.com
WinningDayTraders.com	www.winningdaytraders.com
Zacks.com	www.zacks.com
ZDNet Inter@ctive Investor	www.zdii.com

Chapter 6

AIQ International	www.aiq.com
ASK Research	www.askresearch.com
BigCharts.com	www.bigcharts.com
Big Easy Investor	www.bigeasyinvestor.com
BollingerBands.com	www.bollingerbands.com
ClearStation	www.clearstation.com
DayTraders USA	www.daytradersusa.com
Decision Point	www.decisionpoint.com
Equis International	www.equis.com
Equity Analytics	www.e-analytics.com
Hard Right Edge	www.hardrightedge.com
George C. Lane	www.lanestochastics.com
Market Mavens	www.marketmavens.com
MetaStock	www.equis.com
MurphyMorris.com (John J. Murphy)	www.murphymorris.com
ProphetFinance.com	www.prophetfinance.com
SignalAlert Corporation (Gerald Appell)	www.signalalert.com
Silicon Investor	www.siliconinvestor.com
Stock Cam	www.thestockcam.com
Supercharts	www.omegaresearch.com
Technical Analysis of Stocks & Commodities	www.traders.com
Telescan, Inc.	www.telescan.com
TradeHard.com	www.tradehard.com
Traders Library	www.traderslibrary.com

TradersPressBookstore.com	www.traderspressbookstore.com
Traders World	www.tradersworld.com
Trend Trader LLC	www.trendtrader.com
Wall Street City	www.wallstreetcity.com
Window on Wall Street	www.windowonwallstreet.com

Chapter 7

American Stock Exchange	www.amex.com
Bloomberg.com	www.bloomberg.com
Bond Market Association	www.investinginbonds.com
Bureau of Economic Analysis	www.bea-doc.gov
Bureau of Labor Statistics	stats.bls.gov
CareerDayTrader.com	www.careerdaytrader.com
CBS MarketWatch	www.cbs.marketwatch.com
Census Bureau	www.census.gov
CNBC.com	www.cnbc.com
The Conference Board	www.conference-board.org
The Conference Board's Business Cycle Indicators	www.tcb-indicators.org
Federal Reserve	www.federalreserve.gov
Hard Right Edge	www.hardrightedge.com
Internet.com	www.internet.com
InternetNews.com	www.internetnews.com
MTrader.com	www.mtrader.com
Nasdaq Indexes	www.nasdaqamex.com/reference/IndexDescriptions.stm
Nasdaq Stock Market	www.nasdaq.com
New York Stock Exchange	www.nyse.com
Raging Bull	www.ragingbull.com
Red Herring	www.redherring.com
Russell Indexes	www.russell.com
SmartMoney.com	www.smartmoney.com
SmartMoney University	www.university.smartmoney.com
Standard & Poor's	www.spglobal.com

StockCharts.com	www.stockcharts.com
TheStreet.com	www.thestreet.com
TradingMarkets.com	www.tradingmarkets.com
The Underground Trader	www.undergroundtrader.com
USA Today	www.usatoday.com
Wall Street City	www.wallstreetcity.com
Wall Street Research Net	www.wsrn.com/apps/internetstocks
Wall Street Journal Interactive Edition	www.wsj.com
Wilshire 5000	www.wilshire.com
WinningDayTraders.com	www.winningdaytraders.com

Chapter 8

1-800-Gambler	www.800gambler.org
DayTraders USA	www.daytradersusa.com
Robin Dayne	www.robindayne.com
Mark Douglas	www.markdouglas.com
Linda Bradford Raschke	www.mrci.com/lbr
TraintoDayTrade	www.traintodaytrade.com
Van Tharp's International Institute of Trading Mastery	www.iitm.com

Chapter 9

Ameristock Mutual Fund	www.ameristock.com
CBS MarketWatch	www.cbs.marketwatch.com
CNBC.com	www.cnbc.com
DynamicDayTrader.com	www.dynamicdaytrader.com
InternetNews.com	www.internetnews.com
KCET Public television	www.kcet.org/education/funding
MoneyCentral Investor	www.moneycentral.msn.com/investor
The New York Times	www.nytimes.com
RealMoney.com	www.realmoney.com
SmartMoney.com	www.smartmoney.com
TheSecurityBlanket.com	www.thesecurityblanket.com

TheStreet.com	www.thestreet.com
Trend Trader LLC	www.trendtrader.com
Wall Street Journal Interactive Edition	www.wsj.com

Chapter 10

@Home	www.home.com
1800daytrade.com	www.1800daytrade.com
Adobe Systems, Inc.	www.adobe.com
Ameritrade	www.ameritrade.com
Appian Graphics	www.appiangraphics.com
AT Financial	www.atfi.com
AT&T	www.worldnet.att.net
CableModems.com	www.cablemodems.com
Data Broadcasting Corp.	www.dbc.com
Datalink.net	www.datalink.net
DayTraderTax.com	www.daytradertax.com
DLJdirect	www.dljdirect.com
Dreyfus Brokerage	www.edreyfus.com
DSL Life	www.dsllife.com
DTN.IQ	www.dtniq.com
Earthlink	www.earthlink.com
eSignal	www.esignal.com
Fidelity Investments	www.fidelty.com
First Trade	www.firstrade.com
InterQuote	www.interquote.com
ISDN Tutorial	www.ralphb.net/ISDN
MCI WorldCom	www.wcom.com
Morgan Stanley Dean Witter Online	www.msdwonline.com
MostActives.com	www.mostactives.com
OmniAlert	www.omnialert.com
Palm, Inc.	www.palm.com
PC Quote	www.pcquote.com
PC World Magazine	www.pcworld.com

Phactor.com	www.phactor.com
Phone.com	www.phone.com
Quote.com	www.quote.com
RIM	www.rim.net
RoadRunner	www.rr.com/rdrun
SiebertNet	www.siebertnet.com
Sprint	www.sprint.com
Stock Boss	www.stockboss.com
Stock-Alerts.com	www.stock-alerts.com
TheStreet.com	www.thestreet.com
Symantec.com	www.symantec.com
Telescan Direct	www.telescandirect.com
Townsend Analytics	www.taltrade.com
TraderAccounting.com	www.traderaccounting.com
V90.com	www.v90.com
Wyse Securities	www.wyse-sec.com

Chapter 11

Chatters Dictionaries	www.chatlist.com
CyberInvest.com	www.cyberinvest.com
DayTraders USA	www.daytradersusa.com
Daytrading University	www.trainingaloha.com
Dow Jones University	www.dju.com
Elite Trader	www.elitetrader.com
Internet Relay Chat	www.mirc.com
Legend Trading	www.tradingseminars.com
Motley Fool.com	www.fool.com
MTrader.com	www.mtrader.com
NASD Regulation	www.nasdr.com
Nasdaq Stock Market	www.nasdaq.com
Nasdaq Trader	www.nasdaqtrader.com
National Association of Security Dealers	www.nasd.com
New York Stock Exchange	www.nyse.com

North American Securities Administrators Assn.	www.nasaa.com
Online Trading Expo	www.daytradingexpo.com
Online Trading Academy	www.onlinetradingacademy.com
Phactor.com	www.phactor.com
Precision Buy/Sell Points (PBSP)	www.feargreed.com
Pristine Day Trader	www.pristine.com
Raging Bull	www.ragingbull.com
Resource Link	www.the-resource-link.com
Securities and Exchange Commission	www.sec.gov
Silicon Investor	www.siliconinvestor.com
TeachMeToTrade.com	www.teachmetotrade.com
TeachTrade.com	www.teachtrade.com
TradersEdge.net	www.tradersedge.net
Trading Places	www.trading-places.net
TradingMarkets.com	www.tradingmarkets.com
Tradingschool.com	www.tradingschool.com
The Underground Trader	www.undergroundtrader.com
WinningDayTraders.com	www.winningdaytraders.com

Chapter 12

Nasdaq Stock Market	www.nasdaq.com
Nasdaq-Hong Kong	www.porttracker.nasdaq-sehk.com
Nasdaq Japan	www.nasdaq.co.jp
Nasdaq UK	www.nasdaq.co.uk

Appendix 5

Web Site Addresses Master List

@Home	www.home.com
1800daytrade.com	www.1800daytrade.com
1-800-Gambler	www.800gambler.org
Adobe Systems, Inc.	www.adobe.com
AIQ International	www.aiq.com
Alert-IPO	www.alertipo.com
All-Tech Direct, Inc.	www.attain.com
Amazon.com	www.amazon.com
America-iNvest.com	www.americainvest.com
American Stock Exchange	www.amex.com
Ameristock Mutual fund	www.ameristock.com
Ameritrade	wwwameritrade.com
Appian Graphics	www.appiangraphics.com
Archipelago ECN	www.tradearca.com
Arizona Stock Exchange (AZX)	www.azx.com
ASK Research	www.askresearch.com
AT Financial	www.atfi.com

AT&T	www.worldnet.at.net
Attain ECN	www.attain.com
BestCalls.com	www.bestcalls.com
BigCharts.com	www.bigcharts.com
Big Easy Investor	www.bigeasyinvestor.com
Bloomberg.com	www.bloomberg.com
BollingerBands.com	www.bollingerbands.com
Bond Market Association	www.investinginbonds.com
Boston Stock Exchange (BSE)	www.bostonstock.com
Broadway Trading	www.boadwaytrading.com
Bureau of Economic Analysis	www.bea-doc.gov
Bureau of Labor Statistics	stats.bls.gov
CableModems.com	www.cablemodems.com
CareerDayTrader.com	www.careerdaytrader.com
Castle Online	www.castleonline.com
CBS MarketWatch	www.cbs.marketwatch.com
Census Bureau	www.census.gov
Chatters Dictionaries	www.chatlist.com
Chicago Stock Exchange (CHX)	www.chicagostockex.com
Cincinnati Stock Exchange (CSE)	www.cincinnatistock.com
ClearStation	www.clearstation.com
CNBC.com	www.cnbc.com
Conference Board	www.conference-board.org.
Conference Board's Business Cycle Indicators	www.tcb-indicators.org
CyBerCorp.com	www.cybercorp.com
CyberInvest.com	www.cyberinvest.com
Data Broadcasting Corp.	www.dbc.com
Datalink.net	www.datalink.net
Datek	www.datek.com
Robin Dayne	www.robindayne.com
DayTraders USA	www.daytradersusa.com
DayTraderTax.com	www.daytradertax.com

Day Trading Expo	www.daytradingexpo.com
Daytrading University	www.trainingaloha.com
Decision Point	www.decisionpoint.com
DLJdirect	www.dljdirect.com
Mark Douglas	www.markdouglas.com
Dow Jones University	www.dju.com
Dreyfus Brokerage	www.edreyfus.com
DSL Life	www.dsllife.com
DTN.IQ	www.dtniq.com
DynamicDay Trader.com	www.dynamicdaytrader.com
E*Trade	www.etrade.com
Earthlink	www.earthlink.com
EdgeTrade.com	www.edgetrade.com
Electronic Traders Association	www.electronic-traders.com
Elite Trader	www.elitetrader.com
Equis International	www.equis.com
Equity Analytics	www.e-analytics.com
eSignal	www.esignal.com
The Executioner	www.executioner.com
Federal Reserve	www.federalreserve.gov
Fidelity Investments	www.fidelity.com
First Call	www.firstcall.com
First Trade	www.firstrade.com
Fly on the Wall	www.theflyonthewall.com
GRO Corporation	www.grotrader.com
Hard Right Edge	www.hardrightedge.com
Hoover's Online	www.hoovers.com
IndividualInvestor.com	www.individualinvestor.com
Instinet ECN	www.instinet.com
Internet Relay Chat	www.mirc.com
Internet.com	www.internet.com
InternetNews.com	www.internetnews.com
InterQuote	www.interquote.com
InvestmentHouse.com	www.investmenthouse.com

INVESTools.com	www.investools.com
Investor's Business Daily	www.investors.com
IPO.com	www.ipo.com
ISDN Tutorial	www.ralphb.net/ISDN
Island ECN	www.island.com
JagNotes	www.jagnotes.com
KCET Public Television	www.kcet.org/education/funding
George C. Lane	www.lanestochastics.com
Legend Trading	www.tradingseminars.com
Market Guide Investor	www.marketguide.com
Market Mavens	www.marketmavens.com
MarketXT	www.marketxt.com
MatchBookFX	www.matchbookfx.com
MaxTrade Financial Services	www.maxtrading.com
MBTrading	www.mbtrading.com
MCI WorldCom	www.wcom.com
MetaStock	www.equis.com
MoneyCentral Investor	www.moneycentral.msn.com/investor
Morgan Stanley Dean Witter Online	www.msdwonline.com
MostActives.com	www.mostactives.com
Motley Fool	www.fool.com
MTrader.com	www.mtrader.com
MurphyMorris.com (John J. Murphy)	www.murphymorris.com
Mydiscountbroker.com	www.mydiscountbroker.com
NASD Individual Investors Services	www.investor.nasd.com
NASD Regulation	www.nasdr.com
Nasdaq-Hong Kong	www.porttracker. nasdaq-sehk.com
Nasdaq Indexes	www.nasdaqamex.com/reference/ IndexDescriptions.stm
Nasdaq Japan	www.nasdaq.co.jp
Nasdaq Stock Market	www.nasdaq.com
Nasdaq Trader	www.nasdaqtrader.com
Nasdaq UK	www.nasdaq.co.uk

National Association of Security Dealers	www.nasd.com
National Quotation Bureau	www.nqb.com
New York Stock Exchange	www.nyse.com
New York Times	www.nytimes.com
NewsTraders.com	www.newstraders.com
NexTrade ECN	www.nextrade1.com
North American Securities Administrators Assn.	www.nasaa.com
OmniAlert	www.omnialert.com
Online Investor	www.investhelp.com
Online Trading Academy	www.onlinetradingacademy.com
On-Site Trading	www.onsitetrading.com
OptiMark	www.optimark.com
OTC Bulletin Board	www.otcbb.com
Pacific Exchange (PCX)	www.pacificex.com
Palm, Inc.	www.palm.com
PC Quote	www.pcquote.com
PC World Magazine	www.pcworld.com
PersonalWealth.com	www.personalwealth.com
Philadelphia Stock Exchange (PHLX)	www.phlx.com
Phactor.com	www.phactor.com
Phone.com	www.phone.com
Precision Buy/Sell Points (PBSP)	www.feargreed.com
PreferredTrade.com	www.preferredtrade.com
Pristine Day Trader	www.pristine.com
ProphetFinance.com	www.prophetfinance.com
QuarterMove Securities	www.quartermove.com
Quicken.com	www.quicken.com
Quote.com	www.quote.com
Raging Bull	www.ragingbull.com
Linda Bradford Raschke	www.mrci.com/lbr/index.htm
RealMoney.com	www.realmoney.com
Red Herring	www.redherring.com
REDIBook ECN	www.redi.com

Resource Link	www.the-resource-link.com
RightLine	www.rightline.net
RIM	www.rim.net
RML Trading	www.rmltrading.com
RoadRunner	www.rr.com/rdrun
Russell Indexes	www.russell.com
Salomon Smith Barney	www.salomonsmithbarney.com
Charles Schwab & Co.	www.schwab.com
Securities and Exchange Commission	www.sec.gov
SiebertNet	www.siebertnet.com
SignalAlert Corporation (Gerald Appell)	www.signalalert.com
Silicon Investor	www.siliconinvestor.com
SiXer.cOm	www.sixer.com
SmartMoney.com	www.smartmoney.com
SmartMoney University	www.university.smartmoney.com
Sprint	www.sprint.com
Standard & Poor's	www.spglobal.com
Stock Boss	www.stockboss.com
Stock Cam	www.thestockcam.com
Stock-Alerts.com	www.stock-alerts.com
StockCharts.com	www.stockcharts.com
TheSecurityBlanket.com	www.thesecurityblanket.com
TheStreet.com	www.thestreet.com
SuperCharts	www.omegaresearch.com
SwingTrader	www.swingtrader.net
Symantec.com	www.symantec.com
TeachMeToTrade.com	www.teachmetotrade.com
TeachTrade.com	www.teachtrade.com
Technical Analysis of Stocks & Commodities	www.traders.com
Telescan Direct	www.telescandirect.com
Telescan, Inc.	www.telescan.com
TerraNova Trading	www.terranovatrading.com
Thomson Investors Network	www.thomsoninvest.com

Townsend Analytics (RealTick™)	www.taltrade.com
Tradebook ECN	www.bloomberg.com/products/trdbk.html
TradeCast Securities	www.tradecast.com
TraderAccounting.com	www.traderaccounting.com
Traders Library	www.traderslibrary.com
TradersPressBookstore.com	www.traderspressbookstore.com
TradersEdge.net	www.tradersedge.net
Tradescape.com	www.tradescape.com
Trading Places	www.trading-places.net
TradingMarkets.com	www.tradingmarkets.com
TradingSchool.com	www.tradingschool.com
TrainToDayTrade.com	www.traintodaytrade.com
Trend Trader LLC	www.trendtrader.com
USA Today	www.usatoday.com
V90.com	www.v90.com
Van Tharp's International Institute of Trading Mastery	www.iitm.com
Wall Street City	www.wallstreetcity.com
Wall Street Journal Interactive Edition	www.wsj.com
Wall Street Research Net	www.wsrn.com/apps/internetstocks
A. B. Watley	www.abwatley.com
WhisperNumber.com	www.whispernumber.com
Wilshire 5000	www.wilshire.com
Window on Wall Street	www.windowonwallstreet.com
WinningDayTraders.com	www.winningdaytraders.com
Wyse Securities	www.wyse-sec.com
Zacks.com	www.zacks.com
ZDNet Inter@ctive Investor	www.zdii.com

Notes

Introduction   The Day Trading Game

1. Edwin LeFèvre. *Reminiscences of a Stock Operator*. New York: John Wiley & Sons, Inc., 1994.
2. Harvey Houtkin (with David Waldman). *Secrets of the SOES Bandits*. New York: McGraw-Hill, 1999.

Chapter 1   The Playing Fields: Nasdaq and the NYSE

1. Facts about the New York Stock Exchange obtained from "About the NYSE" at www.nyse.com.
2. Facts about the Nasdaq Stock Market obtained from "About Nasdaq" at www.nasdaq.com.
3. Information on SEC Order Handling Rules obtained from www.nasdaq.com and www.nasdaqtrader.com.
4. Harvey Houtkin (with David Waldman). *Secrets of the SOES Bandits*. New York: McGraw-Hill, 1999.
5. *Wall Street Journal*, December 19, 1997.
6. ECN profiles are gleaned from the ECN web sites and press releases.

Chapter 2   The Tools of the Trade

1. Edwin LeFèvre. *Reminiscences of a Stock Operator*. New York: John Wiley & Sons, 1994.
2. NASD Notice to Members 97-74 at www.nasd.com.

Chapter 3   Electronic Brokers: Cutting Out the Middleman

1. Press release from the NYSE, December 10, 1999.
2. Muriel Siebert, as quoted by SmartMoney.com in "Trading in the Dark," August 17, 1999.
3. Dr. Alexander Elder, as quoted in "Welcome to 24-Hour Wall Street World!" *New York Observer*, August 23, 1999.

4. Matthew Rich, managing director of Kauser Capital, as quoted in "Welcome to 24-Hour Wall Street World!" *New York Observer*, August 23, 1999.

Chapter 5   Define Your Trading Style

1. Alpesh B. Patel. *The Mind of a Trader: Lessons in Trading Strategy from the World's Leading Traders*. London: Financial Times, 1997.
2. An audiotape or CD of this session can be ordered from The Resource Link at www.the-resource-link.com.
3. MTrader.com's home page (www.mtrader.com).
4. G. Douglas Taylor. *The Taylor Trading Technique*. Available through Traders World (www.tradersworld.com).
5. David S. Nassar. *How to Get Started in Electronic Day Trading*. New York: McGraw-Hill, 1999.
6. David S. Nassar. *How to Get Started in Electronic Day Trading*.
7. Ibid.
8. Joe DiNapoli. *Trading with DiNapoli Levels*. DiNapoli, 1998. Available through Traders Press Bookstore (www.traderspressbookstore.com).

Chapter 6   Technical Analysis for the Technically Challenged

1. John J. Murphy. *The Visual Investor: How to Spot Stock Market Trends*. New York: John Wiley & Sons, 1996.
2. J. Welles Wilder. *New Concepts in Technical Trading Systems*. Trend Research, 1978.
3. Kassandra Bentley. *The MACD: An Indicator for All Seasons*. Houston, Texas: Telescan, Inc., 1988.

Chapter 7   When Greenspan Speaks, the Markets Listen

1. "Beige Book: The Basics," by Scott Gerlach, bonds editor, CNBC.com.
2. Marc Friedfertig and George West. *The Electronic Day Trader*. New York: McGraw-Hill, 1998; David S. Nassar. *How to Get Started in Electronic Day Trading*. New York: McGraw-Hill, 1999.

Chapter 8 The Right Stuff

1. Jack D. Schwager. *Market Wizards*. New York: New York Institute of Finance, 1989. *The New Market Wizards*. New York: HarperBusiness, 1992.
2. Mark Douglas. *The Disciplined Trader: Developing Winning Attitudes*. New York: New York Institute of Finance, 1990.
3. Van K. Tharp. *Trade Your Way to Financial Freedom*. New York: McGraw-Hill, 1999.
4. Robert Deel. *Trading the Plan*. New York: John Wiley & Sons, 1997.
5. Mark Douglas. *The Disciplined Trader.*
6. Van K. Tharp. *Trade Your Way to Financial Freedom.*
7. Ibid.

Chapter 9 The Master Plan

1. Michael Turner. *Day Trading into the Millennium*. 1998. Available at Michael Turner's web site at www.tradersresource.com.
2. Van K. Tharp. *Trade Your Way to Financial Freedom*. New York: McGraw-Hill, 1999.
3. If you use a martingale strategy in investing (or gambling), you will increase the size of your bet in a losing streak. An anti-martingale strategy tells you to increase the size of your bet in a winning streak.
4. Robert Deel. *Trading the Plan*. New York: John Wiley & Sons, 1997.
5. David L. Brown and Kassandra Bentley. *CyberInvesting: Cracking Wall Street with Your Personal Computer, Second Edition*. New York: John Wiley & Sons, 1997.

Chapter 10 The Home Office: Setting Up Shop

1. "Cable Modems Overview." www.cablemodems.com.

Chapter 12 The Future of Day Trading

1. Gleaned from the Nasdaq web site at www.nasdaq.com.
2. Taken from a Nasdaq op-ed article that appeared in the *Wall Street Journal* on November 5, 1999.

Glossary

after-hours trading trading after normal market hours, which may be from 4:00 P.M. Eastern Time (when the regular market closes) to 8:00 P.M. Eastern Time. *See* extended-hours trading.

aftermarket performance The trading performance of a stock after it has gone public.

All or none (AON) an instruction that specifies an order must be filled in its entirety or none of it should be filled.

ARCHIP the symbol on the Level 2 quote screen that identifies outside quotes from the Archipelago limit order book.

ask the price at which a market maker, specialist, or ECN is willing to sell a stock. (Also called offer.)

auction market a market in which traders meet on a trading floor to buy and sell securities through a specialist (such as the New York Stock Exchange and the American Stock Exchange).

ax the dominant market maker in a specific stock. (Also called the hammer.) *See* **shadowing the ax.**

backing away a term used to indicate that a market maker is not honoring its displayed quote. As in: *PRUS is showing $107^1/_2$,* but he keeps backing away.

basing trading within a narrow range of prices. In effect, the resistance and support levels have moved close together and the stock is unable to break above resistance or below support.

best ask the lowest price quoted among all competing market makers and ECNs for the sale of a specific stock at a given time. (Also called best offer.) The best ask and best bid make up the inside market or inside quote.

best bid the highest price quoted among all competing market makers and ECNs for the purchase of a specific stock at a given time.

beta a measurement of volatility. With regard to stocks, beta measures how much a stock fluctuates in price, over a specified period of time, compared with the market as a whole. A beta of 1, for example, means that the stock and market move in tandem. A beta higher than 1 indicates that the stock is more volatile than the market; lower than 1, that it is less volatile than the market.

bid the price at which a market maker, specialist, or ECN is willing to buy a stock.

blue chips a term that refers to established companies with large capitalization and a history of good earnings.

broker booth a trading booth.

buy at the bid the ability to buy stock at the inside bid price. Ordinary investors have to buy at the ask, which is higher than the bid.

buy stop order a type of limit order used to buy a stock after the stock has exhibited trading strength. The buy stop order instructs the broker to buy a stock if and only if it reaches a specified price—not at a better (lower) price.

buying power the amount of money available for trading, which is any cash in the account plus the marginable amount of any securities in the account.

chasing a stock continuing to up your bid in order to get an execution on a fast-moving stock. Not a good thing to do.

close the last price at which a stock traded during the day.

closed out exited a position, as in: *I closed out Microsoft.*

cover to buy a stock in order to close out a short position.

crossed market a situation in which the best bid is above the best ask. *See* **locked market**.

curbs in notation on screen that program trading restraints are in effect. *See* **trading curbs**.

day order an order to buy or sell a security that expires at the end of the day.

day trader one who buys and sells securities for short-term gains, usually exiting all positions by the end of the day.

day trading call a demand to deposit additional cash or marginable securities, made when purchases exceed buying power in a margin account.

dealer market a market, like Nasdaq, which has competing broker/dealers who make a market in each stock, each using its own capital and other resources.

decimalization the quoting of stock prices in decimals instead of fractions.

delayed quotes quotes delayed by the stock exchanges, usually for 15 or 20 minutes.

Designated Order Turnaround (DOT) *see* **Super Designated Order Turnaround**.

direct access broker a broker that allows customers direct access to the market through an ECN, as opposed to brokers who sell order flow to market makers. Also referred to as an *electronic broker*.

Dow the Dow Jones Industrial Average, an index that measures the performance of 30 blue-chip stocks.

down-average to buy additional shares of a declining stock in order to lower your average cost per share.

downgrade to change a recommendation on a stock to a less positive rating, as in: *The analyst downgraded IBM from a buy to a hold.*

downtick a quote that is lower than the preceding quote; a trade executed at a price that is lower than the preceding trade.

drawdown a method of calculating cash flow in an account.

earnings estimates projections of future earnings per share (for the next quarter or next fiscal year) made by analysts who write research reports on a company; usually, the consensus estimate (the mean) of all analysts who follow the company.

earnings per share (EPS) a company's net earnings divided by the number of outstanding shares.

earnings surprise when a company's earnings exceed the analysts' consensus estimates.

electronic broker a brokerage firm that allows customers direct access to the markets through an ECN. Also referred to as a direct access broker.

electronic communications network (ECN) a computerized trading system sanctioned by Nasdaq for the display of customer limit orders and integrated into the Nasdaq Level 2 quote system.

emerging growth company a small-cap company in a relatively new high-growth industry.

extended-hours trading refers to trading before and after normal market hours. (Normal market hours are 9:30 A.M. to 4:00 P.M. Eastern Time.) *See* **after-hours trading**.

fair value a mathematically derived relationship of the difference between the S&P futures and the S&P 500 index.

fast markets markets characterized by rapidly changing prices and extreme volatility.

Fed call in a margin account, a demand by the broker to deposit cash or marginable securities to bring the account up to the federally regulated margin requirements. A Fed call (or Reg call) occurs when the purchase of securities exceeds the established margin.

Fibonacci lines technical indicators based on the studies of a twelfth-century mathematician named Leonard Pisano (nicknamed Fibonacci). Fibonacci numbers involve a sequence in which each successive number is the sum of the two previous ones: 1, 2, 3, 5, 8, 13, 21, 34, 55, 89, 144, and so on. The indicators anticipate changes in trends as prices near the lines created by the Fibonacci numbers.

fill order execution. As in: *I got a fill at 20^1/$_2$.*

fill or kill (FOK) a type of order that instructs the broker to cancel the order unless it can be executed within a specified time.

flipping buying shares in an IPO at the offering price and selling soon after the shares start trading in order to cash in on an early profit. This practice is frowned upon by underwriters and brokers.

floor brokers brokers who work on the floor of the New York Stock Exchange, either as employees of brokerage houses (commission brokers) or for themselves (independent brokers). The latter execute orders for both member brokers and nonmember brokers.

fundamentals factors such as earnings, sales, debt, and other balance sheet items that reveal the basic health of a company.

gap a situation that occurs when a stock price skips several price levels between one trade and the next. This usually happens with the release of good or bad news after the market closes and the stock will either gap up (on good news) and open higher than the previous day's close or gap down and open lower than the previous day's close. Intraday gaps can also occur.

good till canceled (GTC) an instruction to leave an order open until it is canceled.

grinder a trader who seeks small profits on dozens or hundreds of trades a day. Similar to scalping.

hard stop an instruction to a broker to sell a stock (if long) or buy a stock (if short) if and when the stock reaches a predetermined price.

index a grouping of securities to track trends in specific market segments.

industry group rotation the movement of industry groups in to and out of favor with institutional investors, due to economic conditions, demographic trends, technological innovations, or other factors.

inflation the rate of the general level of price increases for goods and services; high inflation erodes the purchasing power of the dollar.

initial public offering (IPO) the selling of shares of stock to the public in a privately held company, after which the company becomes a publicly traded company. The IPO is usually underwritten by one or more investment banks that buy the shares from the company and then resell them to the general public.

inside ask the best or lowest quote among all competing market makers and ECNs for the sale of a particular stock. Also called best ask or inside offer.

inside bid the highest quote among all competing market makers and ECNs for the purchase of a particular stock. Also called best bid.

inside market the highest bid and the lowest ask (offer) on a particular stock at any given time.

inside quote the highest bid and lowest ask prices on a particular stock at any given time.

Instinet the oldest electronic communications network. Identified by the symbol INCA on the Level 2 quote screen.

Intermarket Trading System (ITS) the system that electronically links all U.S. stock exchanges.

lagging indicators technical indicators that confirm the trend of a stock, based on its past trading patterns.

leading indicators technical indicators that reveal market extremes (overbought or oversold conditions) and anticipate trend reversals.

Level 1 quotes stock quotes that reveal the best bid and best ask. Level 1 usually includes the last trade, the open, the high and low for the day, and the cumulative volume for the day.

Level 2 quotes stock quotes that reveal the bids and asks of all market participants (market makers and ECNs), along with the number of shares offered at each bid and ask price.

Level 3 quotes available only to market makers, these quotes include Level 1 and Level 2 quotes and allow market makers to enter and change their quotes.

limit order an instruction to a broker to buy or sell a specified number of shares of a stock at a specific price, or better.

limit order book a collection of unfilled limit orders held by an ECN or exchange.

Limit Order Display Rule one of the SEC Order Handling Rules, which states that if a market maker receives a limit order priced better than its current quote for that security, that limit order becomes the best bid or best ask and must be displayed on the Level 2 screen (with the size of the quote).

linear chart a chart that shows the price data on an arithmetic scale, treating each price increment equally.

liquidity having a sufficient amount of trading volume to accommodate the buying and selling of a security without a large bid/ask spread.

locked market a situation that occurs when the best bid is the same price as the best ask.

logarithmic chart a chart that scales stock prices by percentages.

margin the difference between the market value of securities in an account and the amount of money loaned by the broker against those securities.

margin account a type of brokerage account that allows you to borrow funds against the securities in the account in order to purchase more securities.

margin call a demand to deposit cash or additional securities to bring a margin account back to the required level (usually 25 percent of total value of the account). Unlike a Fed call or day trading call, a margin call may be met by selling the securities in your account.

margin rate the rate of interest charged for borrowing funds in a margin account.

marked to market to adjust the value of securities in an account based on the current market price.

market capitalization a measure of the size of a company by multiplying the number of outstanding shares by the price per share; also called market cap.

market impact cost (MIC) the increased cost of acquiring a position due to the rise in the price of the stock that is directly related to the large size of the buyer's orders (usually an institution).

market maker a broker/dealer or investment bank that makes a two-sided market in a Nasdaq security by maintaining a firm quote on both the buy side and the sell side. Market makers are appointed and regulated by the National Association of Security Dealers (NASD).

market maker identifier (MMID) the four-letter symbol that identifies a market maker or ECN on the Level 2 screen.

market order an order to buy or sell a stock at the current market price, whatever that price may be when the order is executed.

marketable limit order a limit order that can be executed because the stock price has reached the limit price.

mental stop a reminder to yourself to consider selling a stock (if long) or buying a stock (if short) if it reaches a predetermined price.

Nasdaq the Nasdaq Stock Market. Nasdaq originally was an acronym for the National Association of Security Dealers Automatic Quotation system.

Nasdaq National Market (NNM) Nasdaq stocks that have market caps of more than $75 million; includes about 4,400 stocks.

Nasdaq SmallCap Market Nasdaq stocks, numbering about 1,800, which have a minimum market cap of $50 million; includes primarily emerging growth companies.

National Association of Security Dealers (NASD) the self-regulating securities organization and parent company of the Nasdaq Stock Market.

negotiated market a market in which prices are negotiated between buyers and sellers.

New York Stock Exchange (NYSE) the largest and second oldest stock exchange in the United States (the Philadelphia Stock Exchange is older) where stocks of more than 3,300 companies are traded.

odd lot a trade of less than 100 shares.

offer *see* **ask**.

offering price the price at which an IPO is priced by the underwriter and the price paid by those who are allocated shares in an IPO. On a hot IPO, the offering price may be significantly lower than the opening price.

open the price at which a stock first traded during the day.

opening price the price at which shares in an IPO start trading.

order flow refers to orders directed by a broker to a market maker for execution. The market maker pays the broker X cents per share for this order flow because it can make a healthy profit on the spread. Electronic brokers do not (for the most part) sell order flow; most Web-based brokers do.

outside market any quote that is inferior to the inside or best quote. Traders may make a trade at the outside market in order to get into or out of a fast-moving stock.

outstanding shares in a publicly held company, the number owned by the public, as opposed to shares in reserve but not issued.

outside quote any quote that is inferior to the inside or best quote; on bid prices, outside quotes are lower than the best bid; on ask prices, outside quotes are higher than the best ask.

overbought a term used in technical analysis that refers to a stock or market having reached a high extreme (a preponderance of buyers) and due for a correction.

oversold a term used in technical analysis that refers to a stock or market having reached a low extreme (a preponderance of sellers) and due for a reversal.

paper trading picking entry and exit points on a stock as if you were actually making a trade and tracking the trades on paper. No money is involved in paper trading. *See* **simulated trading**.

partial fill an order that is not filled in its entirety.

penny stocks stocks that sell for less than five dollars a share; typically, bulletin board and pink sheet stocks.

preferencing directing an order to a specific market maker or ECN.

price improvement refers to making a trade at a price better than the quoted bid or ask.

price-to-earning (P/E) ratio a company's current stock price divided by its earnings per share for the past 12 months.

program trading trades executed automatically by computer programs (used by money managers and other professional traders).

pump and dump a practice whereby a person or firm that holds an interest in a stock promotes (pumps) the stock to the public, and when the price rises due to increased demand, the promoter sells (dumps) its shares, at which point the price usually plummets.

QQQ the index tracking stock for the Nasdaq 100, which is traded on the American Stock Exchange.

Quote Rule a rule passed by the SEC in 1996 (effective January 1997) requiring Nasdaq market makers to display their most competitive quotes on a public quote system, such as Level 2.

range-bound market a market in which the trading is within a general range of prices, with the leaders not moving much.

real-time quotes stock quotes that include the most current bid and ask and the most recent trade.

refresh to restate a quote at the same price. Used when a market maker has filled an order at the bid or offer and remains willing to continue to buy or sell stock at the quoted price.

research alert a notice issued by an analyst who has upgraded or downgraded his or her recommendation on a stock.

retracement a technical pattern on a stock chart made when a stock falls in price and then recovers most or all of its loss. The recovery is the retracement.

risk management having a plan to control your losses and preserve your capital.

round lot a *lot* refers to the number of shares in a single trade; a round lot is a trade of 100 shares or some multiple of 100. *See also* **odd lot**.

round trip the entering and exiting of a single position (i.e., a buy order followed by a sell order for the same stock). Some commissions and other fees are quoted on round trips, rather than on a single trade.

scalper a day trader who makes a lot of quick trades for small profits (often teenies) on each trade.

SEC Order Handling Rules two rules that govern the handling and execution of limit orders (the Limit Order Display Rule) and the display of such orders on ECNs (the Quote Rule). These rules were effective in January 1997 and are responsible for the emergence of ECNs and the flourishing of the day trading industry.

sector an economic grouping of related industries.

sector rotation the movement of sectors in and out of favor with institutional investors, due to economic conditions, demographic trends, technological innovations, or other factors.

securities a general term that encompasses equity instruments (stocks) and debt instruments (bonds), although the term is often used interchangeably with stocks.

Securities and Exchange Commission (SEC) the regulatory body of the securities industry.

SelectNet a nonmandatory electronic order delivery system that allows any subscriber to Level 2 quotes to direct (preference) orders to specific market makers and ECNs or to broadcast orders to all market makers and ECNs.

sell at the ask the ability to sell stock at the inside ask price. Ordinary investors have to sell at the bid, which is lower than the ask.

setup the conditions, dictated by your trading system, that must occur in a stock before you make a trade.

shadowing the ax mimicking the trades of the dominant market maker (the ax) on a stock.

shorting a stock selling a stock you do not currently own (you borrow it from your broker) in the belief that the stock price will drop.

simulated trading using trading software to place mock buy and sell orders and track positions; similar to paper trading in that there is no actual money involved. The purpose is both to practice trading and to become familiar with the trading software.

slippage the difference in the price of the stock that appears on a quote screen at the time you place a trade and the price at which your order is filled. The greatest slippage occurs with non–direct access brokers.

Small Order Execution System (SOES) a mandatory order execution-system that requires Nasdaq market makers to execute limit orders of up to 1,000 shares at their quoted bid or ask.

snap quote a stock quote at a single point in time—a snapshot of a quote—as opposed to continuous or streaming quotes.

SOES short for Small Order Execution System. It is an electronic order delivery system that requires mandatory executions by Nasdaq market makers at the inside quote. Used as a verb, it means to sell shares at the quoted bid or buy shares at the quoted ask. SOES cannot be used with ECNs.

specialist the firm or individual who makes a market in a listed stock and manages all orders for that stock.

specialist market a market, such as the New York Stock Exchange or American Stock Exchange, in which a single firm or individual is assigned the responsibility of maintaining the market and handling the order flow for each stock listed on the exchange.

spread the difference between the bid and the ask prices of a security.

stop the price at which you will sell a stock (if long) or buy a stock (if short) in order to cut your losses.

stop limit order a stop order that limits the price at which the stock will be sold. For example, if the stock gaps down below your stop price, the stock will not be sold. This gives you a chance to evaluate the conditions that caused the gap and give the stock a chance to recover from a temporary setback.

stop order a market order that instructs your broker to sell a stock if it declines to a specified price. (Also called a stop loss order). A stop order will not protect you from a gap down, as the stock will be sold at the first available price, however far that may be below your stop price. *See also* **stop limit order**.

streaming quotes quotes that automatically change on your screen when the actual bid or ask is changed by the market maker or specialist.

Super Designated Order Turnaround (SuperDot) the electronic order handling system used by the New York Stock Exchange, primarily for small orders. It was originally named the Designated Order Turnaround (DOT) system and renamed SuperDot in 1984 after certain enhancements.

swing trading a style of trading in which a position is held for two or more days.

teenie refers to a $1/16$ of a point on a trade.

tick an incremental move in a stock price. There are upticks (plus ticks), downticks, and zero-plus ticks.

timed out a SOES or SelectNet order remains live for only a specified time and then is automatically canceled by the exchange if not filled. When this happens, it is said to have timed out. Time constraints vary for each.

trade ahead refers to a market maker ignoring a customer's order that is priced better than the inside quote and continuing to trade at the inferior quote.

trading booths the structures (about 1,400) along the perimeter of the floor of the NYSE from which member firms and independent brokers operate.

trading curbs restraints initiated by the New York Stock Exchange to prevent program trading if the Dow moves 2 percent in either direction from the previous trading day's closing price. The notation is shown on CNBC as "curbs in."

trading halt a pause in the trading of security, initiated by the specialist, that occurs when significant news is released about the security, to give the market time to absorb the impact of the news.

trading posts the 17 computerized structures on the floor of the NYSE from which specialists trade their securities.

trailing stop a stop that is moved in the direction of the trend to protect profits.

two-sided market a market in which the firm making the market in a security is both buyer and seller and must maintain firm bid and firm ask prices. Nasdaq market makers and NYSE specialists both make a two-sided market in the stocks they handle.

underwriter an investment banking firm that takes a company public by buying the securities from the company and reselling the shares to the public. The primary firm is the lead manager; the other firms assisting in the underwriting are the comanagers or counderwriters.

upgrade to change a recommendation on a stock to a more positive rating. As in: *The analyst upgraded IBM from a hold to a strong buy.*

uptick a quote that is higher than the preceding quote; a trade executed at a price that is higher than the preceding trade.

volatility a measure of a stock's daily price fluctuations. Large swings in stock prices equal high volatility.

wash and rinse refers to a situation that occurs when a stock drops just far enough to clear out your stop and then resumes its upward march. This happens when stops are set at obvious levels, such as support lines; market makers who realize this push the price down to take out the stops.

wash sale rule an IRS rule that states you can't claim the loss if you sell shares at a loss and buy them back within 30 days.

Web-based broker an online discount stock broker whose trading screens are accessed via its Web page on the Internet. Orders placed with Web-based brokers are generally routed by the broker to affiliated market makers for execution.

whisper number an earnings number that is circulated (rumored) on Wall Street a few days before a company announces its quarterly or yearly earnings. The whisper number may be higher or lower than the official earnings estimate for the company, and it is widely regarded as the number the company must meet or exceed in order to retain the favor of the investing public.

zero-plus tick when a stock upticks on a trade and the following trade is executed at the same price level.

Index